6480674

‖‖‖‖‖‖‖‖‖‖‖‖
D1525827

Manners and Southern History

Manners
and Southern History

Essays by
CATHERINE CLINTON,
JOSEPH CRESPINO,
JANE DAILEY,
LISA LINDQUIST DORR,
ANYA JABOUR,
JOHN F. KASSON,
JENNIFER RITTERHOUSE,
AND CHARLES F. ROBINSON II

Edited by Ted Ownby

University Press of Mississippi   *Jackson*

www.upress.state.ms.us

The University Press of Mississippi is a member of the Association of American
University Presses.

First Edition 2007

∞

Library of Congress Cataloging-in-Publication Data

Manners and southern history : essays by Catherine Clinton . . . [et al.] / edited by
Ted Ownby. — 1st ed.
    p. cm.
  Includes bibliographical references and index.
  ISBN-13: 978-1-57806-979-8 (cloth : alk. paper)
  ISBN-10: 1-57806-979-3 (cloth : alk. paper)
    1. Etiquette—Southern States. 2. Southern States—Social life and customs.
I. Ownby, Ted.

  BJ1853.M22 2007
  395.0975—dc22   2006029073

British Library Cataloging-in-Publication Data available

Contents

Introduction

Ted Ownby

The topic of manners is immediately interesting to most scholars in southern history, but the question of how to study manners—or even how to define the term—is not so clear. The literature on manners and southern history is small, with just a few important works showing the potential of investigating manners, if we ask the right questions. The papers in this volume began as contributions to the Porter Fortune Jr. History Symposium at the University of Mississippi. Scholars invited to the symposium had considerable freedom in defining manners and deciding how to approach the topic. As the organizer of the conference, I asked the scholars to consider manners not as customs or mores, but as etiquette, considered broadly and with an eye toward connecting manners to issues central to southern history.

Scholars once tended to define manners as customs or mores or even folkways in which long-held habits and expectations had deep roots in the history of the groups that practiced them. That is rarely the approach of today's scholars. Discussion of the history of manners moved forward with scholars who in the 1970s and 1980s discovered the earlier work of Norbert Elias, whose book *The Civilizing Process* influenced considerable scholarship about how to conceptualize and write about manners. Taking a broad approach to European history, Elias argued that in the Middle Ages, an open approach toward the human body gave way to numerous calls for privacy. Elites in government and outside it tried to set standards about speech, clothing, and especially things like food and sex that set clear lines between classes and established certain forms of behavior as uncivilized and hence undesirable.[1] Notions that human behavior was divided between the civilized and uncivilized, and that people whose manners showed they were uncivilized deserved to be ruled or enslaved or uplifted became crucial to numerous major events in human history, from the coronation of European royalty to the enslavement of millions of Africans.[2] Some but not many American historians have used the start Elias made by analyzing how Americans offered manners either to try to uphold hierarchies or to break them down.[3] Southern historians Jane Dailey, Bertram Wyatt-Brown, Kenneth Greenberg, Stephen Berry, and Stephen Stowe have come to exciting conclusions by analyzing nineteenth-century uses of concepts of manners.[4]

Many historians of the past generation or so, inspired by Michel Foucault, Pierre Bourdieu, and other theorists and by their own imaginations, have been aggressive in analyzing ways people with power tried to make particular, contingent, changeable power relations seem that they were in fact permanent, natural, and not open to question. From such a perspective, the life of a group took the form of a contest among a range of interests and expectations, with one group wishing not merely to win and dominate but to convince everyone else to stop competing and adopt their rules. Manners, from such a perspective, operated as a social construction of people who wanted the world to work smoothly according to their expectations, without repeated contests about how to speak, act, gesture, and do virtually anything else that dealt with other people. Manners thus seemed above all to have served as ways for some people to convince everyone else to accept their rules. To make the point another way, such a perspective suggests that manners represented an attempt to turn politics into something that no longer seemed like politics. Such a conception of manners as a way to support clear structures of power emphasizes how overt expressions of hierarchy such as bowing, ceremony, differences in dress and address, but also more subtle forms of human relations celebrated and reinforced social distinctions.

In most conceptions of manners, having good manners means fitting in by knowing the rules and using them. Bad manners (or the absence of manners) can mean either rebellion—conscious, intentional rejection of the rules—or they can mean not knowing or caring about what some people expect. To study bad manners reminds one of a rare coffee-mug/t-shirt/bumper sticker slogan authored by a historian, Laurel Thatcher Ulrich's often quoted maxim that "well-behaved women rarely make history." The maxim's suggestion that only those willing to deconstruct conventional manners do something important enough to be historically notable seems to undermine the historian's obligation to study all of the human past, including those who embrace and live by the rules, squirm under them, and wonder or worry about them. Studying manners surely means studying the rules and the makers of rules, the breakers of rules, and also the vast range of people who are not sure about the rules or wonder which rules apply to them.

It seems useful to ask if there are other approaches to manners that deserve consideration, and if so, if they are somehow less attuned to issues of power. Many people have tried to live according to egalitarian manners—to act, talk, gesture, and the rest as if their actions do not reflect or certainly do not accept ranks in society. Many parents try to raise children to show respect not just to adult figures of authority, but to all people, with a goal of moving toward notions of universal human decency and understanding. Sometimes respecting all people and all backgrounds means saying there are no rules except the expectation of tolerance and respect, but such an effort creates its own kind of manners. Recent interest in the symbols of personal address—changing Miss and Mrs. to Ms., he to he/she, and many other examples—reflect efforts to create egalitarian manners with hopes of creating a more egalitarian society. And one might ask if there are manners that call for liberation by trying to overturn set rules and embrace new experiences. Perhaps, then, our goal should be to study manners wherever we find them, studying how different people define manners, how they use them, like or dislike them, break them, and change them.

In considering manners in the history of the American South, six issues come quickly to mind. One involves manners and racial segregation. Many of us first thought about the history of manners as an academic subject when we heard teachers lecture about forms of racist etiquette white supremacists hoped to establish and enforce in the late nineteenth-century South. Issues of how to speak, what terms to use when speaking, how to look at people when speaking or being spoken to, what to do with a hat when meeting people on the street, who went first when crossing paths, all seemed especially intriguing as ways for a group grasping for power to try to make that power clear. Another side of the same issue involved discussions of manners in calls for racial uplift. Booker T. Washington was especially vigilant in calling for African Americans to overcome any images of being uncivilized by adopting Victorian manners in speech, comportment, and cleanliness.

A second obvious question in thinking about manners and southern history involves definitions of ladies and gentlemen. The notion that some groups in the South knew how to live as ladies and gentlemen recalls the period when some early Americans wondered if or assumed that upper-class southerners continued British Cavalier traditions. Hospitality, ease, self-confidence in social situations, knowing the rules and living them out without unnecessary worry or uncertainty, the mystiques of the paternalistic male and the gracious female, all suggested that some upper-class southerners were trying to live out manners they associated with an old landed aristocracy. Scholarly discussions of honor, initiated by Bertram Wyatt-Brown's 1984 work *Southern Honor*, depicted men who assumed that certain behaviors were the responsibility of people of their station and then worked hard to live up to expectations of masterly behavior.[5] Scholarship on upper-class women often suggests a greater divide between the rules and the willingness to obey them, but much of that scholarship portrays manners, whether they were goals to admire or frustrating rules to reject, as crucial to women's identities. The works on wealthy women in the antebellum South consistently mention manners as part of an ideal world those women generally did not have and, often, chose to reject.[6]

A third obvious question involves the ways people disagree. Southern history is full of so many claims to hierarchy that questions of how people express disagreement—or do not get to express disagreement or dissatisfaction—are complicated and critical. Is it good manners simply to accept all kinds of dissatisfactions, because to say otherwise seems unkind or selfish? When is raising potentially controversial questions an acceptable form of open discussion, and when is it a dangerous form of sassing people with authority? Have schools and parents raised children to assert their own opinions, or have they encouraged people to accept conventional wisdom, because to do otherwise would be bad manners? The work of Richard Wright, who seems to have been deconstructing manners since early childhood, made particularly vivid the consequences but also the necessity of questioning people who did not want to be questioned.

Another question concerns manners and violence. Have the various forms of violence in southern history been manifestations of certain types of manners, or have some of them violated those manners? Certainly, the perpetrators of whitecappings and some lynchings claimed the privilege of inflicting violence in the name of certain forms of manners—the protection of women, traditional gender roles, community standards. But what happened when that violence became the object of criticism itself? How did the opponents of lynching, for example, use manners as part of their critique of violence? Did violence intend to confirm certain manners, or did the act of turning conflict into violence show that manners had broken down?[7]

A fifth question asks who has taught manners in southern history, and how they taught them. Do parents or other adult authorities teach manners? School teachers? Ministers? People who make and enforce the laws? The question seems especially intriguing, and especially illusive, because the necessity of teaching and enforcing conceptions of manners can call into question that those manners are worthwhile standards of behavior.

A sixth question concerns issues of manners and regional identity. People who claim the authority to make such decisions continue to call Charleston, South Carolina, the most mannerly place in the United States. When and how have certain parts of the South gained such a reputation? William Taylor's 1960 analysis, *Cavalier and Yankee*, argued that it was worried northerners who first characterized upper-class southerners as having ease and manners with long roots in European aristocracy. Since the late 1800s, an array of novelists and promoters of tourism have depicted people in the South as having a set of manners the rest of the country might admire, emulate, or at least enjoy watching.

Studying manners and history can be awkward and uncomfortable, in part because some scholars tend to view the topic as less important than grander questions in history, but in larger part because the subject itself can be illusive. Should we study manners when people write down rules for mannerly behavior, or should we try to study the assumptions behind how people act and write and speak? Should we study manners at moments when they clearly failed to work and thus became points of controversy, or should we study manners when no one seemed to be talking much about them? And how do we study the people who rejected established manners with the same depth and detail we can use in studying those who spoke up for what they saw as good manners?

The papers and comments in this volume address these questions through a range of approaches. Most concentrate on the connections between, and often the impossibility of separating, public behavior and private life. The authors in this volume have rejected older notions that historians should analyze topics like manners separate from issues of power and politics. Few of these authors see themselves as historians of manners, which seems likely to remain a small sub-field in the profession. Most of these papers discuss gender conventions, the purposes those conventions served, and efforts by some people to reject them. All of the papers deal in some way with relationships between manners and race. There are far more questions to raise about manners and how different groups of southerners defined them, used them, or defied them, but these essays seem, for the period since the Civil War, a good beginning.

Anya Jabour's essay begins the volume with the issue of anger. People who were considered ladies in the antebellum South believed they should not become angry. But the Civil War made a lot of women mad, especially at Union armies, so the war that raised so many questions about southern society also raised the issue of proper manners for ladies. Jennifer Ritterhouse's ambitious essay, dealing with definitions, historiography, and historical evidence, proposes that segregation laws emerged in part because white supremacist notions of good manners were falling to African American demands for change.

Lisa Lindquist Dorr's essay details how the behavior of male and female college students at Alabama's public universities in the 1910s enraged both university officials and the Ku Klux Klan. The potential for people to step outside their supposedly proper roles is also important in Catherine Clinton's sweeping paper on Mardi Gras. Emphasizing the fact, little known outside New Orleans, that Mardi Gras festivities climax in debutante balls, Clinton traces the ways Mardi Gras has both elevated young debutantes to the position of queen while at the same time celebrating apparent chaos.

The paper by Charles Robinson raises the question of the differences between standards about interracial sex established by the law and the actual behavior that southern governments chose to prosecute. People who merely had sex rarely faced legal prosecution, but people who had long-term public relationships ran a strong risk of arrest. Also asking questions about the differences between clear rules about white supremacy and issues of manners, Joseph Crespino's paper returns to the issue of how to express discontent. White Mississippians in the Civil Rights years disagreed on whether they should make some allowances to protestors out of a goal of keeping an orderly—mannerly—society or if they should crack down in ways that dramatized that white supremacy had failed to achieve the kind of widespread success its supporters envisioned.

The collection concludes with two comments on the previous papers. Jane Dailey summarizes and critiques each of the papers by pointing out strengths and potential problems. She challenges the entire project by asking if manners, with its implications of internalizing values, is a useful term for scholars who are studying societies that use a great deal of coercive force. Dailey suggests that manners issues might have been especially important during the uncertainties of the Reconstruction period and concludes that "once we are talking about the Jim Crow South we are talking about two codes of manners, not one; about competing and oppositional cultures." Like Dailey, John Kasson notes that the entire project can be a bit uncomfortable for the scholar, because discussing manners and southern history seems to privilege the suggestions of elites who have been claiming something distinctively positive about life in the region since the 1700s. He goes through the essays showing how different groups defined manners and how others often used the uncertainties in those definitions in their own creative ways. His conclusion about one paper that "white paternalists found themselves in a tragicomedy of manners of their own devising" seems a fitting conclusion to the entire volume.

Notes

1. Norbert Elias, *The Civilizing Process: The History of Manners*, translated by Edmund Jephcott (New York: Urizen Books, 1978); Elias, *Power and Civility*, translated by Edmund Jephcott (New York: Pantheon Books, 1982).

2. Winthrop D. Jordan, *White Over Black: American Attitudes Toward the Negro, 1550–1812* (Baltimore: Penguin Books, 1969).

3. Richard Bushman, *The Refinement of America: Persons, Houses, Cities* (New York: Knopf, 1992); C. Dallett Hemphill, *Bowing To Necessities: A History of Manners in America, 1620–1860* (New York: Oxford University Press, 1999); John F. Kasson, *Rudeness & Civility: Manners in Nineteenth-Century Urban America* (New York: Hill and Wang, 1990).

4. Jane Dailey, *Before Jim Crow: The Politics of Race in Postemancipation Virginia* (Chapel Hill and London: University of North Carolina Press, 2000); Bertram Wyatt-Brown, *Southern Honor: Ethics & Behavior in the Old South* (New York: Oxford University Press, 1982); Kenneth S. Greenberg, *Honor & Slavery: Lies, Duels, Noses, Masks, Dressing as a Woman, Gifts, Strangers, Humanitarianism, Death, Slave Rebellions, The Pro-Slavery Argument, Baseball, Hunting, and Gambling in the Old South* (Princeton: Princeton University Press, 1996); Stephen W. Berry III, *All That Makes a Man: Love and Ambition in the Civil War South* (New York: Oxford University Press, 2003); Steven M. Stowe, *Intimacy and Power: Ritual in the Lives of the Planters* (Baltimore: Johns Hopkins University Press, 1987).

5. Wyatt-Brown, *Southern Honor*.

6. See the major works on antebellum plantation women's history and family history: Anne Firor Scott, *The Southern Lady: From Pedestal to Politics, 1830–1930*

(Chicago: University of Chicago Press, 1970); Catherine Clinton, *The Plantation Mistress: Women's World in the Old South* (New York: Pantheon Books, 1982); Jean B. Friedman, *The Enclosed Garden: Women and Community in the Evangelical South, 1830–1900* (Chapel Hill: University of North Carolina Press, 1985); Elizabeth Fox-Genovese, *Within the Plantation Household: Black and White Women of the Old South* (Chapel Hill: University of North Carolina Press, 1988); Jane Turner Censer, *North Carolina Planters and Their Children, 1800–1860* (Baton Rouge: Louisiana State University Press, 1984); Joan Cashin, *A Family Venture: Men and Women on the Southern Frontier* (New York: Oxford University Press, 1991); Marli F. Weiner, *Mistresses and Slaves: Plantation Women in South Carolina, 1830–1880* (Urbana: University of Illinois Press, 1998); Lori Glover, *All Our Relations: Blood Ties and Emotional Bonds Among the Early South Carolina Gentry* (Baltimore: Johns Hopkins University Press, 2000).

7. See Jacquelyn Dowd Hall, *Revolt Against Chivalry: Jessie Daniel Ames and the Women's Campaign Against Lynching* (New York: Columbia University Press, 1993); Grace Elizabeth Hale, *Making Whiteness: The Culture of Segregation in the South, 1890–1940* (New York: Pantheon Books, 1998).

Manners and Southern History

Southern Ladies and She-Rebels; or, Femininity in the Foxhole

Changing Definitions of Womanhood in the Confederate South

Anya Jabour

Tennesseean Ellen Renshaw House exploded with rage against the "blue devils" who occupied her hometown, Knoxville, in Fall 1863, shortly after House's twentieth birthday. Despite repeated resolves to "behave as a lady," House, who described herself as "a very violent rebel," soon discovered that her new identity as a "She Rebel" could not be reconciled with the behavior of a southern lady.[1] House's growing hatred for the invading troops—and her desire to see them come to harm—were incompatible with guidelines for feminine propriety, which counseled gentle submission and a nurturing outlook. "I feel perfectly fiendish," wrote House in her diary in February 1864. "I believe I would kill a Yankee and not a muscle quiver. Oh! the intensity with which I hate them." House predicted that she would soon be forced to do "something devilish," adding, "that is just the word, though not a lady like one."[2]

House quickly earned a reputation as "an outrageous rebel," a term that applied not only to her political loyalties, but to her improper behavior. In January 1864, she and several other young women—a group House described as "Rebel girls"—waved gloves and handkerchiefs at the Confederate prisoners who were on their way to the railroad station. The degree to which this behavior flew in the face of feminine modesty was recognized—if exaggerated—by the Unionist newspaper editor, who reported that the young "she-rebels" had been guilty of "bold, impudent flirting demonstrations." House's behavior toward Yankees was also uncharacteristically "bold." Surrounded by Union soldiers, House refused to treat them with politeness, despite the strictures of southern ladyhood, which required young women to present an amiable appearance at all times. "I cant contain myself," she explained. "I say all sorts of things about all their officers & men . . . and say every thing impudent that comes into my head." "It seems to me sometimes that I feel perfectly reckless of what I say or do," she remarked in March 1864.[3]

So threatening did the Union soldiers find this young woman that in April 1864, they ordered her to leave the state and go south.[4] House's experiences demonstrated that a term she coined in November 1863—"rebel Ladies"—was considered an oxymoron in the war-torn South.[5] Young women in the Civil War era often were forced to choose between their identity as ladies and their identity as rebels, and some, like House, chose the latter.[6]

Ellen House's story dramatically illustrates a growing trend in the Confederate South: young white women's willingness to surrender their status as proper young ladies in order to defend their beloved Confederate nation. Like this "very violent rebel," many elite young women in the Confederate South weighed the value of ladylike behavior against the ethos of southern nationalism and concluded that Confederate loyalty was of greater worth than good manners. Earning a reputation as southern spitfires, these southern-ladies-turned-she-rebels simultaneously challenged conventional gender roles and revealed the fragile underpinnings of slaveholding society.

The Civil War forced a major crisis in southern culture, pitting the ideals of southern ladyhood and southern independence against one another. Prior to the conflict, southern femininity and regional loyalty were not only consistent with each other, but mutually reinforcing. Pro-slavery theorists defended the supposedly "natural" hierarchy of white over black by comparison with another so-called "natural" hierarchy: the subordination of women to men. Moreover, they argued that the presence of slavery elevated the position of white women, placing "the southern lady" on a pedestal that rested on the bent backs of enslaved African Americans. The presence of southern ladies, then, demonstrated the alleged superiority of southern society and its "peculiar institution," slavery. By accepting their own position in southern society—simultaneously honored and oppressed—elite white women literally embodied the southern defense of slavery.[7]

The Civil War changed this situation. In their display of Confederate—as opposed to simply southern—loyalty, southern white women often acted in ways that contradicted their assigned role as symbolic supporters of the system. As southern women demonstrated their commitment to maintaining

the Confederacy, including slavery, they abandoned their pedestals and rebelled, not only against the Union, but also against prescriptions of southern
femininity. This was particularly true for the South's young women—those
between the ages of fifteen and twenty-five. While their mothers counseled
patience, these daughters of the Confederacy chafed under Yankee rule and
struggled with the rules of ladylike propriety. Often, like Ellen House, they
concluded that the display of southern loyalty was more important than the
ideal of the southern lady.[8]

Young white women's behavior during the Civil War reveals that the Confederate South was a society at war with itself. To defend the Confederacy—
and the South's "peculiar institution" of slavery—southerners had to sacrifice propriety—and the ideal of "the southern lady" that was integral to the
defense of slavery.

In the Old South, what Kent Anderson Leslie has termed "the myth of
the southern lady" was central not only to ideals of femininity but to the defense of slavery.[9] As intellectual historian Michael O'Brien points out, "the
defense of slavery mandated the repudiation of egalitarianism"—and egalitarianism included women's rights. Indeed, the antebellum movement for
women's rights met with a particularly hostile reception in the slaveholding
South, as southerners rightly understood the connection between rights for
women and freedom for blacks. This connection was both philosophical—
a commitment to equality of all people was antithetical to both female subordination and racial slavery—and practical: for many northern women's
rights activists, feminism was a logical (and sometimes necessary) extension
of abolitionism.[10] Whereas northern activists tied the struggle for women's
rights with the movement to end slavery, southern writers on woman's
proper role linked feminine submissiveness with racial slavery. Placing the
white woman on a pedestal thus made it defensible to place African Americans in chains.[11]

Southerners countered the equation between abolitionism and feminism
with the assertion that white women's position as dependents within the
family justified African Americans' positions as slaves in the South. Both
black slaves and white women were expected to submit to the benevolent
rule of the planter-patriarch—a figure that Christopher Memminger, in a
lecture to the Young Men's Library Association in Augusta, Georgia, in 1851,
called "a ruler in his household." For all other members of the household,
Memminger continued, "obedience and suburdination become important
elements of education."[12]

Submission was central to the ideal of the southern lady. To deserve protection, white women—like black slaves—had to admit their absolute dependence on the husband or master and obey him implicitly. According to the renowned proslavery author George Fitzhugh, submissiveness was both the essence and the salvation of the southern lady: "Her weakness is her strength, and her true art is to cultivate and improve that weakness. . . . In truth, woman . . . has but one right and that is the right to protection. The right to protection involves the obligation to obey. . . . If she be obedient she stands little danger of maltreatment."[13]

While Fitzhugh was anomalous in some ways—O'Brien writes that he was "a man half-in, half-out of what his world thought"—his negative views on "individualism," his commitment to "patriarchalism," and his adherence to the "Victorian notions of domesticity and separate spheres" were entirely "unoriginal." When Fitzhugh wrote on gender issues, in particular, he said, according to O'Brien, "things that many other Southerners had argued before him," although with a style that was uniquely Fitzhugh.[14]

Many other southerners—both producers and consumers of prescriptive literature—echoed Fitzhugh's notions about the *sine qua non* of the southern lady: submissiveness. Indeed, submissiveness was one of the four "cardinal virtues" recommended to northern women in what Barbara Welter termed "the cult of true womanhood" in her classic essay. But it was only in the South that feminine submissiveness was linked to racial slavery; as a result, southerners' emphasis on this trait was particularly marked. According to Anne Firor Scott's landmark work, *The Southern Lady*, "the need to maintain the slave system contributed to the insistence upon perfect, though submissive, women."[15]

Scott might have said *perfectly* submissive, given the emphasis that southerners laid on this trait. Female advice-givers as well as male pro-slavery theorists recommended submissiveness to southern white women. Caroline Gilman, author of *Recollections of a Southern Matron* (1839), admitted the difficulty of achieving this ideal when she wrote: "To repress a harsh answer, to confess a fault, and to stop (right or wrong) in the midst of self-defence, in gentle submission, sometimes requires a struggle like life and death." Nonetheless, Gilman firmly reminded her readers that "gentle submission" was essential to "domestic happiness."[16]

Young women in the Old South translated such prescriptions into an ideal of southern ladyhood that equated good manners with gentle submission, and both with southern femininity. What Virginian Mary Jefferson

Randolph called "the deportment principles and manners that constitute a lady"[17] illustrated a young woman's gentle birth and breeding and established her claim to the status of a southern lady. Schoolgirl Sally Lucas revealed the link between possessing good manners and being a southern lady when she boasted to her father in 1850: "I have one thing to tell you dear Father which I know will give you . . . much pleasure and gratification. . . . It is that Mrs Wilner thinks I am a young lady of very good manners."[18] Young women in the Old South strove to attain the status of "a young lady of very good manners" by acquiring and displaying all "the deportment principles and manners that constitute a lady." In so doing, they upheld and perpetuated the ideology of southern ladyhood and the system of slavery that it justified.

The coming of the Civil War challenged this orderly arrangement. The Civil War was not only a conflict between North and South, freed labor and racial slavery, industry and agriculture; it was also a war of manners. Nineteen-year-old Louisiana resident Sarah Morgan called attention to this aspect of the conflict when she resolved that military conflict and Union occupation "shall not make me less the lady." Morgan was well aware that the war provoked many southern women to abandon their prewar standards of behavior, and she was resolved to adhere to the conventional definition of ladylike propriety. She decried women's political talk—"I hate to hear women on political subjects," she declared, as "they invariably make fools of themselves"—and refused to take part in the gatherings of women who met to discuss the war in her hometown of Baton Rouge. When news reached her of the rude behavior of "the so called *ladies* of New Orleans," who publicly insulted General "Beast" Butler's men when they occupied the town, Morgan criticized them for their "ugly" and "unladylike" behavior. "In my opinion," she reflected, "the Southern women . . . have disgraced themselves by their rude, ill mannered behavior. . . . 'Loud' women, what a contempt I have for you! How I despise your vulgarity!" Yet in her own efforts to show herself a lady—which took the form of conversing politely with a Union officer encountered on a train late in the conflict—Morgan worried that "in behaving like a lady I have forfeited my self-respect" as a southerner.[19]

Sarah Morgan's anxiety over whether to behave "like a lady" or to "glory" in her identity as "a rebel, body and soul"[20] neatly summed up young women's dilemma in the Confederate South: a lady was submissive; a rebel was, well, rebellious. The two identities could not be reconciled. As Ellen House recognized, "rebel ladies" were engaged in a war with themselves—a war that was just as critical for young southern women as the Civil War was for the Confederate nation. Ultimately, many southern girls and young women concluded that "self-respect" was more important than good manners. To defend southern nationalism, it proved necessary to abandon southern ladyhood. When young women did so, they shook the very foundations of the culture that they so desperately wished to defend.

The precise definition of southern ladyhood was as elusive as the ideal was difficult to achieve. Proslavery author George Fitzhugh described the perfect southern lady as "nervous, fickle, capricious, delicate, diffident and dependent."[21] Southern novelist Caroline Gilman recommended gentleness, submissiveness, and cheerfulness to her readers.[22] In their discussions of "what makes a true lady," southern girls and their parents offered a long list of ladylike attributes that included cleanliness, neatness, patience, industry, kindness, cheerfulness, modesty, politeness, respect for elders, and obedience.[23] Perhaps most important, however, were what we might call the three M's: a young lady was expected to be mild, meek, and modest—or, to put it another way, young women were supposed to abjure anger, accept hardship, and act behind the scenes. When young women in the Confederate South embraced an identity as southern rebels rather than as southern ladies, however, they rebelled against southern ladyhood as well as against the United States. Their fierce commitment to the Confederacy led them to replace mildness with rage, meekness with outrage, and modesty with outrageous behavior.

White southerners frequently used the words amiable, mild, soft, and gentle when describing the ideal woman.[24] Praising his student Mary Whitfield for her conduct, Salem, North Carolina schoolmaster John Jacobson commented on her "mild & amiable deportment."[25] In letters to her daughter Susan, a student at Mrs. Carrington's girls' school in Richmond, Virginia, Susanna McDowell prompted her twice in less than a month to be "gentle."[26] Rachel Mordecai's father typified prevailing sentiments when he wrote to his daughter: "I wish to see you an Amiable Woman, esteem'd by your acquaintants & belov'd by your Relatives & Friends for the Gentleness of your Manners."[27]

When parents and other adults urged southern girls to be mild, soft, and gentle, they were also telling them what *not* to be. Above all, a young woman who wished to be esteemed "for the Gentleness of [her] Manners" had to avoid anger. Parents and guardians repeatedly warned young women to subdue their tempers. "Avoid fretfulness & passion," Rachel Mordecai's father advised her. According to this North Carolina father, anger was absolutely unacceptable for women. Anger "in ev'ry person is unbecoming," he admitted, "but in a female [it] is truly disgusting."[28] But it was not simply "in a female" that anger was anathema; it was southern ladies—elite, white women—to whom southern society prohibited anger. South Carolinian Rose Ravenel learned the importance—and the significance—of governing her temper in an exchange with her black nursemaid, "Maum Katy." While washing up dishes, young Rose became annoyed when she broke some glasses. As Ravenel later wrote in her reminiscences, her servant assumed responsibility for instructing her in ladylike behavior:

> Maum Katy: "Miss Rose you ought not to get vexed"
> Rose: "Maum Katy dont you get vexed some times, every one gets vexed sometimes"
> Maum Katy: "Miss Rose I get vexed, it dont hurt no one no harm for me to get vexed [but] you are old Miss daughter, a lady ought not to get vexed."[29]

"A lady ought not to get vexed"—this was a message repeated over and over in southerners' correspondence. And if a young woman felt anger, she must never, ever display it. Southern girls were warned repeatedly to contain and conceal their feelings. North Carolina father James Ramsay sternly warned his daughter Margaret to repress her feelings, particularly strong, negative emotions that might cause others discomfort. A woman, he reminded her, should exert "self control, especially over her feelings, emotions, and temper." Most importantly, she should avoid "anger and vexation." "My dear child," he counseled, "you should never allow yourself to get angry . . . but if you should, you must strive not to show it, either in your looks words or actions."[30]

Young women took these lessons to heart. In a short essay on "The deportment principles and manners that constitute a lady," Virginia student Mary Jefferson Randolph used the phrase "soft and gentle" no less than three times in a single page.[31] The "Rules for This Summer" that thirteen-year-old Mississippian Anna Rosalie Quitman and her younger sisters established for themselves in 1852 also demonstrated girls' attempts to repress anger. While the rules included such practical matters as dressing oneself in the morning, feeding the family dog, keeping belongings in order, and going to bed by ten o'clock, the majority of rules focused on keeping the girls' personal desires and passionate tempers under wraps. These included injunctions to avoid quarreling, calling names, or saying "ugly words" as well as the order to "be obliging" and its closely allied reminder to avoid "getting in a passion."[32] In their private writings, as well, young women excoriated themselves for both feeling and displaying anger. Maryland student Alice Ready began a diary entry about her anger with a teacher who she believed had treated her unfairly by criticizing herself for her temper: "I have been a very bad girl," she wrote.[33]

The Civil War, however, prompted even the most proper young ladies to expressions of anger. "This war has brought out wicked, malignant feelings that I did not believe could dwell in woman's heart," Sarah Morgan remarked regretfully. "O woman! into what loathsome violence you have debased your holy mission! God will punish us for our hardheartedness," she predicted.[34] Morgan's comments indicated both the thoroughness with which young women had imbibed the lesson to avoid anger—what Morgan called "wicked, malignant feelings"—and the difficulty of adhering to such codes—especially in the midst of war. Young women in the Old South had also struggled to subdue their tempers. As North Carolinian Lizzie Kimberly mourned in the 1850s, "it is so hard . . . to be meek submitting and unmindful of self."[35] But whereas girls in the antebellum era had been more likely to repress their anger (and suffer from depression), young women in the Confederate South found at least a provisional cultural sanction for the expression of anger—at least so long as it was directed toward the South's declared enemies, and not toward the South's own culture.

During the Civil War, young women filled their diaries with expressions of unladylike rage. Tennessean Nannie Haskins, responding to the Battle of Fredericksburg in late 1862, was bursting with anger: "I feel as if I could fight myself," she wrote. "[I] never see [a Yankee] but what I roll my eyes, grit my teeth, and almost shake my fist at him, and then bite my lip involuntarily and turn away in disgust—God save us!"[36] Furious when her beloved plantation, Bel Air, was invaded by Union soldiers in May 1862, nineteen-year-old Virginian Lucy Buck pronounced herself "so weary and exhausted with rage that I could scarcely drag myself up to my room tonight." While her mother counseled restraint, Buck was unable to suppress her anger at the idea of having "a houseful of Yankees." "Ma tells me it is so wicked to allow my passions to get such an ascendancy over my better feelings," she worried, "but I cannot help it—it seems as if I am *possessed* of an evil spirit as well as *surrounded* by them."[37]

Clearly, these young women were not fully comfortable with their own anger—they bit their lips to hold back angry retorts and referred to strong, negative emotions as evil spirits, after all—but the fact that they admitted their feelings, even in the privacy of their own diaries, and that they refused to subdue or conceal their tempers suggests that young women in the Confederate South considered their anger at occupying troops a form of righteous rage. Thus, the Civil War provided these young women with an appropriate outlet for previously unacceptable anger.

Rage at occupying troops translated into outrage at Yankee depredations. Like young women's expressions of anger, their responses to invasion contradicted antebellum codes of ladylike conduct. According to antebellum authorities on southern gender norms, ladies exhibited patience in the face of hardship, calmly and quietly accepting difficulties and maintaining a cheerful facade no matter how trying the circumstances. As advice author Caroline Gilman explained, it was imperative for southern women to "smile amidst a thousand perplexities."[38]

Southern parents and other family members echoed these messages. Tennessean Ignatius Brock's advice to his younger sister, Orpah, was typical; he urged her to "be obliging and kind . . . and cultivate a spirit of forgiveness toward those whom you think do you wrong."[39] Young women took such recommendations to heart. Virginia schoolgirl Janet Henderson wrote a composition titled "A Perfect Woman" that praised this rare creature as "one of Gods noblest works." "A perfect woman," she explained, "must be amiable kind & affectionate." Devoting herself to promoting the happiness of those in her family circle, the perfect woman never had the bad grace to feel, much less to display, bad temper: "She does not fret herself about all the petty annoyances," Henderson explained, "but tries to look cheerful all the time."[40] Young women in the Old South, then, thoroughly imbibed the lesson that women were made "to suffer and be strong."[41]

During the Civil War, however, young women found it impossible—and even undesirable—to suffer in silence. Instead of patiently submitting to the hardships of war, they angrily demanded justice, even violent retribution. Sarah Morgan recognized this shift at the same time that she decried it. Convinced that women should display kindness under all circumstances, she was concerned by women's abandonment of "charity" for "Politics"— and by the bloodthirsty sentiments that many women expressed. "Let historians extol blood shedding," she wrote; "it is woman's place to abhor it." Yet Morgan knew that many women abhorred Yankees even more than they abhorred violence. "This is a dreadful war," she reflected in May 1862, "to make even the hearts of women so bitter! I hardly know myself these last few weeks. I, who have such a horror of bloodshed, consider even killing in self defense murder, who cannot wish them the slightest evil, whose only prayer is to have them sent back in peace to their own country, *I* talk of killing them!"[42]

Like Sarah Morgan, many young women in the Confederate South shocked themselves with the strength of their hatred for the enemy. Hatred quickly translated into violence, or at least the desire to do violence: Georgian Eliza Andrews, who witnessed the destruction of General Sherman's (in)famous "March to the Sea" first-hand, was not the only young woman to exclaim: "I almost felt as if I should like to hang a Yankee myself."[43] Andrews's comment was particularly problematic for this well-bred young lady in light of her own criticism of a southern soldier's "savage" behavior; the "coarse" soldier, who shared her carriage in 1864, had both amused and horrified Andrews with his tales of "losin'"—that is, summarily executing—Yankee prisoners in the woods.[44] Although she professed herself to be horrified at her traveling companion's casual violence, Andrews's antipathy for Yankees led her to adopt his uncouth and "savage" views, if not to imitate his actions.

Other young women displayed similar savagery. Virginian Lucy Buck, whose Bel Air plantation was overrun by Union soldiers, acidly remarked that she would not "object much" if one of the occupying Yankee soldiers were to break his neck.[45] South Carolinian Emma LeConte was more direct. When she heard a report that "a great many Yankees" had been wounded by exploding shells and an ensuing fire, the seventeen-year-old confided to her diary: "How I rejoice to think of any of them being killed. . . . If only the whole army could have been roasted alive!"[46]

Such bloodthirsty pronouncements were in sharp contrast to the meekness expected of southern girls before the Civil War, as Tennessean Alice Ready recognized. Since the war broke out, she remarked, she used "many harsh expressions." Not only Ready's expressions, but her sentiments, were indeed harsh. "There are a great many sick," she wrote of Union prisoners in 1862. "I rejoice to hear of their dying, because then our men will have fewer to kill." While Ready realized that her sentiments were "hard hearted, unwomanlike . . . even unChristian," she did not repent, instead writing: "O! how I wish I was a man."[47]

Young women's "hard hearted" attitude toward invading soldiers was in sharp contrast to the "gentle submission" that southern ladies were expected to display under all circumstances.[48] Rather than meekly accepting their situation as they were advised to do in the antebellum era, young women in the Confederate South angrily denounced their oppressors. While southern girls usually limited such expressions of outrage to their private writings, their sense of being wronged sometimes led them to engage in public protests. Such actions violated prescriptions of womanly modesty and turned enraged Confederate girls into outrageous "she rebels."

"Woman naturally shrinks from public gaze," wrote George Fitzhugh,[49] and most antebellum southerners concurred. Modesty—a term that connoted social invisibility as well as sexual innocence—was an indispensable requirement for young women in the Old South. Southerners frequently compared modesty to gold, jewels, and other forms of wealth; in value, this quality surpassed them all. As North Carolina student Kate Landing expressed it in a school composition, "modesty . . . is cultivated and considered as one among the precious jewels of true ladyhood."[50]

It was not enough for a woman simply to *be* modest, however; to be a lady, she had to be *known* as modest. In other words, she had to have a good reputation. As North Carolina father Cary Whitaker counseled his daughter Anna in 1831, "the best legacy a girl can have, is a pure and spotless reputation." To earn (and keep) the requisite reputation, young women had to avoid even the appearance of impropriety. "I wish you to be discreet in your conduct," Papa Whitaker reminded his daughter, "never act so, as to give the least room for censure."[51] A. M. Baker advised her daughters: "Conduct yourselfs [sic] in such a manner, as that the World may have nothing to say to your disadvantage."[52] Indeed, the world could be harsh in its judgments of female reputation: "One false, imprudent step will blast the reputation of a female forever," exclaimed Alabama resident Elizabeth Ruffin Cocke.[53] In general, then, southerners agreed with Virginia mother Elizabeth Noland's assessment in an 1846 letter to her daughter: "My dear little Ella, you cannot be too circumspect in your deportment."[54]

Being "circumspect" meant being quiet. North Carolinian John Steele congratulated his daughter Ann on her decision not to discuss politics, reminding her that "a lady" should not seek "to be distinguished."[55] Alabama father Richard Brumby urged his daughter Ann to be "unobtrusive" while in company. "I know this is not the way to attract attentions," he admitted, "but attentions gained by any violation of the rules of modesty, is a loss to her who gets it."[56] Marylander William Wirt reminded his daughters to avoid any *"ostentatious* display" in the strongest language, explaining that for "a young lady," any forward behavior was "revolting."[57]

During the Civil War, however, young women revolted against prescriptions of feminine modesty—at least where Union soldiers were concerned. Just as the Civil War offered a degree of license to young women to express anger, the presence of enemy troops gave them an excuse to act out their resistance. In their interactions with northern officers and soldiers, young women in the Confederate South routinely violated the rules of ladylike behavior.

In May 1861, Sarah Morgan marched with a group of other young women to the State House to wave the Confederate banner in front of the occupying Union troops. Afterward, Morgan was overcome with a sense of shame at her "conspicuous"—and immodest—appearance. "I—I am disgusted with myself," she wrote. Morgan's "unladylike display of defiance," and her shame at being involved in "such a display," she hoped, would "be a lesson . . . always to remember a lady can gain nothing by such displays." "Never again!" she vowed.[58]

Although Morgan expressed shame at her "unladylike display," other young women in the Confederate South engaged in similar actions—and not all of them shared Morgan's regret. When soldiers invaded her New Orleans home in 1865, Emma Holmes spent forty-five minutes giving the officers who stayed to watch her a severe tongue-lashing. "Oh how I enjoyed being able to relieve my bottled wrath and show the spirit which animates the Southern women," she rejoiced. Holmes attempted to convince herself that it was possible to reconcile patriotism with propriety; "I did not forget my character as a lady," she reassured herself. But the young woman knew that she had behaved immodestly; Holmes admitted to herself that the men she spoke to so insultingly might judge her "bold, conceited and impudent."[59]

Certainly the Union soldiers found Mississippian Victoria Batchelor "bold, conceited and impudent." Forced to apply repeatedly to the troops that occupied Vicksburg (and raided the Batchelor home) for aid in obtaining necessary supplies, Batchelor quickly earned a reputation for her "long tongue," which she employed with striking effect during each of her encounters with Union soldiers. Indeed, "Miss Vic" attained fame—or infamy—when a Union commander published an article in "a Yankee paper" about this "stubborn traitor." "Vic is 18, and by no means pretty," the disgruntled officer wrote, "but her people think so, and are happy in her accomplishments. She can sing and play and do worsted work and use her tongue very glibly; and she is peculiar in the employment of sarcasm and [a] thorough enumerator of hate." Victoria Batchelor let no opportunity slip to "openly denounce and abuse" the occupying forces, the author explained; she invited the soldiers into the family parlor only to sing them Confederate anthems, predicted their ultimate defeat, and laughed in their faces when she drew her rations. Indeed, the Mississippi teenager was "a fair specimen of a she rebel," the author wryly concluded. Far from feeling shame at her conspicuous behavior, the young "she rebel" received affirmation for it; "her people gazed at her with the utmost admiration," commented the astonished officer, "laughing heartily at her every denunciation of Yankees."[60] When a young woman received "admiration" and applause instead of criticism and ostracism for patently rude behavior, it became clear that the Civil War had ushered in significant modifications in the definition of southern ladyhood.

In his study of children in the Civil War era, James Marten writes that "living in a war zone . . . seemed to free children . . . from prewar restraints on their behavior and limits on their imaginations."[61] Although Marten suggests that this was most true for boys—and northern ones at that—southern girls also experienced this expansion of horizons. Southern girls' unwavering support for the Confederate cause often led them to abandon their efforts to behave as southern ladies. Indeed, in many instances, young women's fierce desire to protect the Confederacy provoked—or perhaps simply sanctioned—a wish to cast aside the limitations of gender entirely.

Many young women in the Confederate South echoed Louisianan Sarah Wadley's complaint that "my spirit often makes me chafe at the regulations . . . a woman should submit to."[62] A startling number of young women, weary of the strictures of ladyhood, expressed a desire to become men.[63] "I never before wished I was a man," Tennessean Alice Ready reflected in 1862, but "now I feel so keenly my weakness. and dependence. I cannot do or say anything—for 'it would be unbecoming in a young lady'—How I should love to fight and even die for my Country—our glorious beautiful South—what a privilege I should esteem it, but am denied it because I am a woman."[64]

Despite—or perhaps because of—her difficulty in reconciling her political loyalties with her sense of propriety, Sarah Morgan was particularly fervent in her desire to escape the strictures of southern ladyhood by adopting a male persona. Morgan's reflections on the gender wars that accompanied the

Civil War shed light both on the continuing power of conventional definitions of southern femininity and on the increasingly tenuous status of the
myth of the southern lady in the Confederate South.

Even as she deplored southern women's—and her own—"unladylike"
thoughts and actions and attempted to uphold antebellum ideals of femininity, Morgan lamented the fact of her womanhood, repeatedly express-
ing her desire to be a man so that she could fight—and even die—for the
Confederacy.[65] Fascinated by weapons and by her brother's gray uniform,
Morgan used her diary to express her dissatisfaction with her passive role
in the war and her desire to free herself of the restrictions of feminine propriety. As a woman, she explained, she would have to "repent for ever after
in sack cloth and ashes" if she harmed anybody, even an invading and "in-
solent" Union soldier. But if she were a man, she speculated, the situation
would be very different. "O if I was only a man!" she cried. "Then I could
don the breeches, and slay them with a will!"[66]

Over and over, Morgan expressed her regret at her limitations as a woman.
Denied even the option of nursing ailing soldiers, Morgan declared herself "a chained bear." Rather than being the "coward, helpless woman that
I am," she wished to be "free"—and the freedom and "independence" that
she longed for, Morgan associated with men.[67] "We worthless women," she
believed, were "of no value or importance to ourselves or the rest of the
world."[68] "What is the use of all these worthless women, in war times?"
she demanded. "Why was I not a man?"[69] Morgan knew that her sentiments
were shared by many others. "If I was only a man!" she repeated her old war
cry. "I dont know a woman here who does not groan over her misfortune in
being clothed in petticoats," she added.[70]

Ultimately, even as she struggled to uphold feminine propriety, Morgan
concluded that the traits traditionally associated with southern femininity
were not always desirable. Submissiveness—the *sine qua non* of the southern
lady—became anathema to loyal Confederates who described the Civil War
as a war for southern self-determination. Morgan recognized the dissonance
between her old identity as a southern lady and her new one as a southern
rebel when she proclaimed: "Bondage, woman that I am, I can never stand!"[71]
Small wonder, then, that she imagined being able to cast aside the bonds of
womanhood. "Pshaw!" she exclaimed in May 1862. "There are *no* women
here! We are *all* men!"[72]

Morgan could not literally become a man—indeed, she could not even bring herself to try on her brother's breeches—but she and other young "she-rebels" did substantially modify and challenge conventional gender roles during the Civil War.[73] According to that antebellum authority on ideal femininity, George Fitzhugh, women gained men's love, affection, and protection by being "weak, helpless, and dependent"; any woman who became "masculine or rebellious" forfeited her claim to protection.[74] Yet in wartime, many southern girls rebelled not only against the Union, but also against this definition of ideal womanhood. To borrow Fitzhugh's terminology, as southern girls became "rebellious," they also became "masculine"—or, at least, markedly less ladylike.

The experiences and observations of young Confederate women revealed a fundamental flaw in southern society. Although young women in the Old South also struggled to adhere to the demanding role of the southern lady, it was commitment to southern independence that prompted—and permitted—young women to act contrary to the dictates of southern ladyhood—and, ultimately, to criticize the entire concept of southern ladyhood. Ironically, in their efforts to preserve what sixteen-year-old Tennessean Sally Broyles, in the last days of the war, called "our Sunny South,"[75] these southern-ladies-turned-she-rebels chipped away at a vital foundation of the defense of slavery: the myth of the southern lady.

Notes

1. Daniel E. Sutherland, ed., *A Very Violent Rebel: The Civil War Diary of Ellen Renshaw House* (Knoxville, TN: University of Tennessee Press, 1996), 4, 5, 13, 25, 113.

2. Ibid., 43, 108, 113. See also pp. 117, 119.

3. Ibid., 85, 90, 113, 118, 123.

4. Ibid., 127–28 (quotation).

5. Ibid., 38.

6. Ibid., 123.

7. Kent Anderson Leslie, "A Myth of the Southern Lady: Antebellum Proslavery Rhetoric and the Proper Place of Woman," *Sociological Spectrum*, vol. 6 (1986), 31–49; and Anne Firor Scott, *The Southern Lady: From Pedestal to Politics, 1830–1930* (Chicago and London: University of Chicago, 1970), 16–21. On the peculiar position of white southern women in the South's social hierarchy, see

Drew Gilpin Faust, *Mothers of Invention: Women of the Slaveholding South in the American Civil War* (Chapel Hill and London: University of North Carolina Press, 1996), Introduction.

8. Although Faust's *Mothers of Invention* uses many of the same sources utilized here, she does not distinguish between young women and mature women. The importance of age is central to my work-in-progress, a study of young women in the nineteenth-century South. Also on young women in the Confederate South, see Giselle Roberts, *The Confederate Belle* (Columbia and London: University of Missouri Press, 2003).

9. Leslie, "Myth of the Southern Lady."

10. Michael O'Brien, *Conjectures of Order: Intellectual Life and the American South, 1810–1860, 2 vols.* (Chapel Hill and London: University of North Carolina Press, 2004), II, 948. See also Dorothy Ann Gay, "The Tangled Skein of Romanticism and Violence in the Old South: The Southern Response to Abolitionism and Feminism, 1830–1861" (Ph.D. dissertation, University of North Carolina, 1975).

11. Scott, *Southern Lady*, 14–17.

12. Ibid., 17.

13. Ibid.

14. O'Brien, *Conjectures of Order*, 972, 974, 977.

15. Barbara Welter, "The Cult of True Womanhood, 1820–1860," *American Quarterly* XVII (Summer 1966), 151–74; Scott, *Southern Lady*, 17. The centrality of submissiveness to northern women's ideals of femininity has been challenged recently in Laura McCall, "The Reign of Brute Force Is Now Over': A Content Analysis of Godey's Lady's Book, 1830–1860," *Journal of the Early Republic*, IX (Summer 1989), 217–36.

16. Scott, *Southern Lady*, 8–9.

17. Mary Jefferson Randolph Commonplace Book, 1826, Virginia Historical Society, Richmond, Va.

18. Sally Lucas to William Lucas, May 22, 1850, Lucas Family Papers, VHS.

19. Charles East, ed., *Sarah Morgan: The Civil War Diary of a Southern Woman* (Athens, GA: University of Georgia Press, 1991), 73–74, 76, 122, 609.

20. East, ed., *Sarah Morgan*, xxiii. See also 611.

21. Scott, *Southern Lady*, 17.

22. Ibid., 8–9.

23. For quotation, see Ann Steele to John Steele, February 11, 1801, John Steele Papers, Southern Historical Collection, University of North Carolina, Chapel Hill, NC. For examples of discussions of ladylike behavior, see Richard Trapier

Brumby to Ann Eliza Brumby, April 3, 1858, Ann Eliza Brumby Paper, SHC; Mary
Jefferson Randolph Commonplace Book, VHS; Judith McGuire to Mary Anna
McGuire, August 22, n.d., Claiborne Family Papers, VHS; Kate Landing, "What
Makes a True Lady," May 7, 1872, Thomas M. Smith Papers, SHC; Janet Hender-
son Randolph, "A Perfect Woman," April 11, 1862, Randolph Family Papers, VHS;
Father to Rachel Mordecai, July 3, 1798, and Father to Rachel and Ellen Morde-
cai, March 18, 1799, Mordecai Family Papers, SHC; William Polk to Mary Polk,
March 18, 1822, and Leonidas Polk to Mary Polk, January 12, 1823, Polk, Badger,
and McGehee Family Papers, SHC; Cary Whitaker to Anna Whitaker, August 1,
1831, William Henry Wills Papers, SHC.

24. See for example J. Price to Isabella Price, May 29, 1853, Charles B. Simrall
Papers, SHC.

25. John Jacobson to Mr. Bryan, January 3, 1840, Whitfield Family Papers,
Special Collections, Auburn University Libraries, Auburn, AL.

26. Susanna McDowell to Susan McDowell, January 2, n.d., and n.d., McDowell Family Papers, VHS.

27. Father to Rachel Mordecai, July 3, 1798, Mordecai Family Papers, SHC.

28. Father to Rachel Mordecai, July 3, 1798, Mordecai Family Papers, SHC.
See also Mary R. Kenan to Mary Kenan, September 2, 1839, Kenan Family Papers,
SHC.

29. Rose P. Ravenel Reminiscences, South Carolina Historical Society, Charleston, SC.

30. James Ramsay to Margaret Ramsay, February 13, 1865, James Graham Ramsay Papers, SHC.

31. Mary Jefferson Randolph Commonplace Book, 1826, VHS.

32. "Our Rules for This Summer," [1852], Anna Rosalie Quitman Journal,
Quitman Family Papers, Records of Ante-Bellum Southern Plantations: From the
Revolution Through the Civil War. Series J: Selections from the Southern His-
torical Collection. Part 6: Mississippi and Arkansas.

33. Alice C. Ready Diary, May 21, 1861, SHC.

34. East, ed., *Sarah Morgan*, 65, 122–23, 607.

35. Emma Kimberly to John Kimberly, [April] 10, 1858]; Lizzie Kimberly to
John Kimberly, November 20, 1858, John Kimberly Papers, SHC.

36. Betsy Swint Underwood, "War Seen Through a Teen-ager's Eyes," *Tennessee Historical Quarterly* XX (June 1961), 181.

37. Elizabeth R. Baer, ed., *Shadows on My Heart: The Civil War Diary of Lucy
Rebecca Buck of Virginia* (Athens, GA, and London: University of Georgia Press,
1997), 62, 77, 109. See also p. 70.

38. Scott, *Southern Lady*, 9.

39. Ignatius Brock to Orpah Brock, April 6, 1861, Ignatius W. Brock Papers, Duke.

40. Janet Henderson Randolph, "A Perfect Woman," April 11, 1862, Randolph Family Papers, VHS.

41. Scott, *Southern Lady*, 9.

42. East, ed., *Sarah Morgan*, 65, 122–23, 607.

43. Eliza Frances Andrews, *War-Time Journal of a Georgia Girl, 1864–1865*, edited by Spencer Bidwell King Jr. (1908; rpt. Macon, GA: Ardivan Press, 1960), 32. Andrews was twenty-four years old at the time.

44. Andrews, *War-Time Journal*, 29, 30, 37.

45. Baer, ed., *Shadows on My Heart*, 62, 77, 109. See also p. 70.

46. Miers, ed., *When the World Ended*, 55.

47. C. Alice Ready Diary, April 8, 19, 1862, SHC. This was a common theme in women's Civil War writings. Drew Faust writes: "Nearly every female Confederate diarist at some point expressed the desire to be a man." See *Mothers of Invention*, 231.

48. Scott, *Southern Lady*, 8.

49. Ibid., 16.

50. Kate Landing, "What Makes a True Lady," May 7, 1872, Thomas M. Smith Papers, Special Collections Library, Duke University, Durham, NC.

51. Cary Whitaker to Anna Whitaker, August 1, 1831, William Henry Wills Papers, SHC.

52. A. M. Baker to Daughters, n.d., William Henry Wills Papers, SHC.

53. Elizabeth Ruffin Cocke to Tariffa Cocke, January 24, [1848?], Henry Harrison Cocke Papers, SHC.

54. Elizabeth Noland to Ella Noland, December 25, 1846, Ella Noland MacKenzie Papers, SHC.

55. John Steel to Ann Steele, December 27, 1800, John Steele Papers, SHC.

56. Richard Trapier Brumby to Ann Eliza Brumby, April 3, 1858, Ann Eliza Brumby Paper, SHC.

57. Wiliam Wirt to Laura, Catharine, and Elizabeth G. Wirt, May 23, 1829, William Wirt Papers, Maryland Historical Society, Baltimore, MD.

58. East, ed., *Civil War Diary of Sarah Morgan*, 51, 68–69.

59. John F. Marszalek, ed., *The Diary of Miss Emma Holmes, 1861–1866* (Baton Rouge and London: Louisiana State University Press, 1979, 1994), 402, 407.

60. Gordon A. Cotton, ed., *From the Pen of a She-Rebel: The Civil War Diary*

of Emilie Riley McKinley (Columbia: University of South Carolina Press, 2001), 30, 61.

61. James Marten, *The Children's Civil War* (Chapel Hill and London: University of North Carolina Press, 1998), 103.

62. Sarah Wadley Diary, April 21, 1861, SHC.

63. See for instance East, ed., *Sarah Morgan*, 65, 77, 166, 410–11, 491, 504; Elizabeth Collier Diary, August 26, 1861; April 11, June 28, 1862, July 31, 1864; April 25 and July 9, 1865, SHC; C. Alice Ready Diary, April 19, 1862, SHC; Sarah Wadley Diary, September 29, 1861, SHC.

64. C. Alice Ready Diary, March 31, April 15, 1862, SHC.

65. In addition to the examples that follow, see East, ed., *Sarah Morgan*, pp. 410–11, 491, and 504.

66. Ibid., 65.

67. Ibid., 123–24.

68. Ibid., 77.

69. Ibid., 166.

70. Ibid., 77.

71. Ibid., 141.

72. Ibid., 65.

73. She turned aside at the last moment for fear of being seen—by her pet canary. See Ibid., 167.

74. Quoted in Leslie, "Myth of the Southern Lady," 42.

75. Sally E. Broyles Diary, May 1, 1865, William Johnston Cocke Papers, Duke.

The Etiquette of Race Relations in the Jim Crow South

Jennifer Ritterhouse

In July 1939, an African American domestic servant named Eloise Blake was fined fifteen dollars by the recorder's court of Columbia, South Carolina. Her crime was "disorderly conduct over the telephone." As the Associated Negro Press reported, Blake had asked to speak to "Mrs. Pauline Clay," rather than simply "Pauline," when she called the white home where her friend Pauline Clay worked as a servant. Clay's employer, a white woman named Hadden, was so incensed by Blake's impudence that she called the police and filed charges. Blake hired a lawyer, and William Pickens, the Director of Branches for the National Association for the Advancement of Colored People (NAACP), also picked up on the case, but ultimately nothing ever came of it—except that Eloise Blake was out fifteen dollars, perhaps three weeks' wages for a black southern domestic worker in 1939.[1]

Eloise Blake's case is surprising only because it went to court. Historians have long recognized that unwritten rules of racial "etiquette," such as the one that reserved the titles "Mr." and "Mrs." for white men and women, were the chief form of everyday social control in the segregated South. Blacks and whites alike knew what was expected of them as they interacted across the color line and, for the most part, they lived by those expectations—whites primarily because to do so reinforced their own sense of superiority and blacks because whites would punish them if they did not. As important as this method of social control was, historians have barely scratched the surface of what racial etiquette can tell us about the South's racial culture, about the cultural significance of segregation, and about continuity and change. Looking broadly at the period from emancipation to World War II, we see a persistence in racial etiquette that indicates not only *that* white southerners tried to enforce continuity in race relations but also *how* and *where* (in white households, on farms, in towns and cities), as well as where they were successful and where they were not. Understanding the how and where of racial power relations is key to understanding that segregation was only part of white southerners' broader effort to maintain dominance and that whites expanded the Jim Crow system after 1890 largely because they were *unable*, especially in cities, to command blacks' deference through other more traditional means (although they still tried, expecting blacks to be polite rather than surly, for example, as they made their way to the back of the bus). Blacks always had minds of their own—the double consciousness that W. E. B. Du Bois wrote about and that Jane Dailey emphasizes in her comments at the end of this volume[2]—and they challenged white dominance when and where they felt they could, a calculation that varied for individuals as well as according to individual circumstances. For much of the twentieth century, however, and in much of the South—especially in rural areas and small towns and, significantly, in the white households, both rural and urban, where black women and men worked in close proximity to their white employers and where white children learned their earliest lessons about race—older patterns of domination and deference prevailed. Only by exploring the relationships between urban and rural, public and private, segregation and racial etiquette can we map change and continuity in the South with precision.

The outlines of racial etiquette are already fairly clear. Analyzing dozens of little incidents like Blake's run-in with Hadden as well as the observations of autobiographers, travelers, and other contemporaries, historians such as Leon Litwack, Neil McMillen, and David Goldfield have detailed the social code that governed day-to-day encounters between black and white southerners.[3] Whites did not call blacks "Mr.," "Mrs.," "Miss," "Ma'am," or "Sir," but insisted that blacks use these honorifics for white adults, and even adolescents, at all times. If a white southerner did not know the first name of the black person he was addressing—or even if he did—he used "boy" or "girl" or the somewhat more respectful (from the white point of view) "uncle" or "aunt." "Doctor" and even "professor" were also acceptable terms for blacks whose positions seemed to warrant greater respect—unless they got "uppity" and then they too were "boy" or, even more bluntly, "nigger." White men did not tip their hats to blacks, including black women, but black men were expected to remove their hats in whites' presence, and they also had to be very careful about where they rested their eyes. Making eye contact or looking too long or with too much interest at a white woman could get a black man in trouble, and black women, too, were expected to *show* their deference to whites through a bodily performance of humility that included not dressing too well or taking up too much space. Black men and women were to enter white homes by the back door, like servants, and those who were servants could expect to eat their meals by themselves in the whites' kitchen or on the back porch, never in the dining room or with any but the youngest members of the white family—since relaxing the otherwise hard and fast rule against blacks and whites eating together was convenient for white southerners who relied on blacks to take care of their children. In less intimate spaces like sidewalks and stores, blacks were supposed to get out of whites' way, a rule that was so ingrained in whites' minds in the early twentieth century that some southern cities even banned black motorists from the public streets.

"All told, this was a social code of forbidding complexity," McMillen concludes. Individual whites' expectations varied, as did local customs, yet blacks who failed to meet those expectations and abide by those customs faced punishments ranging from verbal and physical abuse to arrest and imprisonment to lynching. Even so, racial etiquette embodied a certain unjust logic. As McMillen explains, "If violence was the 'instrument in reserve'— the ultimate deterrent normally used only against the most recalcitrant— social ritual regulated day-to-day race relations." Racial etiquette "assured white control without the need for more extreme forms of coercion."[4]

Historians' tendency to call this pattern of behaviors the "etiquette" of race relations seems to stem from early social scientists' use of the word, most notably in Bertram Wilbur Doyle's oft-cited 1937 book *The Etiquette of Race Relations in the South*. Doyle described customary forms of deference and paternalism between slaves and masters and traced the continued observance of those customs, with some changes, up to his own day. "Separation of the races is relatively more prominent" in the twentieth century, he noted, but all in all, relations had "changed so gradually that only here and there are differences made obvious."[5] Doyle attributed much of this continuity to a black preference for clear-cut, if unjust, social relations—a part of his argument that historians have not tended to embrace and that seems all the more difficult to account for considering that Doyle was himself a black southerner, born in Lowndesboro, Alabama, in 1897.[6] But he was also a student of pioneering sociologist Robert E. Park at the University of Chicago and was undoubtedly influenced by Park in accepting British philosopher Herbert Spencer's definition of etiquette as the "earliest kind of government, the most general kind of government and the government which is ever spontaneously recommencing." "This kind of government," argued Spencer, "besides preceding all other kinds, and besides having in all places and times approached nearer to universality of influence, has ever had, and continues to have, the largest share in regulating men's lives."[7] No wonder, then, that Doyle subtitled his book *A Study in Social Control*.

Although historians have shared Doyle's understanding of racial etiquette as a truly fundamental form of social control, their analyses have rarely said much more than that, with only a couple of important exceptions.[8] This is unfortunate because one of the great advantages of approaching the past through an examination of everyday interactions and the etiquette that governed them is that it allows us to see the activities of people who are usually marginal in other kinds of studies. This includes not only African Americans, but also white women and children. Indeed, black and white southerners' autobiographical accounts of how they learned racial etiquette in childhood are among the best sources documenting both racial etiquette's content and its function. Meanwhile, as Hadden's behavior illustrates, the enforcement and perpetuation of racial etiquette was one of white women's chief forms of collusion in the Jim Crow system. Unlike the legal and political dramas of segregation and disfranchisement, which were enacted primarily by white men, the daily dramas of racial etiquette involved men, women, and children equally. Hadden could not sit on a jury in South Carolina in 1939, but she could persuade the police and the courts to punish Eloise Blake for her insolence.[9] Or she could have done it herself, scolding Blake or trying to get her fired, which would have been much more typical responses on the part of a white southern woman and which she may well have done. Unable to find out anything more about this case, I have often wondered why she felt it necessary to call the police.

The fact that racial etiquette provided a script for all members of southern society—black and white, young and old, male and female—is just as important as the violence that made it perilous for blacks and, to some extent, whites to depart from that script by very much. In short, we need to recognize that racial etiquette was not merely regulatory, but formative. That is, it did not simply reflect the culture, but helped to *make* it. This insight, which I first encountered in white Virginian Sarah Patton Boyle's autobiography, *The Desegregated Heart*, and which I read with considerable skepticism *because* it came from a white source, is, to my current way of thinking, a highly valuable one, but only if handled with care. Blacks did not have to buy into racial etiquette to find their lives, and to some extent their minds, shaped by it. This was, at least in part, why their consciousness was double: "a peculiar sensation, this double-consciousness, this sense of always looking at one's self through the eyes of others, of measuring one's soul by the tape of a world that looks on in amused contempt and pity."[10] Meanwhile—and ironically, as Dailey emphasizes in her comments—internalizing racial etiquette allowed many whites to convince themselves that theirs was an honorable society and that blacks *did* believe in a natural racial hierarchy, despite overwhelming evidence of black resistance. Recognizing the power of racial etiquette to shape individuals' sense of the world and their place in it—to paraphrase one of John F. Kasson's observations below—ought not to obscure the coercion and violence at the heart of southern society. It ought not to make us lose sight of the material and governmental and other many facets of *racism*, a word that historians must not let slip from our vocabulary, as Barbara J. Fields has recently reminded.[11] On the contrary, we need to foreground the fact that etiquette and segregation and violence, both individual and state-sponsored, were all part of the same system of oppression, the system that had created southern notions of race in the first place and continued to recreate them on a daily basis. As J. William Harris argues in one of the most sophisticated discussions of racial etiquette to date, "It was not the presence of two races in the South that created a boundary between them, but the presence of a boundary that created two races. Like the levees that held back the Mississippi River, that boundary had to be constructed, but the materials at hand were symbolic, not physical." This was all the more true in the late nineteenth century, when "the Civil War and Reconstruction had wiped out the legal and even much of the economic basis for racial subordination." As white southerners reimposed their dominance over blacks, they found it imperative to draw the color line in new ways, strengthening taboos against interracial sex, intimidating and ultimately disfranchising black voters, and expanding and eventually codifying existing patterns of exclusion into the system of segregation. "Racial subordination also was continually recreated in the routine actions of the everyday world," adds Harris. "In that world, racial etiquette and violence served to mark a new color line."[12]

As much as I admire Harris's article, especially for its efforts to grapple with what it really *means* when we say that race is "socially constructed," I think this idea of a "new color line" requires further examination. Based, as

Bertram Wilbur Doyle tells us, on the performance of deference required of slaves, post-emancipation racial etiquette seems to me to have a lot more to do with continuity than with change. In fact, racial etiquette seems to defy change; David Goldfield not only describes the racial etiquette of the 1930s and 1940s in much the same terms other historians have used for the 1880s and the 1910s, but also suggests that a "subtle, unofficial residue" continued to operate in the late 1960s and beyond.[13] Nevertheless, I am convinced that analyzing racial etiquette can help us connect a timeline to the color line that black and white southerners were constantly renegotiating from their respective positions of unequal socioeconomic and cultural power. Detailing change over time within the South's racial culture is important because, as Glenda Gilmore has observed, "Even though history without chronology may be about the past—even though it may tell us *how* people did the things they did—without chronology it cannot tell us *why* they did the things they did. . . . Without change over time, we might have anthropology, or sociology, or political science, or literary criticism, or post-modern cultural analysis, but we do not have history."[14]

As a historian whose favorite questions almost always begin with "how," I find Gilmore's words chastening. Even continuity unfolds, and even if racial etiquette remained remarkably consistent, as well as persistent, over many decades, no one would mistake the South of 1940 for the South of 1880 (leaving aside Goldfield's observations about the workings of racial etiquette in an even later period). So what can a study of racial etiquette—supposedly fundamental and, I argue, formative—tell us about the changing nature of southern culture? Simply put, by emphasizing the *how* and the *where*, it can help us understand what Gilmore defines as the historian's chief concerns: the when and the why.

Jane Dailey's excellent article on the Danville massacre is a good starting point. In "Deference and Violence in the Postbellum Urban South," Dailey recounts the story of an 1883 dispute in Danville, a booming industrial town in southern Virginia, that began with a black man bumping into a white man on the sidewalk but quickly "escalated into a massacre when a white mob shot into a crowd of unarmed black men, women, and children." Five men—four black and one white—died, and gangs of white men patrolled Danville's streets for the rest of that Saturday evening and night, terrorizing the black population. In statewide elections held just three days later, the Democratic Party recaptured the state from the Readjusters, a biracial third party that had dominated state politics for the previous four years. "But the importance of the Danville Riot lies less in its effect on the 1883 election than in the stories told about it," Dailey argues. Claiming that the black crowd had been armed and aggressive and that the white men had fired in self-defense, white Democrats in Danville and beyond added the Danville massacre to a litany of complaints about black behavior in public that whites would have to do something about. Shortly after the massacre, the Danville city council proposed one possible solution: a new city ordinance that would levy a fine against anyone, black or white, who failed to yield to the pedestrian on his or her right when walking on the sidewalk. But this ordinance "was diametrically opposed to the hierarchical predispositions of Danville's white residents," Dailey explains, "and the proposal was rejected by the Committee on Public Ordinances as unenforceable." Undoubtedly, the members of this committee recognized how few white southerners would be willing to give up this important point of racial etiquette, and they also hoped that no change would be necessary. Whether or not they were consciously evaluating the effects of the violence in intimidating Danville's black population, the committee felt confident " 'that in future the general rules of common politeness will be observed and that we will not need such an ordinance.' "[15]

Indeed, white southerners had been making blacks observe "the general rules of common politeness"—a.k.a. racial etiquette—in precisely this way ever since freedom. When northern journalist Whitelaw Reid toured the South in 1865 and 1866, he found many white southerners ready to kill black men and women who violated the code that had governed interracial encounters during slavery. A conversation Reid had with a member of the Mississippi state legislature in 1865 is telling. "A nigger's just as good as a white man now," the legislator observed argumentatively in the midst of a crowded barroom, "but I give my Sam t'other day to understand that he wasn't a d—d bit better." The trouble had started when Sam came into the white man's room without removing his hat. " 'Take off your hat, you dirty black scoundrel, or I'll cut your throat,' " the legislator had shouted. "D—n him, he had the impudence to stand up and say he was free, and he wouldn't do it unless he pleased. I jumped at him with my knife, but he run. Bimeby, he came sneakin' back, and said he was sorry. 'Sam,' says I, 'you've got just the same rights as a white man now, but not a bit better. And if you come into my room without takin' off your hat I'll shoot you.' " It seems obvious that the legislator would not have threatened a white man who simply failed to take off his hat, despite his supposed acceptance of the idea that African

Americans were "just as good" and had "just the same rights." His talk of equality, perhaps emphasized for the sake of the northern observer, could not disguise his unshakeable commitment to maintaining racial etiquette. "This Bowie-knife and pistol style of talk pervaded all the conversations of these people about their late affectionate bondsmen," Reid remarked. "Nothing less gunpowdery, it seemed, would serve to express their feelings."[16]

Making blacks adhere to racial etiquette in public was all the more urgent, since white southerners, especially men, had long measured their personal honor in terms of how much respect they were accorded by the people around them.[17] Black novelist William Wells Brown told two stories in his autobiography, *My Southern Home*, that illustrate how whites enforced racial etiquette on city streets. Standing in front of a landmark building in Knoxville, Tennessee, one day in 1880, Brown saw a "good-looking, well-dressed colored man" approach a white man "in a business-like manner" and start talking to him. Before the black man had finished a sentence, the white man "raised his walking stick, and with much force, knocked off the black man's hat, and with an oath said, 'Don't you know better than to speak to a white man with your hat on, where's your manners?'" Although he must certainly have been angry, the black man merely "picked up his hat, held it in his hand, and resumed the conversation." Upon inquiry, Wells learned that the white man was a real estate agent and the black man was the "Hon. Mr. —, ex-member of the General Assembly."[18] Clearly, Mr. — knew that he had to control himself to prevent further violence, but his ability to do so still seems remarkable.

An incident in Huntingdon, Tennessee played out somewhat differently but had just as much to do with white conceptions of honor, specifically the requirement that honorable white men defend their wives and other dependents. In this case, the wife of John Warren, whom Brown described as a "two-fisted, coarse, rough, uncouth ex-slaveholder," was accidentally bumped by a young black schoolteacher named Florence Hayes. Although Miss Hayes apologized profusely, Mrs. Warren was unsatisfied and John Warren took it upon himself to go to Hayes's home, where he beat her senseless. Hayes was so badly injured that she had to return to her parents' home in Nashville to recuperate for several weeks. Meanwhile, the white Huntingdon *Vindicator* described Warren as a "gentleman" and advised "white men everywhere to *stand up for their rights*" as he had.[19]

Incidents like the ones Reid and Brown describe took place every day in the post-emancipation South as white southerners attempted to regain control over a black population that was adapting to life after slavery—whether assertively, as in the case of Sam, who refused to take off his hat; passive-aggressively, like the ex-legislator who seemingly "forgot" to take off his hat; or non-confrontationally, like Florence Hayes, who really did bump into Mrs. Warren by accident (although her very *existence* as an educated, middle-class African American was an affront to many white southerners' sensibilities). The dispute that sparked the Danville massacre was equally commonplace and might not have amounted to much except for the fact that, as Dailey explains, "tempers were running high that Saturday" in anticipation of the upcoming election that would result in the Readjusters' downfall. Most street-level conflicts over racial etiquette ended with either a black person's apology or an individual white person's aggression, but a few erupted in communal acts of violence. Often, the difference lay in how much political influence blacks had at a given moment and thus in how calculated whites perceived black "insolence" to be. For, as Dailey concludes, "The point here is not that black and white southerners could not understand each other because they spoke different social languages, but just the opposite. . . . It was the convergence of black and white opinion on markers of status and face in the postwar urban South that turned public behavior into a zero-sum game where one person's gain was another's clear loss."[20]

The interesting thing about Danville, as far as questions of continuity and change are concerned, is that some whites were clearly starting to feel a need to change the rules of the game. The proposed ordinance to make all pedestrians yield to the right was not workable, either logistically or culturally, from white southerners' point of view. Instead of this colorblind alternative, whites would move to mark the color *line* more clearly in public space. Now, some kinds of space are easier to regulate than others, and sidewalks would continue to be a contested terrain long after segregation became formalized. In Danville, for example, white complaints about black children taking up the whole sidewalk on their way to and from school would lead the police to implement a new rule in 1915 limiting black children's use of the sidewalk when white children were coming or going the other way.[21]

The comparison between 1883 and 1915 is illuminating because, by 1915, attempting to resolve day-to-day conflicts through segregation was routine for white southerners, whereas a few decades earlier, it had been a *necessary new approach*. Culturally, segregation is best understood as a fall-back position for white southerners, indicating that their efforts to command respect from African Americans were not working or were costing too much in the way of disorder and violence. Unable to move through space in a clear vertical hierarchy of whites on top and blacks on bottom, white southerners had to divide space horizontally, albeit unequally, both to minimize conflict and to define blacks' "place" in a new way.

The newness of segregation has, of course, been a subject of much scholarly debate ever since the publication of C. Vann Woodward's *The Strange Career of Jim Crow* in 1955. Noting the relative absence of segregation laws prior to 1890 and citing evidence of blacks using various public facilities on a non-segregated basis in the 1870s and 1880s, Woodward argued, in what became known as the Woodward thesis, "first, that racial segregation in the South in the rigid and universal form it had taken by 1954 did not appear with the end of slavery, but toward the end of the century and later; and second, that before it appeared in this form there occurred an era of experiment and variety in race relations of the South in which segregation was not the invariable rule."[22] Almost immediately, new scholarship emerged that challenged this contention, including books by Leon Litwack, Richard C. Wade, and Joel Williamson that found segregation, including legal segregation, in the antebellum North, in the cities of the antebellum South, and in Reconstruction-era South Carolina, respectively.[23] Even more challenging, Howard Rabinowitz not only found considerable segregation in southern cities prior to 1890, but also determined that segregation often replaced *exclusion*, making it somewhat of an improvement for blacks.[24] John Cell's comparative study of the origins of segregation in the South and apartheid in South Africa extended Rabinowitz's argument to conclude that segregation, while certainly in place earlier than Woodward had claimed, was primarily an urban and modern phenomenon.[25]

Despite these challenges, the Woodward thesis has maintained considerable appeal among southern historians, an appeal I attribute not only to a boxer-like elusiveness on Woodward's part, but also to a sense that Woodward was really talking about *culture* in an era before cultural history.[26] The litmus test for Woodward was not what was most common, but what was *conceivable*. Writing about instances of interracial fellowship during Reconstruction, Woodward insisted: "It is not that such occurrences were typical or very common, but that they could happen at all that was important." And again: "It is impossible to conceive of innumerable events and interracial experiments and contacts of the 1860's taking place in the 1900's." Woodward's point about the variety and experimentation of the 1870s and 1880s is similar. "To appreciate the significance" of his examples of "forgotten alternatives" to segregation, Woodward wrote, "one has only to attempt to imagine any of them occurring in any of the states concerned at any time during the first half of the twentieth century."[27] To say that Woodward's was a poetic rather than a factual truth might be damning in the eyes of some historians, but his most poignant message does seem to be one about culture: namely, that sometime between 1890 and 1940 the vast majority of white southerners settled comfortably enough into what we might call a "culture of segregation" that they lost their ability even to imagine a world in which black and white were not separated in the public sphere.

I use the words "culture of segregation" on purpose because Grace Elizabeth Hale's *Making Whiteness: The Culture of Segregation in the South, 1890–1940* remains the most ambitious cultural history of the Jim Crow era yet published. Hale argues that white southerners turned segregation—the physical separation of blacks and whites—into culture in a variety of ways in the late nineteenth and early twentieth centuries. One way they did so, in her view, was to depict "integration" as an impossible ideal, either lost to the past, in the literature of the old plantation with its faithful slaves, or possible only in childhood, in tributes to "mammy" and dealings with her twentieth-century counterparts. "Segregation was the way of adult white southerners who learned to love and then separate from mammy in an integrated island of time, childhood, and space, the white home," Hale writes. "As the Lost Cause made integration and the 'family white and black' the past of southern culture, the white home made integration and 'me and my mammy' the past of the individual."[28] The "multiplying spaces" of consumer culture also "became key sites for the white southern middle class's creation of and African Americans' resistance to the culture of segregation," in Hale's view.[29] On the one hand, stores and shopping districts were scenes of racial mixing and could never be wholly segregated, lest whites segregate themselves from blacks' money. On the other hand, visual culture and advertising disseminated racial imagery widely throughout the region and the entire United States.

How southern racial culture contributed to American whiteness—the unspoken conflation of national identity with whiteness not as a race but as "the norm"—is a driving concern throughout Hale's book, and undoubtedly her work's most significant contribution is to position the South within modernizing America. But to what extent the cultural developments she describes were wholly southern (in the case of racist advertising, for example) or centered on *segregation* is not entirely clear. Much of her most interesting work focuses on what, in a "culture of segregation," must be considered exceptions: the white household, the sales floor, and even spectacle lynchings, which she says "symbolically and physically subverted segregation, separation as culture, in order to strengthen it."[30] To my mind, such interesting and important exceptions make the whole concept of a "culture of segregation" problematic. I take Woodward seriously when he suggests what white southerners could and could not imagine by the mid-twentieth century, and I know enough about massive resistance to know that many white southerners cared deeply about segregation by the mid-1950s. But I still think southern racial culture is more accurately described as a "culture of" something other than segregation. And I think that, more than a label, we need a nuanced historical analysis—one that is more sensitive to chronology than Hale's and that recognizes that we can gain a true understanding of the South's racial culture only if we look forward from the past as well as backward from the present.

Separation was not white southerners' first choice for how race relations should operate in the New South, as their protracted efforts to enforce a racial etiquette rooted in slavery demonstrate. If this older method of social control had worked—if blacks had been willing to abide by racial etiquette in all times and places even as the South urbanized and modernized technologically—then whites would not have needed or wanted segregation. Instead, blacks continued to strive for political representation and social and economic advancement long after Reconstruction ended, and the etiquette itself even changed slightly in response to their efforts, as, for example, in the substitution of "Boss" or "Mister" where the slave had once been compelled to say "Master."[31]

"It is now clear that something highly significant happened in southern race relations during the 1890s," Howard Rabinowitz concedes in an important essay on the Woodward thesis. "Though many segregation laws were already on the books, Woodward is right about the importance of post-1890 legislation."[32] Those laws reflect—not, I would argue, a "capitulation to racism," as one of Woodward's chapters in *The Strange Career of Jim Crow* has it—but a capitulation to change and an admission that, short of engaging in endless violence both personal and communal, white southerners could not keep blacks "in their place" through old familiar means.

This is where questions of *where* and *how* become crucial to answering questions of *when* and *why*. Woodward himself recognized this by 1988, when he responded to critics of the Woodward thesis one last time. Work on the origins of segregation "got started off on the wrong foot," he admit-ted, because of his decision "to put the question of *when* before the ques-tions *where* and *how*, giving to time priority over circumstance and placing the chronology before the sociology and demography of the subject."[33] This is, ironically enough, the very opposite of what newer books like Hale's *Mak-ing Whiteness* and Leon Litwack's *Trouble in Mind* do, in Glenda Gilmore's opinion, prompting her reflection on the importance of chronology that I quoted above and suggesting how much cultural studies approaches have influenced the discipline.[34] Back in 1955, the question of *when* had been paramount both historiographically and, even more important, politically, so that Woodward's "first concern" had been "to overcome the prevailing impression—and in southern ideology the firm conviction—that . . . race relations in the South remained basically unchanged, that changes in law, whether associated with slavery, emancipation, Reconstruction, or segre-gation, had been superficial and resulted in no real change in relations be-tween races. No changes, no history," Woodward, like Gilmore, reminds us. Yet this sense of timelessness was shared, in 1955, "by those who wished to keep things the way they were and by many who wished to change things but despaired of ever being able to do so."[35]

From the vantage point of the 1980s, Woodward could see that the "sig-nificant thing was not *when* [segregation] appeared but *where*, not the time but the circumstances"—although my point in this essay, ultimately, is that both are significant: the *when* and the *where* as well as my own abiding in-terest, the *how*. Woodward had long before pointed out that segregation was incompatible with plantation slavery, "given the necessities of policing, su-pervising, and exacting involuntary labor, receiving slave services, and at-tending to slave needs." The same was true, for the most part, in rural areas after emancipation, as former slaves became tenants and small farmers still tied intimately, if rarely easily, to individual whites. For, if whites wanted "to maintain racial dominance and discipline, that was handled in the coun-try by direct, personal, or 'vertical' control—whether by the 'boss man' or by any white who chose to keep blacks in their place. They were personally identifiable and rarely beyond white surveillance." Although Woodward did not use the words "racial etiquette" in this passage, this, surely, is part of what he was describing, along with other aspects of blacks and whites' eco-nomic and social relationship, such as the establishment and supervision of work routines, the accounting of debts over the course of a season, and the rituals of settling up. Woodward went on to suggest that it was the insufficiency of racial etiquette that encouraged whites in cities to embrace segregation. The "countryside reliance on direct or 'vertical' control did not work well enough in urban conditions," where "blacks enjoyed more autonomy and anonymity," he wrote. "To supplement the old methods, white urbanites added the 'horizontal' system of segregation, an impersonal complex of interlocking economic, political, legal, social, and ideological components designed not only to separate the races but also to maintain white dominance and keep blacks in their place."[36]

Even as I quote that last sentence, however, I am troubled by the idea of an interlocking segregation "complex" springing, fully formed, from white city dwellers' heads. Drawing on the work of Rabinowitz and others, we know that different southern cities adopted segregation to different degrees and at different rates.[37] Given that, I think we need to ask a larger question about the nature and pace of change, which is: How do we get from segregation as fall-back position to, if not segregation as culture, at least a cultural moment by the early 1950s when, as Woodward observed, neither conservatives nor progressives could conceive of a desegregated South? To put it another way, if white southerners traditionally preferred a vertical, face-to-face means of social control—as I think both the extensive work on the culture of "honor" in the antebellum South and whites' efforts to reassert racial etiquette in the postbellum years indicate they did—then when and why and how did a younger generation of white southerners come to have, if not a preference for the horizontal system of segregation, at least an inability to imagine anything else?

Again, I think we need to ask questions of *where* and *how* to get at questions of *when*. In terms of where, we need to explore differences not only between urban and rural, but also between public and private. The complexity of race relations in rural and small-town communities even in the mid-twentieth century challenges the idea that segregation came to define white southerners' thinking on race—at least not with any great speed.[38] The same is true, and maybe even more so, of relationships within white households. White southerners continued to rely heavily on domestic servants, almost all of them black, throughout the first half of the twentieth century. They did so because they *could*—because black men's low wages and frequent unemployment meant that black women and girls had to work in one of the very few jobs open to them. But whites also *preferred* having servants, so much so that historian David Katzman suggests that "the Southern preference for hiring servants retarded the development of commercial laundries" in the South until after World War II.[39] Low wages also meant that black laundresses, maids, cooks, child nurses, and yardmen were within reach of a broad segment of the white population—especially those middle-class urbanites who systematized segregation.[40] Exploring the region in the wake of the Atlanta race riot of 1906, northern journalist Ray Stannard Baker was surprised to find whites hiring black domestic workers even in an Atlanta mill neighborhood that he had visited specifically "to see how the poorer classes of white people lived." One family "hired a Negro woman to cook for them, and while they sent their children to the mill to work, the cook sent her children to school!" he wrote, astounded at the irony.[41] Among "genteel" white southerners, however strapped for cash, the propensity to hire servants was even greater. "No white family ever did its own washing," asserted Polly Stone Buck, whose father, a professor, had died, leaving his widow and children to support themselves by renting rooms to Emory College students. "Even at the time when we were poorest, the soiled clothes were regularly 'counted out.'"[42]

Autobiographical accounts like Buck's can tell us a great deal about what whites' continued reliance on black labor in their homes *meant*, in cultural terms. Sarah Patton Boyle's autobiography, *The Desegregated Heart*, is particularly revealing. Having grown up with servants on her family's farm in Virginia, Boyle not only hired a maid while she was in art school in the late 1920s, living alone in a "room in a second-class Washington, D.C. boarding house," but also determined to have help after she married in 1932. "It was in the depth of the Great Depression," she recalled, and her husband was lucky to have a job as a University of Virginia drama instructor at the pay of a graduate assistant. All told, they were making less than one hundred dollars a month. "I liked the challenge of making ends meet," Boyle remembered, and she "contentedly collected such data as that rice was cheaper per serving than potatoes, tea per cup than coffee, and that I could entertain a room full of people for one dollar if only I invited them to tea, not dinner or cocktails." Nevertheless, "foregoing a maid entirely was one sacrifice to poverty which I didn't propose to make. . . . My plan was to have an untrained teenage girl drop by for an hour after school each day, clean my tiny flat and wash the dishes. . . . In exchange, I could offer the girl the experience of her first job, my cast-off clothes and one dime an hour, or fifty cents a five-day week." Times being what they were, there was no shortage of applicants. "The mother of the girl I finally engaged even stopped by to beg me please not to throw away any garment, regardless of its condition,"

Boyle added. "The pathos eluded me. Poverty in Negroes was a racial trait. I felt only a pleasant glow, knowing that I had nothing to give which couldn't be worn at least a dozen times before it fell apart."[43]

Boyle's lack of empathy is telling. Race relations within white households not only operated according to older, face-to-face, vertical methods of social control, but also partook of the myth, suggested in Herbert Spencer's very definition of etiquette, that racial etiquette reflected the natural order of things. "My requirements were that the girl know her place, do her work quickly, and show appreciation of the opportunity I was offering by making a real effort to learn what nice people expected of their maids," Boyle wrote, providing a pretty good checklist of what most white southerners wanted out of their relationships with black domestic workers, despite the fact that Boyle herself was, by the time she wrote her autobiography, a born-again white liberal.[44] An earlier source makes the emotional and cultural work expected of domestic servants even more clear. In 1913, University of Georgia master's student T. J. Woofter Jr. surveyed black life in Athens, then a city of about 15,000. To find out about domestic work, Woofter sent a questionnaire to every white family in Athens that was thought to employ servants—some 310 households. He received 143 replies commenting on 175 female and 80 male workers, or 72 percent of the total number of black household workers, excluding laundresses, in the city.[45]

Given this golden opportunity to complain, Woofter's survey respondents did so in abundance. Their servants were lazy, dirty, dishonest, wasteful, and almost more trouble than they were worth. "If we Southern people would build our houses with more conveniences we would not be compelled to worry with the negro," one white employer wrote. Yet the most contented of her fellow respondents were clearly those who had kept the same servants the longest, indicating reasonable satisfaction with their work, of course, but also suggesting that efficiency and even honesty were not employers' only criteria. "The old man on my lot is in his 7th year of service to me. He is old and slow, but has never failed once to come in the morning in good time," one informant wrote. Another reported that her maid "is sickly, or pretends to be a great part of the time. Has been absent a month, but sends word each week that she will be back." "Above I said that servant is honest," noted a third informant, "yet I [claim] $75 per year for food 'taken.' Nobody expects a negro's honesty to extend to food." "I never discharge them," a fourth employer confided. "I allow them to discharge me, if I wish to be rid of them. Then they give me a good name, and to get servants is easier. The reason I let any of them go is that they get 'trifling'—they all do in time. Some of them have admitted it themselves. Negroes have intellects of the type of children's and the only way to get along with negro servants is to humor them and command them just as you would children."[46]

Perhaps it is too much to say that white southerners *enjoyed* "worrying with" black domestic servants, but it is clear that they continued to do so and, whether those relationships proved comparatively satisfactory or disastrous to the black and white individuals involved, whites generally understood them in ways that reinforced notions of a natural racial order. Hortense Powdermaker saw this in Indianola, Mississippi, in the mid-1930s, noting that white women talked "indulgently or regretfully" about their black servants' dishonesty, regarding any evidence of lying or theft "as proof that the Negro is unstable, incompetent to fend for himself, and actually better off under white domination." Furthermore, white employers' "constant opportunity to be indulgent" reaffirmed their belief that they were "not only right, but also kind and good," an emotional reassurance that, Powdermaker added, is "valuable in the circumstances."[47] Precisely because they did help white southerners feel good about themselves, the dynamics in "integrated" white households are best understood, not as an exception within a culture centered on segregation, but as evidence of the unevenness of cultural change. "Worrying with" blacks who kept their place (or could be fired if they did not) was more emotionally satisfying to white southerners than mere mechanistic, anonymous segregation. That this was so and that whites were loath to give it up is also indicated in white child rearing practices, arguably one of the cultural processes in which ordinary people's understanding of their world becomes most distilled.

To the extent that white southern parents consciously instructed their children in racial matters, racial etiquette is what they most often taught. Certainly, much parental teaching was indirect and unconscious; as Lillian Smith explained in *Killers of the Dream*, white southern children "learned the intricate system of taboos, of renunciations and compensations, of manners, voice modulations, words, feelings, along with our prayers, our toilet habits, and our games. I do not remember how or when, but by the time I had learned . . . that all men are brothers with a common Father, I also knew that I was better than a Negro, that all black folks have their place and must be kept in it." Even though she learned these lessons early and largely unconsciously, however, Smith also learned that keeping blacks "in their 'place'" meant conscientiously following various "bleak rituals" and "steel-rigid decorums." Of these, the most specific and immutable were that no "well-bred southerner" would "call a Negro 'mister' or invite him into the living room or eat with him or sit by him in public places."[48] So we do see sensitivity to segregation by the time Lillian Smith was growing up in the early 1900s, but as part of a broader pattern of racial etiquette premised on the notion that blacks and whites *would interact*, often quite intimately, but never as equals.

This broader pattern would persist in white child rearing for decades. When sociologist Olive Westbrook Quinn interviewed white Memphis high school and college students about their racial attitudes in 1944, she found that, like Smith, few remembered direct lessons except in the use of the word "lady," which white children had to learn to withhold from blacks. "I remember when I learned that lesson," one informant told Quinn. "I told Mother the washlady was here. She said to say 'woman,' and I asked why. Mother explained that you never say 'Negro lady.' She said 'lady' was a term of respect applied to few white ladies and to no Negroes at all." Clearly, this was a particularly touchy subject for white southerners, who used the sanctity of white womanhood to justify much of their most brutal behavior toward blacks. But this anecdote also tells us that white parents did correct their children when they made mistakes in racial etiquette, and they did so even when the children were quite young. "One time when I was leaving to go to kindergarten, I kissed my nurse," one of Quinn's informants recalled. "Father waited until I was in the car with him, and then he told me not to. I asked why, but Father is very domineering, and he told me I was too young to understand and that I'd just have to do as he said."[49] By the time they started school and certainly by the time they were old enough to read and understand segregation signs, white children like this informant had already learned a great deal about how blacks and whites were and were not supposed to relate to one another. In contrast to black parents, who often taught their children to avoid whites as much as possible, many white parents continued to teach timeworn scripts of domination and paternalism. "You know, I think from the fact that I was told so often that I must treat colored people with consideration, I got the idea that I could mistreat them if I wanted to," one of Quinn's informants reflected.[50]

As Quinn's interviews suggest, white parents continued to teach racial etiquette in the 1940s, but by this time, change was coming to the South in a variety of ways. Government assistance programs and mechanization were transforming rural life and resulting in the displacement of thousands of black sharecroppers and tenants. More than a million African Americans had already left the region in the Great Migration of the 1910s and 1920s, and some two million more would follow in the 1930s and especially the 1940s, as opportunities opened up with mobilization for World War II.[51] Meanwhile, the entire South was participating much more fully in a national consumer culture that traded heavily in Old South nostalgia and other racist imagery but also brought new influences into cities and towns and even crossroads communities. And, most important in terms of racial etiquette, blacks themselves were changing, including those domestic servants with whom whites interacted most intimately. In my own research, I have seen examples of domestic workers challenging racial etiquette much more forcefully than their mothers or grandmothers dared. Fourteen-year-old Olivia Cherry is a case in point. Born in Hampton, Virginia in 1926, Cherry worked as a maid when she was in high school because, as she put it, "basically . . . that's all I could get." But she refused to answer when white employers tried to call her by any name but her own—"They loved to call me Susie," she complained—nor would she go to the back door of white employers' homes. "My reason was [that] my mother had to go to the back door to keep her job," Cherry told an interviewer. "Not that I was better than my mother, but I was avenging my mother, and I said, 'I'm not going to the back door.'" Her refusal ended up costing her a job one Saturday when she was really too sick to be working anyway because of severe menstrual cramps. After walking across town, Cherry "knocked and rang . . . and called" for her employer to let her in the front door. "She never did come, because she was determined for me to come to the back. I went home and went to bed, and that was the end of that job."[52]

Cherry's youth and the fact that she did not have a family to support made it easier for her to risk being fired. As black employment opportunities expanded during and after World War II, older, more settled domestic workers would come to share some of her relative autonomy. Whites, in turn, responded with exasperation and with the theory that black household workers were forming "Eleanor Clubs," named after First Lady Eleanor Roosevelt, to insist on higher wages and easier work or else, according to one rumored Eleanor Club slogan, to "put a white woman in every kitchen by 1943."[53] As in Danville in 1883, whites thought they were seeing a pattern in blacks' growing "uppitiness"—as indeed they were, to the extent that blacks understood the rules of the "zero-sum game" of racial etiquette and felt more able to challenge them, even on an individual basis, when material and political circumstances were going their way. Perhaps this is why Mrs. Hadden found it necessary to call the police on Eloise Blake in 1939.

Not so many years later, the police would be called on extensively to defend segregation against a civil rights movement that not only mobilized the black masses but also gained federal government support. That segregation is what blacks challenged in the 1950s and early 1960s makes perfect sense, for it was the legal, institutional edifice of white supremacy. It was what could be forcibly changed through federal court orders and Supreme Court decisions. That whites rose to defend segregation is also clear, although historians have only just begun to write the intellectual history of massive resistance. As they do so, they may find that segregation, especially if defined in appropriately narrow terms as the spatial separation of black and white, was less definitive of the South's racial culture than has usually seemed to be the case when we look back from a post–civil rights movement perspective. Understanding that should help us to understand the movement's successes and failures, as well as what came after—whether, to what extent, and why a "subtle, unofficial residue" of racial etiquette might have survived into the late 1960s and 1970s, as David Goldfield suggests. It might also help us to answer Elizabeth Lasch-Quinn's recent charge that "sensitivity training" and other therapeutic approaches have "hijacked" the civil rights movement's revolutionary potential by imposing a new kind of racial etiquette rather than allowing for true egalitarianism.[54] Well-intentioned "race experts" have not been the fiercest of the many enemies the civil rights revolution has faced in the last thirty or forty years, but Lasch-Quinn's work is nonetheless valuable for making us think about codes of interracial conduct in our own day, codes that must be understood in relation to other forms of power, both political and economic, in our own time as much as in the past. As Glenda Gilmore argues, and as C. Vann Woodward argued before her, what we need is a timeline detailing shifts within the South's racial culture, but it must be one that establishes whens in conjunction with hows and wheres. That is, we need to identify whites' methods of racial dominance and where they used them (on farms, in homes, or in public spaces), then we can look for change in these methods and these places. The result of such a study will not be timelessness or even simple continuity but a history in

which, to use J. William Harris's words, "racial subordination . . . was continually recreated"—further confirmation of the very real, in the sense that it affected people, yet wholly constructed nature of race itself.

Notes

1. William Pickens to Rev. James M. Hinton, July 27, 1939, in *The Papers of the NAACP*, Part 12: Selected Branch Files, 1913–1939, Series A: The South (Frederick, Md.: University Publications of America, 1982), 530–31, microfilm. Hinton was the president of the Columbia, South Carolina branch. The letter includes a typescript identified as Associated Negro Press copy. On domestic workers' wages in the 1930s, see Jacqueline Jones, *Labor of Love, Labor of Sorrow: Black Women, Work, and the Family, From Slavery to the Present* (New York: Basic Books, 1985), 206–7; and Susan Tucker, *Telling Memories Among Southern Women: Domestic Workers and Their Employers in the Segregated South* (New York: Schocken, 1988), 104–5.

2. I am grateful to Jane Dailey and John F. Kasson for their very helpful comments on this essay at the fall 2004 Porter L. Fortune Jr. History Symposium at the University of Mississippi. In my revisions, I have tried to indicate where their insights have been most important in helping me to refine my arguments. I also want to thank Ted Ownby for organizing the symposium and Jacquelyn Dowd Hall and Molly Rozum for their suggestions and support.

3. See Leon F. Litwack, *Trouble in Mind: Black Southerners in the Age of Jim Crow* (New York: Knopf, 1998), 327–36; Neil R. McMillen, *Dark Journey: Black Mississippians in the Age of Jim Crow* (Urbana and Chicago: University of Illinois Press, 1989), 23–28; and David R. Goldfield, *Black, White, and Southern: Race Relations and Southern Culture, 1940 to the Present* (Baton Rouge and London: Louisiana State University Press, 1990), 2–9. For a brief, but perceptive and early account of the rules and function of racial etiquette, see also Jacquelyn Dowd Hall, *Revolt Against Chivalry: Jessie Daniel Ames and the Women's Campaign Against Lynching*, rev. ed. (New York: Columbia University Press, 1993), 141–42. James C. Cobb's approach to racial etiquette is also interesting for the extent to which he foregrounds material aspects of blacks' and whites' relationships. See *The Most Southern Place on Earth: The Mississippi Delta and the Roots of Regional Identity* (New York and Oxford: Oxford University Press, 1992), 163–64.

4. McMillen, *Dark Journey*, 28.

5. Bertram Wilbur Doyle, *The Etiquette of Race Relations in the South: A Study in Social Control* (Chicago: University of Chicago Press, 1937), 169.

6. On Doyle's background, see G. James Fleming and Christian E. Burckel, *Who's Who in Colored America*, 7th ed. (Yonkers-on-Hudson, N.Y.: Christian E. Burckel, 1950), 162.

7. Herbert Spencer, quoted in Doyle, *Etiquette of Race Relations*, 5. On Spencer's influence on Park and Park's influence on Doyle, see Gary D. Jaworski, "Park, Doyle, and Hughes: Neglected Antecedents of Goffman's Theory of Ceremony," *Sociological Inquiry* 66 (May 1996), 160–74.

8. The primary exceptions are the articles by Jane Dailey and J. William Harris discussed below, but it is also worth noting David Goldfield's especially broad conception of racial etiquette, which seems to encompass segregation and other forms of discrimination, in *Black, White, and Southern*.

9. According to the South Carolina Information Highway website, the General Assembly amended the state's constitution to allow women to serve on juries on March 1, 1967. See *http://www.sciway.net/hist/governors/mcnair.html*.

10. W. E. B. Du Bois, *The Souls of Black Folk* (1903; New York: Dover Publications, 1994), 2.

11. Barbara J. Fields, "Whiteness, Racism, and Identity," *International Labor and Working-Class History* (Fall 2001), 48–56. See also Fields, "Origins of the New South and the Negro Question," *Journal of Southern History* LXVII (November 2001), 811–26.

12. J. William Harris, "Etiquette, Lynching, and Racial Boundaries in Southern History: A Mississippi Example," *American Historical Review* 100 (April 1995), 388, 390. Joel Williamson makes a similar point in *The Crucible of Race: Black-White Relations in the American South Since Emancipation* (New York and Oxford: Oxford University Press, 1984), 258: "There was a black country and a white country, and the frontier between them was not clearly marked and was ever-shifting as if in some undeclared and usually quiet war. The location and nature of the frontier were much more a function of mind than of matter, of white minds and black minds rather than white bodies and black bodies."

13. Goldfield, *Black, White, and Southern*, 2–9, 207.

14. Glenda Elizabeth Gilmore, "Dating Jim Crow: Chronology as a Tool of Analysis," *Georgia Historical Quarterly* 83 (Spring 1999), 59.

15. Jane Dailey, "Deference and Violence in the Postbellum Urban South: Manners and Massacres in Danville, Virginia," *Journal of Southern History* 63 (August 1997), 556, 581, 584–85. A version of this article appears as Chapter Four in Dailey's *Before Jim Crow: The Politics of Race in Postemancipation Virginia* (Chapel Hill and London: University of North Carolina Press, 2000).

16. Whitelaw Reid, *After the War: A Tour of the South, 1865–1866* (Cincinnati

and New York: Moore, Wilstach & Baldwin, 1866; rpt. New York: Harper & Row, 1965), 419–20.

17. On the culture of "honor" in the antebellum South, see Bertram Wyatt-Brown, *Southern Honor: Ethics and Behavior in the Old South* (New York and Oxford: Oxford University Press, 1982) and *The Shaping of Southern Culture: Honor, Grace, and War, 1760s–1880s* (Chapel Hill and London: University of North Carolina Press, 2001); Edward L. Ayers, *Vengeance and Justice: Crime and Punishment in the 19th-Century American South* (New York and Oxford: Oxford University Press, 1984); Elliot J. Gorn, "'Gouge and Bite, Pull Hair and Scratch': The Social Significance of Fighting in the Southern Backcountry," *American Historical Review* 90 (February 1985), 18–43; and Kenneth S. Greenberg, *Honor & Slavery: Lies, Duels, Noses, Masks, Dressing as a Woman, Gifts, Strangers, Humanitarianism, Death, Slave Rebellions, The Pro-Slavery Argument, Baseball, Hunting, and Gambling in the Old South* (Princeton: Princeton University Press, 1996).

18. William Wells Brown, *My Southern Home: or, the South and Its People, in From Fugitive Slave to Free Man: The Autobiographies of William Wells Brown*, ed. William L. Andrews, (Columbia and London: University of Missouri Press, 2003), 245–46.

19. Brown, *My Southern Home*, 246–47.

20. Dailey, "Deference and Violence," 576, 586.

21. Litwack, *Trouble in Mind*, 235.

22. C. Vann Woodward, *The Strange Career of Jim Crow*, 3rd rev. ed. (New York: Oxford University Press, 1974). All references are to this edition. Woodward offered the concise statement of the Woodward thesis quoted here in *American Counterpoint: Slavery and Racism in the North-South Dialogue* (Boston: Little, Brown, 1971), 237. My discussion of the Woodward thesis and its critics relies heavily on Howard N. Rabinowitz, "More Than the Woodward Thesis: Assessing The Strange Career of Jim Crow," *Journal of American History* 75 (December 1988), 842–56.

23. Leon F. Litwack, *North of Slavery: The Negro in the Free States, 1790–1860* (Chicago: University of Chicago Press, 1961); Richard C. Wade, *Slavery in the Cities: The South, 1820–1860* (New York: Oxford University Press, 1964); and Joel Williamson, *After Slavery: The Negro in South Carolina during Reconstruction, 1861–1877* (Chapel Hill: University of North Carolina Press, 1965).

24. Howard N. Rabinowitz, *Race Relations in the Urban South, 1865–1890* (New York: Oxford University Press, 1978).

25. John W. Cell, *The Highest Stage of White Supremacy: The Origins of Segregation in South Africa and the American South* (Cambridge, New York and other cities: Cambridge University Press, 1982).

26. Rabinowitz uses a boxing metaphor to describe Woodward's elusiveness in "More Than the Woodward Thesis," 846. For evidence of the continued appeal of the Woodward thesis among historians, see for example, Glenda Elizabeth Gilmore, *Gender & Jim Crow: Women and the Politics of White Supremacy in North Carolina, 1896–1920* (Chapel Hill and London: University of North Carolina Press, 1996), esp. 255, n.10; and Dailey, *Before Jim Crow*, 6–7. Another recent work that emphasizes contingency in race relations in the late nineteenth century is Suzanne Lebsock, *A Murder in Virginia: Southern Justice on Trial* (New York and London: Norton, 2003).

27. Woodward, *Strange Career*, 26–27, 29, 35.

28. Grace Elizabeth Hale, *Making Whiteness: The Culture of Segregation in the South, 1890–1940* (New York: Pantheon, 1998), 118–19.

29. Hale, *Making Whiteness*, 123.

30. Hale, *Making Whiteness*, 238.

31. On the shift away from "Master" and "Mistress" as forms of address, see Leon F. Litwack, *Been in the Storm So Long: The Aftermath of Slavery* (New York: Vintage, 1979), 253.

32. Rabinowitz, "More Than the Woodward Thesis," 849.

33. C. Vann Woodward, "Strange Career Critics: Long May They Persevere," *Journal of American History* 75 (December 1988), 857.

34. See Gilmore, "Dating Jim Crow," in which she reviews Hale's *Making Whiteness* and Litwack's *Trouble in Mind*.

35. Woodward, "Strange Career Critics," 860.

36. Woodward, "Strange Career Critics," 858–59.

37. On this point, see Woodward, "Strange Career Critics," 859–60, and Rabinowitz, *Race Relations in the Urban South*.

38. On the complexity of rural race relations, see Jack Temple Kirby, *Rural Worlds Lost: The American South, 1920–1960* (Baton Rouge and London: Louisiana State University Press, 1987), esp. ch. 7; Jacqueline Jones, "Encounters, Likely and Unlikely, Between Black and Poor White Women in the Rural South, 1865–1940," *Georgia Historical Quarterly* 76 (Summer 1992), 333–53; Melissa Walker, "Shifting Boundaries: Race Relations in the Rural Jim Crow South," in *African American Life in the Rural South, 1900–1950*, ed. R. Douglas Hurt (Columbia and London: University of Missouri Press, 2003), 81–107; and Mark Roman Schultz, *The Rural Face of White Supremacy: Beyond Jim Crow* (Urbana and Chicago: University of Illinois Press, 2005).

39. David M. Katzman, *Seven Days a Week: Women and Domestic Service in Industrializing America* (New York: Oxford University Press, 1978), 62.

40. In fact, Katzman suggests in *Seven Days a Week* that "the employment

of domestics in the South was even more heavily urban than in the North, and that the association of the Southern white life-style with servants was more of an urban pattern than a universally Southern one" (60). However, his reliance on census data to establish servants-per-family ratios for urban vs. rural areas may underestimate rural white southerners' use of black household labor, which may have been more casual and occasional than in cities.

41. Ray Stannard Baker, *Following the Color Line: American Negro Citizenship in the Progressive Era* (1908; New York, Evanston, and London: Harper and Row, 1964), 53.

42. Polly Stone Buck, quoted in Tera W. Hunter, *To 'Joy My Freedom: Southern Black Women's Lives and Labors After the Civil War* (Cambridge and London: Harvard University Press, 1997), 109.

43. Sarah Patton Boyle, *The Desegregated Heart: A Virginian's Stand in Time of Transition* (1962; Charlottesville and London: University Press of Virginia, 2001), 39, 43–45.

44. Boyle, *Desegregated Heart*, 45.

45. T. J. Woofter, Jr., "The Negroes of Athens, Georgia," *Bulletin of the University of Georgia* 14 (December 1913). For these statistics, see p. 45.

46. Woofter, "Negroes of Athens," 59–62.

47. Hortense Powdermaker, *After Freedom: A Cultural Study in the Deep South* (1939; Madison: University of Wisconsin Press, 1993), 39.

48. Lillian Smith, *Killers of the Dream* (1949; New York: Norton, 1994), 27–28.

49. Olive Westbrook Quinn, "The Transmission of Racial Attitudes Among White Southerners," *Social Forces* 33 (October 1954), 42, 43.

50. Quinn, "Transmission of Racial Attitudes," 44.

51. For the numbers of black migrants in each decade, see Dernoral Davis, "Toward a Socio-Historical and Demographic Portrait of Twentieth-Century African-Americans," in *Black Exodus: The Great Migration from the American South*, ed. Alferdteen Harrison (Jackson and London: University Press of Mississippi, 1991), 10–11.

52. Olivia Cherry, interviewed by Blair L. Murphy, August 10, 1995. From *Behind the Veil: Documenting African American Life in the Jim Crow South*. Center for Documentary Studies at Duke University, Rare Book, Manuscript, and Special Collections Library, Duke University. See unedited transcript, 4, 9–10.

53. Goldfield, *Black, White, and Southern*, 37.

54. Elisabeth Lasch-Quinn, *Race Experts: How Racial Etiquette, Sensitivity Training, and New Age Therapy Hijacked the Civil Rights Revolution* (Lanham, Md.: Rowman & Littlefield, 2001).

Fifty Percent Moonshine and Fifty Percent Moonshine

Social Life and College Youth Culture in Alabama, 1913–1933

Lisa Lindquist Dorr

"The only time a girl does not want the spotlight on her is when she is on a wild party," remarked a short entry in the first edition of the *Rammer Jammer*, the University of Alabama's new student humor magazine. Introduced in 1924 during Prohibition, the *Rammer Jammer* confirmed the connection between alcohol and the social relationships between men and women.[1] After alluding to young coeds partying with abandon, the entry continued, "All she wants then is moonshine, fifty percent moonshine and fifty percent moonshine."[2] Dating, college life, and getting "tight" walked hand in hand on the University of Alabama campus, placing Alabama in the mainstream of the youth culture of the 1920s.[3]

This is not to say that all college students, much less all women, went on "wild parties," nor that they all engaged in the new social customs of youth. Manners and morality were contested issues in college towns across the country. As Paula Fass has shown, in the 1920s, college youth created new forms of heterosocial interaction that caused parents, administrators, clergymen, and even fellow students endless concern.[4] Alabama was no different from elsewhere. Nevertheless, the forms of social interaction that characterized relationships between southern men and women in the 1920s were not solely the result of the dislocations of World War I and the rise of modernism thereafter. Such activities appeared in 1913 and 1914, and illuminate the transition away from traditional forms of courtship. By the 1920s, the white students who attended Alabama's major white state universities consciously saw themselves as part of a national college scene characterized by dating, petting, and drinking, but one that had a peculiarly southern cast.[5] Alabama's college dating rituals redefined the calculation of white women's value, believing that it no longer resided solely in their virtue. Instead, college attitudes suggest that women could increase their sexual capital, and thus their worth as desirable women, by spending it, rather than saving it. To adults, however, women's virtue was a fragile commodity that required protection, not only from the black beast rapist, but also from white college men and college women's own desires. Sexualized behavior rendered women common and cheap and needed to be controlled at all costs if respectable white women were to continue to be self-evident proof of white superiority. While Alabama reflects well-established patterns of the youth culture of the 1920s, the distinctive racial and class environment of the segregated South during prohibition shaped Alabama's college life, as well as the efforts adults—parents, college administrators, and the Klan—exerted to contain their seemingly wayward youth.[6]

By the 1920s, the youth culture on college campuses openly celebrated dating and rituals of physical intimacy like necking and petting. While the sexual component of dating relationships seemed to blossom after World War I, the diary of one female student at the University of Alabama between January 1913 and September 1914 suggests that the "promiscuous" dating and dancing of the 1920s was nothing entirely new. Daphne Cunningham rated and dated with the best of them.[7] She lived at home with her parents within walking distance of the University. She was a member of the Kappa Delta sorority, took classes in history, Latin, and English, and received a bachelor of arts degree in 1916.[8]

Her life, or at least the aspects of it she deemed worth recording for posterity, however, centered on dating, a word that she herself used. In both 1913 and 1914, she listed social activities with fifty-five different men. Virtually every day a variety of men walked her home from classes, spent time with her at her home, took a meal with her family, and accompanied her to some form of commercial entertainment. She frequently attended movies with men—fifty-three times in 1913, and forty-three times in the first nine months of her 1914 diary. Most Sundays, a young man took her for Sunday dinner at a local hotel, though she rarely attended church unless it was on a date. She attended twenty-four university dances in 1913, and nineteen in 1914. She took rides with men, both in buggies and in cars. She went to University athletic events, concerts, and plays, went "to town" in the late afternoon or evening (or both), played bridge, had picnics, and even made candy on a few occasions all accompanied by a male companion. It was not uncommon for her to do several of these activities all with different men on the same day. For example, on January 9, 1914, a Friday, she wrote that Hargrove Vander Graaf (a famous member of the football team) walked her home from classes. She then went to the picture show with Frank Greenhill at four in the afternoon, and then Richard Foster took her to the Alpha Tau Omega dance in the evening. On May 30, she wrote, "Frank came down at ten and nothing unusual happened. DeVane and Hargrove took Clare and me riding from two to three, and Hargrove asked me to lead the hop with him. Mr. Gosa came then and stayed until five when Arthur and Jimmie came to see me. That night Merrill took me to a dance."

The competition for her attention seemingly caused no confusion or controversy. Daphne was one of 91 women in the 1915–16 school year, out of a total enrollment of 774 (just under 12 percent), so her popularity was in part a function of scarcity.[9] As rare commodities, successful competition for women was one marker of status for men, and women were eagerly pursued. In an article about her experiences as a college student that appeared in the Tuscaloosa *News* in 1966, Daphne commented that women were so rare that at University dances in Clark Hall, "we could hardly dance a few feet before someone cut in."[10] The men surely knew they did not have her exclusive attention, nor did they likely expect it. The careful coordination required to keep her social events on schedule required the cooperation of her male companions. As she wrote on May 10, she went to the McLester Hotel for dinner on Sunday, "and had such a good time we were almost late for my date with Arthur."

Not all dates were equal, however. In the 1914 diary, she began to include more editorial comments on her various companions. She had "a pleasant time generally" on her walk with Frank on May 14. When she went to town with Jimmy and Pete, "of course I had a good time."[11] On June 1, after taking her riding at nine in the morning, "Mr. Joplin took her to his Skull dance, and he proved to be a wonderful partner." Of course between the morning ride and the dance in the evening she attended another morning dance with Jimmie and then went riding again with Frank who took her to the McLester Hotel for dinner afterwards, but neither outing merited additional comment. Other men, by comparison, were less exciting. On May 29, "Joe Peeler came down during the morning and I thought he would never leave." It did not stop her from seeing him again, however. And while she enjoyed eating at the McLester with Charlie and Kid Aldridge because "we cut up shamefully," when she went out with Aldridge to the movies in July, she grudgingly admitted that she "liked him better than usual."[12] Still other men thought entirely too much of themselves. When Hargrove brought Lawrence Foster to see her, she laughingly noted that Foster thought by bestowing his attention on her he was "giving [her] a rare treat."[13]

Daphne Cunningham had clear favorites, but they did not receive her exclusive attention. When Edwin Goodhue called her up for a date she noted that "I had a date with Mr. Aldridge, but *of course* I broke it for my 'buddy' . . . [I'm] crazy about him." When he left the next day to return home, she noted she "would have gone with him."[14] Fond as she was of Goodhue, she also seemed crazy about Hugh Sherman. When he returned to Tuscaloosa from Columbus, Mississippi, over the summer to spend the day with her she wrote, "there is no use to write it down because I shall always remember it, about how happy I was." When she spent two hours with him in Mississippi traveling to see her relatives she wrote, "he was the best looking thing I ever saw!" She met him later to travel together to Tuscaloosa, and they "fussed most all the way home." A few weeks later, however, she noted that Hugh "has gotten into a bad habit lately of fussing,"[15] suggesting that her ardor was cooling.

Daphne Cunningham's diary stopped abruptly in late September of 1914. At its conclusion, she seemed most enamored with Hugh Sherman and Edwin Goodhue. Surprisingly, perhaps, in 1930 she married a hometown friend, Merrill Smith, whom she described as "too nice to be interesting," and "dear old monotonous Merrill."[16] After they married, they remained in Tuscaloosa, where he was an engineer for Alabama Power. In 1981, they still lived in the home in which Daphne was born.[17]

Daphne Cunningham's social life, however, serves as a bridge between the courtship rituals of the nineteenth century and the sexual intimacy and dating of the 1920s. Privacy was more elusive and perhaps less desired, as most of her dates involved spending time at her home, going to movies, or walking to town. While the automobile was starting to allow private time for couples, for Daphne, rides were often in groups. Living at home also facilitated the supervision of her parents, who could determine the suitability of the men she entertained. Parental control, however, was neither absolute nor uncontested. Daphne's father refused to allow her to go to Birmingham for the day after she returned home six hours late from her visit with Hugh the previous day.[18] Moreover, despite the numerous entries describing who took her where and when, in which her date was named (and occasionally even described a bit), she also referred every Sunday to unnamed "boys" who came "calling." Both dating and calling appeared to occur simultaneously, but with different meaning and import assigned to each. While she was clearly pleased at being the object of attention, callers were not worth the detailed entry that a true date deserved. While nameless boys called in the afternoon, she still noted by name those who took her to dinner at the McLester, and those who took her to the picture show later in the evening.

A picture of the class of 1916's five-year reunion in 1921 accompanied the 1966 article in which Daphne described her experiences as a coed. It shows twenty-eight members of the class posing for a formal portrait. Daphne Cunningham stands front and center, one of only two women who returned for the reunion. By the time this picture was taken, the dating culture of the University had changed. Dates were still common, and competition for women remained stiff, as male students outnumbered female students by more than three to one (women were approximately 17.6 percent of the total enrollment in 1921). But heterosocial interactions in the 1920s were more likely to involve illegal alcohol consumption and expectations of physical intimacy. Daphne Cunningham mentioned alcohol only once in her diary, when she noted that Charlie Fitts came in the evening "and we talked about how he was drinking."[19] She noted fifty years later that back then, "boys who were drinking didn't come around nice girls."[20] By the 1920s, humor in University publications played on alcohol as a social lubricant and suggested it was embraced by both male and female students. And, while Daphne's elaborate dating culture may have been distinctive in the 1910s, by the 1920s, a more generalized version of these intimate rituals governed student socializing. In this context, the value of white women's virtue was a contested commodity—adults believed it should be hoarded while students saw it as a means of exchange. Dating rituals now explicitly challenged University limitations on female students, while simultaneously illuminating the struggles over women's power and agency, as well as their need for protection.

In the 1920s, most universities enforced parietal rules controlling social interactions between students. At Alabama, all freshman were not supposed to date until they had passed their first set of exams. Additionally, the University, under the guise of the Women's Council, established another set of regulations concerning women's activities outside of class. Female students were required to get special permission from the dean of students if they desired to leave Tuscaloosa or spend a night off campus, visit a fraternity house, attend an evening dance, concert, or theater performance, or eat at a

restaurant, hotel, or boarding house, and then only if an appropriate chaperone was present. Underclass coeds could receive male visitors two times
per week (seniors three times per week), and had to submit their plans on
a "date card" well in advance. Women were prohibited from riding with a
man at night without a chaperone, though riding was acceptable during the
day on several main streets adjacent to campus. The rules governing women
students even prohibited where they could walk. They certainly could not
loiter outside fraternity houses, but the margins of campus were also off
limits, as was the river, unless they were in groups. Finally, female students
were not permitted to smoke on campus or in University buildings.[21] At Auburn, female students living in university housing had to be in their rooms
on weeknights by 7:30, by 10:30 on weekends. And in an effort to discourage "late dates" (defined by the president as dates "between the close of the
dance and breakfast") the Dean of Women timed the walk from the gymnasium where dances were held to the women's dorm, and stood at the door
with a stopwatch to make sure women returned on time.[22] University administrators thus circumscribed women's mobility, supervising female students
under the guise of adult protection. The potential independence of coeds
caused parents, and other adults, to worry that college life would make their
daughters disreputable. One father, writing Alabama's President Denny for
advice, asserted that his daughter was "a quiet, nice girl of good reputation
which I wish her to retain."[23] Restricting women's movements theoretically
limited the trouble they could get into, protecting them from their own desires, as well as the predations of the men around them.

Rules for male students were far less explicit, and followed the mandates
of the college's Honor System. Nevertheless, parents of boys also expressed
concern about the effect of college on their son's character. One father wrote
both President Denny and the local Baptist preacher inquiring about "the
moral conditions of your town . . . and what are the temptations for young
boys, have you the obscene places as most towns?"[24] One mother's concern that "there is considerable dissipation among the students" was sufficient reason to consider sending her son elsewhere.[25] Despite frequently expressed fears that University life actually caused otherwise respectable sons
to degenerate into immorality and bad behavior, there was no suggestion
that the mobility of male students should be restricted like the movement
of female students, or that they should be protected from contact with possible vice. Adults expressed concern about the vulnerability of men's character, but protection was not the antidote. Instead, parents relied in part

on threats of punishment or expulsion to control their sons. There is also some suggestion that adults resigned themselves to allowing young white men's natural proclivities to flow in acceptable directions, toward African American women or lower-class women. This piece of doggerel made it past faculty censors in the *Rammer Jammer*, suggesting the wide acceptance of its sentiment: "The browner the berry / The sweeter the juice, / I want a colored lady / For my personal use!"[26] At Auburn, the college surgeon's annual report to the Board of Trustees included the numbers of college men treated for venereal disease, usually numbering between ten and sixteen, indicating that at least some college men were sexually active. Turning to cheap or common women, of course, maintained the value of virtuous (and rare) white women.[27]

Adults who worked with college students also tried to influence men's behavior with and towards coeds, calling on codes of chivalry to remind students of their duty as white men toward white women. The *Crimson-White* quoted a YMCA speaker in 1920, chastising men who had neglected to attend: "To you fellows who did not hear this talk, you should have heard it. If you do not know, you should know to what degree you are bound by your honor to respect the girls, not alone here at the institution, but everywhere."[28] President Knapp at Auburn took a more direct approach. In 1928, he wrote the fraternities before the mid-term dances, reminding male students that they must adhere "to the dictates of good society and to the behavior of a gentleman under all circumstances." He warned them to engage only in conduct which they "would be willing to recite in full detail to your own mother." Such reminders seemed necessary, as the previous president had complained that he was continually fighting "whiskey and immorality." By 1930, Auburn's dean of women and social director was pleased to report that "The attitudes of the young men towards young women students has changed almost unbelievably. . . . This changed social attitude has brought about a better and finer relationship between men and women students and as a result, co-education is more popular on the campus than ever before."[29]

Whatever the efforts of adults, students bent college regulations, and codes of honor as well, to craft a system that facilitated social interaction and emphasized the mutual interests and attractions of the opposite sex. One humorous comparison of male and female students noted that both drank, cussed, flunked exams, and got caught in autos.[30] Socializing was a particularly enjoyable part of college life. It was a common topic of discussion and humor, and talk about it openly challenged formal codes of conduct. In 1924, the *Crimson-White* listed the joys of summer school for female students as follows: "Slipping to a dance at 12:30. Ford Coupes at night with a big, strong, wonderful man. Pinned and kissed—on five minutes' acquaintance—for five cents. Coming in at sunrise. That eight o'clock class!"[31] Three of the five joys specifically violated rules regarding women's conduct but were sufficiently shared to be openly acknowledged in the newspaper. Some editorials suggested that women attended college for purely social reasons, and lowered the level of intellectual debate, making college "little more than a succession of proms, petting parties, and heavy dates." Most debates about coeds, however, ultimately ended by retorting patronizingly, "Anyway, won't you agree that coeds are worth the trouble?"[32] For students, the rewards of heterosociality were worth the risks and inconveniences.

College students, indeed, increasingly defined their environment in terms of their interactions with the opposite sex. Unlike Daphne Cunningham, who lived with her parents, by the 1920s most female students at Alabama resided at Julia Tutwiler Hall. Both men and women routinely referred to Tutwiler as "the Ranch" and its residents as "chickens," a designation that allowed for plenty of jokes about feeding chickens "corn," an obvious reference to moonshine.[33] Dating thus involved more than spending time walking a woman home from class or eating a meal with her family. It now was woven into the web of student life. Students checked each other out on a series of benches located outside the main classroom hall, and they also used trips to the post office to ogle potential dates. They sought out the dim recesses of the Gorgas Oak to find privacy, and sat around other trees to watch the girls go by. As one poem noted, "I love to sit beneath the trees / Where cool sweet breezes blow / And watch them bare our coeds' knees / As they pass to and fro."[34] Students at Alabama met at Roy's Place for drinks and attended the picture show at the Belvedere. At Auburn, the café at Toomer's Corner was popular, as were the movies at Langdon Hall.

Inculcating new male students into the etiquette of dating was a staple of college publications. Written facetiously, discourses on dating etiquette (as opposed to college regulations) often implied that women were more trouble than they were worth, while playing heavily on gender stereotypes. Instructions on how to get a date provided detailed warnings about the near-impossibility of actually contacting a desirable coed by phone at the Ranch. Other rules warned men that women were perpetually late, or so covered with cosmetics that men would need to brush the rice powder from their suits the moment they dropped their date back at the dorm.[35] One article played on the popularity of football, telling male students that they needed to become "knockout 'linesmen'" if they hoped to attract coeds. Striking up a conversation with a female student required a catchy line and was the necessary first step in "rushing" (or pursuing) a desired date.[36] Auburn's 1927 yearbook included a facetious "Code of Etiquette for Auburn Collegians," subtitled, "How to Gain Popularity in Six Weeks," that included techniques for "breaking" (cutting in) during a dance, and suggested "lines" to use on desirable women.[37] Maintaining a woman's interest without losing out to an enterprising male competitor also required careful attention. The *Crimson-White* published a day-by-day list of suggested dates and gifts, including flowers, candy, stationery, and jewelry, that would supposedly ensure the continuing affections of the desired woman, but also guaranteed the man would find himself broke by the end of a week.[38] The *Crimson-White* even offered an article on the etiquette of the stag line, through which men without dates at dances acquired dancing partners. Cutting in usually required little more than "slap[ping] her dancing partner viciously on the back," and could serve as a form of formal introduction. Picking one's partner, however, was important, as an undesirable partner could be disastrous. After all, "a self-respecting stag cannot afford to be stuck."[39]

By the 1920s, automobiles provided one of the most favored venues for dates. Not solely the province of the rich, any student with some spare change could rent one, as the song "Meet her in a Drive-It" (sung to the tune of "Nothing Could Be Finer") celebrated. "Nothing could be sweeter than to run downtown to meet her in a drive-ii-ve-it! They are good for parking, You can do a little sparking, So just try-I-I-it."[40] For men, cars could be the ticket to popularity, as "the road to a co-ed's heart is traveled best with a drive it."[41] Cars offered the best opportunity for privacy and thus intimacy, and jokes frequently referred to the possible consequences. The *Crimson-White* warned, "The great danger of driving with one hand is that one-handed steering often leads one right up to a church."[42] Sexual activity might also leave evidence that created momentary embarrassment, ribbing, or adult chastisement, but did not necessarily lead to marriage, as the following example suggests. "Frat: What's the matter? Worrying about your footprints in the sand of time? Brother: No! I'm worried about those footprints upside down in my car."[43] Petting also might leave other telltale evidence, that modern fashion could eliminate. One man stated that he "liked bobbed hair because he didn't have to fish hairpins out of his car the next morning." Another joke highlighted the disapproval of adults, as a male student fondly recalled the enticing young woman he met at a dance, and the trouble he got into when his father found her hairpins in the car.[44] It was a risk that men seemed willing to take, and women desired as well. Riding in cars after hours without a chaperone was reportedly one of the most common ways that University of Alabama women violated the Honor Code.[45]

For all the stereotypes and all the seeming superficiality around fostering relationships with women, men eagerly helped their dates evade restrictions supposedly designed to protect female students. Much of the joking about dating concerned tricks to flout restrictions on women's movements. For example, told that couples could not be in the parlor without a light, the woman quickly obtained a book of matches, playing on their need to light their cigarettes.[46] Another couple pretended they had fallen asleep to justify being caught in a lounge after hours with the lights off.[47] These ruses might not have been successful anywhere but in the *Rammer Jammer*, but they attest to the creativity with which students strategized to outwit the administration. Students even developed a vocabulary for their efforts. "Slipping a date," for example, meant going out after curfew, a serious violation of the rules, but one, as the following vignette suggests, that was commonly accepted by students: "All was dark in the vicinity of Tutwiler Hall except Tutwiler Hall itself. A figure slipped noiselessly out the side door and became part of the darkness. Gay, is it you? Nobody else. . . . Then she shivered. I'm frightened to death, Clarence. This is the first date I have ever slipped, you know. . . . They stole silently to a bench away from the maddening throng— after they had tried six and found them occupied. On Thursday night too, she scandalized. The shameless creatures!" The couple then found a bench, leaned back into the hedge, and enjoyed their date.[48] Men were both instigators and co-conspirators in women's efforts to fool the watchful eyes of the administration. Women who were caught in violation of the rules faced social probation, or being prohibited from dates and socializing for anywhere from a month, to a semester, to the entire academic year. It is unclear whether men were punished along with their dates.

Despite their enjoyment of college youth culture, men's and women's expectations nonetheless came into conflict. In April 1924, the *Crimson-White* printed a satirical piece entitled "Student Draws Date Contract with Coed," as an attempt to reconcile male and female interests and ensure a fair exchange. The article revealed much about the nature of dating and male students' attendant complaints. A. P. Phillips Jr., who wrote the article, argued that such a contract was necessary because female students (who were in the minority) had far too much control over the dating process. By signing the contract, the coed waived the right to cancel the date because of the arrival of an unexpected out-of-town friend; the sudden recollection of a forgotten date with another man; sickness, either her own or her roommate's; her required presence at a different social function; or the promise of better food. In return, the male date agreed to furnish appropriate transportation (no Fords unless rented and with consent of the date, Cadillacs and Lincolns not required except with five years' prior notice); to maintain an "artistic" haircut; to take her to an acceptable place of entertainment specified later in the contract; to buy her an appropriate refreshment; and finally, "to whisper such sweet nothings as eminate directly from dator's heart of hearts, inspired only by datee's presence, but to use no line or standard system that is dog-eared or second run." At the same time, the male dator agreed to waive his right to use the following male excuses to break the date: that he was broke; must go out of town on business; that his car was in the shop; or that "he has sprained his ankle, broken his back, swallowed his tongue, or is sick in any degree from stomach ache to leprosy." The contract also specified exactly what constituted a date—dances were technically not dates because the male was "a mere convenience or necessity." Bridge parties might be considered dates, but only when very little bridge was actually played. And the length of a date could be determined later—as long as the female remained enthusiastic and did not mention the weather.[49]

While certainly meant in jest, the "contract" outlined both men's complaints about dating and their perception of women's complaints. Women, in men's eyes, were fickle, and held the upper hand in the tight competition for dates. It was standard fare in the humor magazine for men to bemoan women who accepted dates only to leave them stranded:

Have you ever had a date with that one whom you regarded as the very epitome of all that's good and dependable . . . and after spending two hours in an effort to appear to the best possible advantage, you gayly walked up to her house with a smile on your face and heaven in your heart, blithely whistling your favorite tune, only to be told that she had just gone out with your best friend, and the only message she left was that she would not be back in time to see you, and there was nothing for you to do except turn around and go back and dully wonder where Cleopatra got that damned asp?[50]

Not only were women able to humiliate men in front of their friends and other women, men's desire for women destroyed male solidarity, even among friends. It was an uncomfortable role reversal. Other jokes reveled in the possible pitfalls of feminine popularity, encouraging women to "gather ye frat pins while ye may!" but also warning, "Maid, if you would wear his pin / You'll always careful be— / If you date with Delta Phi / Don't pin on SPE."[51] In the face of feminine power, the wise man maintained his reserve. A poem in Auburn's 1929 yearbook, the *Glomerata*, described all the virtues of a man's "new gal," but with a noted qualification in every verse. While she was fine, wore "swell clothes," and "calls me her man," he wasn't sure, "And I won't take chances, 'Cause she's been to the Auburn dances."[52]

While women's affections were unreliable, their consumption habits were predictable. Numerous jokes highlighted college men's continual need to write to parents asking for money, and men blamed the expectations of their female dates for their poverty. "Greek: I'd like to date with some of your freshmen some night. Greekess: Fine. I'll introduce you to Margaret. She's a sweet girl. Greek: No thanks. The last sweet girl I went with kept me broke."[53] According to one critic, women's insistence that dates provide them with car rides worked to deprive less wealthy men of access to women's affections. Men joked that women were little more than gold-diggers, judging the merit of a date by the make of the car he drove.[54] One poem in particular, entitled "Men—The Co-ed's Version," written by "George" emphasized women coeds' mercenary approach to dates, but mingled women's appetites for material goods and popular entertainment with their sexual appetites: "These men are simple folk / I like 'em / They take me out until they are broke, / I like 'em. / I like them naughty, tall and lean, / And short and fat and good and green, / And many other kinds I've seen, / I like 'em. / They take me to the show, / They take me to the candy store— / I like 'em. / But when they show that they don't care, / and hug me roughly, like a bear, / and crack my ribs and muss my hair— / Oh man—I love 'em."[55] Gold-diggers they might be, but modern coeds relished physical intimacy and saw little value in keeping men at arm's length. Men, in turn, tolerated fickle and greedy women in exchange for physical intimacy.

George's poem indicated a generational shift in estimations of the value of women's virtue. Adults believed women only retained their virtue, which was, of course, virtually their only sexual capital, by protecting it from men. The youth increasingly assessed women's sexual capital by their willingness to spend it, legitimating women's sexual desire. Student writings (probably written by men and conceivably representing some wishful thinking) insisted that women expected and desired kisses and petting during dates. Auburn's yearbook in 1929 insisted that while "A little loving now and then / Is relished by the best of men. / But if the truth you only knew, / We'd find the women love it, too."[56] A cartoon in the *Rammer Jammer* showed a man and woman in evening dress, with the woman crying. The man sought to ascertain the reason for her tears, asking "I haven't said anything out of the way, have I? . . . Or done anything?" To which she replied "N-no," asking, "Then why did you bring me out here?" suggesting that his failure to press for intimacy was a rejection of her charms.[57] Spending one's sexual capital, in fact, was an investment, ensuring continued desirability in the eyes of men. Bluntly put, "Some girls pet; others don't have dates."[58] Humor suggested college women appreciated a good kisser, and intimacy set them apart from previous generations. *Rammer Jammer* offered several different definitions of "neck" that helped to define college students as a distinct group. To fathers a "neck" was something tortured by a collar, to mothers it was a body part rarely cleaned, to "big brother it is that part of a bottle which will not go completely out of sight in your pocket." To big sister, however, "it's something her date last night could surely do."[59] Indeed, a willingness to pet implied an acceptable celebration of promiscuity. Exclusivity was derided. As one vignette put it, "Isn't it awful the way she pets? Sure is—always the same man."[60] Men who did not meet these expectations themselves became the butt of jokes. Students redefined a dumbwaiter as "a guy that asks for a kiss and then waits for it,"[61] and slyly criticized shy men saying, "he was like the horizon . . . he never got any closer."[62] The culture of college youth so naturalized women's sexual desire, in fact, that it simultaneously excused male aggression.

Men were encouraged to believe that all women wanted to pet, and sanctioned the exclusion of reluctant women from the dating scene. On the one hand, some vignettes suggested that women's refusal was feigned when they rejected advances. "Do you get angry when men get fresh? Of course, but I usually protest in arms." Such an attitude could allow men to believe women desired intimacy despite their protests. Other jokes, however, suggested that fending off unwanted advances required considerable female effort: "He thought his girl had love light in her eyes, but after she slapped him for the 46th time, scratched one eye out, and ruined a good shin, he realized it must have been [a] stop light."[63] The youth culture even encouraged men to believe that they could deduce women's consent by the clothes they wore or their style of make-up. In one poem, the narrator dumped his date Mary because her garters were red, an indication she forced him to stop when his petting reached her garters. His new date Louise was not as pretty as Mary, but her garters were green, implying she did not stop his fumblings as Mary had. The *Glomorata* also used driving as a metaphor, writing, "A traffic light / Means 'stop' when red; / But lips that are / Mean 'Go Ahead.' "[64] A woman's style was thus a scrutable indicator of her modernity, her morality, and her acceptance of dating fashions as well.

Unsurprisingly, men's desire for intimacy could evolve into coercion, especially on dates in cars. A woman who refused intimacy on a car date might be punished by being forced to walk home, an abandonment by her supposed protector that, if the sheer number of references to it are any indication, male and female students saw as justified. Walking home was another term students understood. "Joe: Say, sis, you know why girls walk home? Joena: No. Joe: Well, that's the reason."[65] The following poem darkly wove together the seclusion cars provided, the alcohol dates included, and the expectation of intimacy: "Ah Love! I would with you conspire / To find a quart and a car for hire / Would we not ride and park?—and then / You'd be my sweet or walk home again."[66] Plays on nursery rhymes also took on a sinister hue: "Mary Mary quite contrary / Kept on saying No. / Changed her mind when she found / There were twenty miles to go."[67] "The Tired Girl's Diary" implied that a willingness to be intimate not only guaranteed a ride home, but also insured a wealth of future dates: "Tuesday—Auto ride. Walk back. Saturday—Auto ride. Walk back. Tuesday—Auto ride. Wednesday—Auto ride. Thursday—Auto ride."[68]

Indelibly connected to the pleasures and dangers of dating was the consumption of alcohol. There is little dispute that college students drank heavily during prohibition.[69] The University of Alabama was no different. The Board of Public Health, for example, notified President Denny that when it cleared a vacant field adjacent to campus it found "several bottles of whiskey hidden in the vines," suggesting that the area was the headquarters of a local bootlegger, likely one who sold to college students.[70] Many of the letters between President Denny and the parents of students concerned drinking and its effect on academic work. One mother's reply to the news that her son had been recommended for suspension because of his drinking was only unusual in that she blamed the university for "permitting whiskey to be sold to University students away from their Mothers."[71]

Some observers of college life worried that school administrators either condoned the consumption of alcohol by students or turned a blind eye to it. An anonymous student sent a letter to the governor alerting him that a professor had enabled a student to obtain cash, knowing that the student intended to purchase whiskey. Making the connection between drinking and sexual immorality, the student then noted that the same student "a few nights later went to bed with a co-ed in one of the Frat Houses."[72] Fraternities were frequent targets of allegations of alcohol abuse. It was a common joke that an ideal pledge was one who was the son of a bootlegger. Things apparently got so bad in Tuscaloosa that the U.S. district attorney in Birmingham wrote President Denny concerned about the reports of liquor at fraternity houses and at social events.[73] But drinking was not solely the purview of students. Carl Carmer, in *Stars Fell on Alabama*, his memoir of teaching at the University of Alabama in the 1920s, recounted that shortly after he arrived in Tuscaloosa, one colleague took him for a drive during which they drank moonshine and a second colleague offered him homemade wine before dinner.[74]

While drinking was common, the extent to which women participated is less clear. Amy McCandless argues that alcohol consumption was largely confined to men. She writes, "There is little evidence, however, that Southern College women had the same access to illegal drink as their Northern sisters. . . . Even at coeducational institutions where alcohol flowed freely, women students were forbidden to imbibe." As evidence she cites Auburn University's 1963 handbook which specifically prohibited women's consumption of intoxicating beverages.[75] Both Alabama and Auburn in the 1920s prohibited all their students from consuming alcohol, but as with regulations on women's conduct, student humor suggests that students believed such rules should be flouted. Definitive evidence of drunken co-eds, however, is elusive. President Denny's correspondence occasionally expressed concern about women's behavior but did not contain any specific references to named female student drinking.[76] Rumors about a drunken female student being carried into a fraternity house at Auburn caused such a scandal that they reached the governor's office.[77] Both Alabama and Auburn proudly reported that while there were some violations of the rules by women students, none were sufficient to merit expulsion, perhaps seeking to reassure concerned adults that alleged coed indiscretions were fears and fantasies rather than fact.[78] Nevertheless, the sheer number of allusions to women students drinking, and enjoying drink, suggests that women's participation in illegal alcohol consumption, even in the South, was an accepted part of college life. And while humor might not be an exact representation of reality, as the *Rammer Jammer* suggested, it represented "the truth in an intoxicated condition"—meaning an exaggeration, but not necessarily a fabrication.[79]

The *Crimson-White*, for example, pointedly reminded men that when taking a woman on a date, "Thou shalt always be mindful of her hunger—and thirst."[80] A joke in the *Rammer Jammer* played on generational differences: "Old Lady: Shame on you smoking here in a public place. Why, I would as soon be drunk! Hard-Hearted Hannah: Well, who wouldn't?"[81] Other jokes pointed to connections between women's access to alcohol and their relations with men. "He: Didja ever take a drink? She: 'Twas never necessary. They always offer it to me."[82] Women who shared men's flasks, rather than obtaining alcohol on their own, represented merely another iteration of the requirement that men must provide for their female dates. Women did not merely sip politely. Some apparently got "tight," a 1920s euphemism for drunk.[83] Fictional coed Ruby told her friend she had the grandest time the previous night even though she could not remember anything after eleven p.m. When asked how she knew she had fun, she replied, "Oh, I heard a cop tell the judge about it this morning."[84] According to the *Glomerata*, the usual coed smoked, chewed, cussed, wore rouge and powder, danced, went out with beaus, attended dinner parties, cards, and shows, craved silk "undies" and, notably, bootleg booze.[85] Most students likely agreed with the following version of the myth of Pandora's box, which suggested that modern girls, on their own initiative, drank. Pandora, of course, had been forbidden to open the box, "but [she] was a modern young thing and didn't give a damn about orders. So she snapped the lock and took out the two bottles of Old Crols." [86] Perhaps flirting with evil, modern Alabama coeds snapped their fingers at the possible dangers of alcohol, and enjoyed it with their dates.

While college administrators confronted abstract concerns about student drinking, conduct at University dances drew particular attention. Certainly dances on their own had caused controversy. The new, modern forms of music and dancing were shockingly immodest to members of the older generation. In 1919, for example, Auburn University formally banned several "vulgar" dances including the shimmy dance, the cheek dance, the tickletoe, and others like them. The administration denounced the willingness of young people to adopt what it saw as racially degraded behavior, writing that the "wriggling and writhing" of dancing couples was "an indifferent imitation of a colored cake walk . . . struggling to make decent and respectable an exhibition that was never intended to be such."[87] Alcohol, however, interacted with intimate dancing, leading inexorably it seemed to immorality. In 1921, the student body at Alabama began the Cotillion Club in an effort to control the drinking at University dance functions. It required male students to pay for advanced tickets, and by doing so, agree to "refrain from drinking or becoming intoxicated" at the dance.[88] At Auburn, the president's report to the board of trustees stated that while the "mid-year dances were not so free" from misbehavior, Auburn had instituted a surveillance system by which "each one who goes on the dance floor takes a solemn pledge that he has not taken a drink of liquor during the twelve hours preceding the opening of the dance, and that he will not take a drink during the dance season, nor within twelve hours after the close of the final dance." It also noted that women attending the dance were checked every time they went on the dance floor.[89] At Alabama, women who left the dance hall without a chaperone were forbidden from returning. Evidence from the *Rammer Jammer*, however, suggests this was another rule women and their dates routinely worked to evade.[90]

Efforts to control drinking at dances were a mixed success at best. One local minister wrote President Denny in 1922 that he thought the drinking had decreased admirably, while in 1923 a Birmingham businessman wrote that he had heard that the drinking was getting so heavy at the midterm dances that he thought they should be done away with entirely.[91] There were also problems with drinking at dances that were held off campus. In 1921, the owner of the McLester Hotel in downtown Tuscaloosa responded to Denny's concerns that students had been drinking and disorderly at a dance in his dining room. The interchange did not end favorably, as Denny eventually accused the hotel's proprietor of being seen drunk at a fraternity house.[92] A concerned public school superintendent also wrote Denny about rumors that women were drinking and dancing immorally at University functions. The writer insisted, however, that it was the visiting women, not the coeds, who were to blame.[93] Finally, students at Alabama publicly chastised several students for attending a dance visibly drunk, calling it "a very offensive and disgraceful thing to do" but confirming it occurred nonetheless.[94]

Other sources reiterate that drinking was an integral part of University dances. Carl Carmer believed that most male students were at least "slightly inebriated" at dances.[95] President Knapp at Auburn saw fit to remind fraternities that "there is strictly and absolutely to be no drinking . . . during the period of dances." He also sought to squelch rumors that his decision to crack down on late dates meant he intended to be more lenient when it came to drinking. The use of alcohol, he reiterated, "during the dancing period is just as definitely prohibited as anything can be."[96] Student humor, however, alluded to the extent to which students tried or hoped to violate the rules. One cartoon at Alabama showed a male student inquiring, "Going to the dance tonight?" His male companion replied, "Nah, I'm gonna get drunk at home." Another vignette suggested that it was a blessing that students drank to the point of amnesia: "No one remembers who was there or what happened at the dance last night, and, as a result, many reputations will be saved."[97] A poem implied as well that coeds drank alongside their male dates: "Full many a flask of whitest corn indeed / The gay and polished floors of midterm bear, / Full many a flower becomes the wildest weed, / But not from the spirits in the fragrant air."[98] Alcohol allowed women to let loose, and male students seemed to find particularly attractive a woman who saw herself as modern and uninhibited.

The criticism about drinking on campus was part of a larger debate about the reasons why young people attended college in the first place. The University of Alabama frequently faced charges that its students attended not for the benefits of an education, but for its dissipated social environment. Critics insisted that college was little more than a pleasure resort for wealthy whites who could afford not to work, and that higher education was ultimately harmful. Alabama supporters, for example, howled in protest when a speaker at a small anti-tax rally in the southern part of the state criticized the state's system of higher education and the University of Alabama in particular, saying "the worst service a father could render his son was to send him to the University of Alabama as there he would be taught to be a drunkard, a craps shooter, and an infidel."[99] The letters that parents wrote to George Denny confirmed that many believed evidence of drinking on campus was sure proof that colleges failed to encourage or teach good character. Denny, for example received notice that at least one father "had intended sending his son to the University, but had changed his mind because he had heard there was much drinking and immoral dancing among the students."[100]

For many adults, rumors about college students' antics merely confirmed that American society's moral fabric was beginning to fray. College administrators sought to counter such allegations, responding to reports about student misbehavior, as well as seeking to rid themselves of students who too openly violated rules against drinking and carousing, or for whom such activities overshadowed academic pursuits. Behaviors among college students were not evidence that the youth had become untethered from the moorings of civilized society, however. Instead, as the president of Auburn insisted to his board of trustees, "they are more independent, more ambitious, more self-reliant, and more resourceful than young people ever were before, and that this is due not to deterioration in character or intelligence, but to self-discovery which leads to the recognition of personal responsibility."[101]

College students were not silent in this debate. They recognized that their actions shaped how they and their institutions were viewed by the state at large. They joked that those who believed all college students were little more than drunk dancers in cheap cars spouting revolutionary ideas had probably never met a college student in the flesh.[102] But they also warned their fellow classmates before major dances that their behavior would reflect on their University, and even its ability to raise much needed funds.[103] At the same time, students insisted that the behaviors that the older generation found most objectionable were really not so significant after all. As one student wrote, "Most of the glaring immoralities of our co-eds pointed out by the super-pious and those lacking in understanding and sympathy are not to my mind immoralities at all, but merely matters of taste. I refer especially to smoking, dress or lack of it, and familiarity with men." [104] Students defended their evolving moral code and their reliance on their own sense of propriety. Nevertheless, while debates over how to control student behavior occasionally appeared in local newspapers, others in the South took it into their own hands to police and reform the seemingly immoral and wayward youth. Even for white southerners, flouting moral conventions in Alabama in the 1920s could carry specific dangers, especially with the rise of the second Ku Klux Klan.

Moral regulation was a hallmark of the second Klan. Concerned not only with bootleggers, prostitution, and derelict husbands, the Klan also sought to put an end to new social practices taken up by middle-class white youth. In Georgia, the Klan offered to police the secluded areas that young couples used as "places of assignation," hoping to eliminate immorality by shaming young couples caught in indiscretions. Publicizing their names, the Klan argued, would quickly put an end to such practices.[105] Popular literature also picked up the theme of Klan as moral enforcer.[106] Like their fictional counterparts, Alabama's white knights sought to enforce their version of morality on a wayward population. Especially in 1927, the Klan targeted whites who flouted the Klan's codes regarding sexuality and alcohol, flogging them to encourage better behavior.[107] Much of the flogging aimed at reputed bootleggers or women suspected of sexual improprieties, but even respectable couples did not feel immune. Virginia Durr, the future civil rights activist from a well-known Montgomery family, recalled that she and her future husband did most of their courting in a car parked in the garage to avoid the attention of the Klan. In 1926 and 1927 Klan groups in the Birmingham area raided couples parked on dates on well-known lover's lanes, without resorting to the violence of the lash.[108]

The Klan's efforts as moral guardian elided easily into their desire to protect white supremacy. In the eyes of many whites, young and old, the new social and cultural forms of college youth freely toyed with racial boundaries. Adults condemned modern dances for their roots in African American styles, as we saw. But students wove racialized behavior into many aspects of college culture. One sorority, for example, in 1921, received much favorable commentary in the *Crimson-White* after it had conducted its spring program in blackface.[109] Another newspaper issue likened female summer school students' enthusiasm for social life during summer school to "negroes" and religion. College social life softened women's moral code, it suggested and "makes 'em love everybody."[110] Student humor even flirted with the idea of mistaken racial identity. One poem recounted a fictional male student's attempts to sneak into his paramour's yard for a rendezvous, only to find himself embracing her family's black cook.[111] Adherents to white racial superiority shuddered as students openly abandoned the high standards associated with whiteness.

The Klan stood ready to step in where other white adults failed. Tuscaloosa, home of the University of Alabama, had an unusually active Klan.[112] It routinely provided Saturday night excitement by burning crosses along the Black Warrior River just blocks from the University campus.[113] It also emphasized the Klan's position as a surrogate moral guardian. A 1924 publication, *The Fiery Cross*, described the Klan as the "haunting dread of the depraved and the hated Nemesis of the vicious . . . [and] the foe of Vice." More specifically, an address by a Tuscaloosa Klansman noted increasing numbers of daughters "out automobiling on lonely country roads" late at night, warning, "if the mothers of the town did not prepare to look after their daughters the Klan would."[114] There are no reports of actual floggings of students out on dates, but there is other evidence that Tuscaloosa residents feared the Klan's moral enforcement. Carl Carmer, when taken to drink moonshine on his first night in Tuscaloosa, became uneasy when his companions wondered aloud whether the Klan would find them in the woods, suggesting it was something that had happened before.[115] Alabama's students displayed some gallows humor about the Klan's efforts at moral enforcement, especially as it targeted modern women. In a poem entitled "Dollie Goes to College" the *Rammer Jammer* suggested the consequences women might face for imbibing too indulgently in the social activities of college. "Dollie Dingle went out to play / She never played her games by day / Dollie Dingle went away— / Klu Klux.[sic]"[116]

Ominous as Dollie's come-uppance might appear, however, when the Klan did chastise moral delinquents, it punished either the men alone, or the couple together. Nevertheless, it illustrates that the social etiquette of youth, the manners and morals that shaped interactions between men and women were not limited to the man and the woman together on a date. Beliefs and expectations about the culture of dating and social life on campus caused social friction precisely because they sought to blur visible differences that many thought provided the foundation for the southern social order. The rituals of dating in college allowed the youth to bridge supposedly immutable gender differences through potentially erotic interactions. They simultaneously highlighted the differences between students and those supervising their college experience. For some adults, the behavior of youth even erased racial difference, bringing the vice and immorality that was thought to be the exclusive province of African Americans into the dorms, the back seats, and the gymnasium dances of white college students. The addition of alcohol further compromised cherished social norms, turning respectable white, middle-class youth into irresponsible, pleasure-seeking law-breakers who mirrored racist stereotypes of blacks. To the Klan, fearful of modern culture, such elisions were unacceptable, making their efforts to return to a time when men and women, blacks and whites knew their places all the more imperative. To those concerned about the coed on the wild party that began this paper, who desired fifty percent moonshine and fifty percent moonshine, both parts of the equation spelled her ruin, and perhaps that of society as well. To college youth, however, wild parties merely represented a new estimation of women's value and a new commodification of dating. Pandora's Box was open. Women had tasted freedom and desire along with

their two bottles of Old Crols. They invested their sexuality with new meaning, as something to be savored, rather than hoarded. There was little sense
in trying to close the box again.

Notes

1. For information on Prohibition, see John Kobler, *Ardent Spirits: The Rise
and Fall of Prohibition* (New York: Da Capo Press, 1993). For information on women
and alcohol, see Catherine Gilbert Murdock, *Domesticating Drink: Women, Men,
and Alcohol in America, 1870–1940* (Baltimore: Johns Hopkins, 1998). Works that
explore prohibition in Alabama specifically include, Mary Martha Thomas, *The
New Woman in Alabama: Social Reforms and Suffrage, 1890–1920* (Tuscaloosa:
University of Alabama Press, 1992) 10–40; Arthur F. Howington, "John Barley-
corn Subdued: The Enforcement of Prohibition in Alabama," *The Alabama Review*, (July 1970), 212–25; and James Benson Sellers, *The Prohibition Movement in
Alabama, 1702–1943* (Chapel Hill: University of North Carolina Press, 1943).

2. *Rammer Jammer*, vol. 1, no. 1, 36.

3. There are numerous allusions to women and alcohol in Alabama's student
publications that reflect the larger culture of the 1920s. For example, references
to "tight skirts" played both on flapper fashions and on drunk women. See, for
example, *Rammer Jammer*, vol. 7, no. 3, 6.

4. This paper builds on the wonderful work of Paula Fass, who, while focusing primarily on northern schools, does include information from southern
schools like LSU. In many ways, what I have found in Alabama fits well within
her analysis of youth culture in the 1920s. One notable difference, however,
is that while Fass argues that much of the socializing of youth, with its attendant forms of sexual expression, was a result of the dislocations of war, my evidence suggests many aspects of the youth culture of the 1920s were present before World War I. Paula Fass, *The Damned and the Beautiful: American Youth in
the 1920s* (New York: Oxford University Press, 1977). Another work that touches
on southern higher education, youth culture, and the older generation's discomfort with the attitudes of college students is Lawrence J. Nelson's, *Rumors of In-
discretion: The University of Missouri "Sex Questionnaire" Scandal in the Jazz Age*
(Columbia: University of Missouri Press, 2003).

5. Several contemporary novels explore the national culture of college youth,
including F. Scott Fitzgerald, *This Side of Paradise*, L. and L. S. Montross, *Town and
Gown*, and Percy Marks, *The Plastic Age*, which Alabama students considered re-

quired reading. In each novel, dating, the ubiquity of alcohol, and the joys and perils of petting play prominent roles.

6. I am certainly not the first historian to comment on the commodification of dating, as well as the commodification of women in the early twentieth century. Beth Bailey spends much time exploring economic metaphors in dating. See Beth Bailey, *From Front Porch to Back Seat: Courtship in Twentieth-Century America* (Baltimore: Johns Hopkins University Press, 1988).

7. The term "rating and dating" was popularized in 1937, by Willard Waller, and referred to a system of dating in which one's status was determined by the quantity and quality of one's dating partners. It was characterized by what Beth Bailey described as a kind of promiscuous popularity, where success was determined by the sheer number of dates one had rather than having a single steady boyfriend or girlfriend. It is clear that this system shaped how young people understood dating in the 1920s and 1930s. But Daphne Cunningham's diaries suggest that it took shape much earlier. While she never discussed whether her dates rated, quantities of dates seemed to override the relative quality of dates. Admittedly, while it is difficult to argue that her experiences alone are sufficient to make this claim, they are nonetheless suggestive, not least because they seemed so acceptable to those around her. For an analysis of the system of rating and dating, see Willard Waller, "The Rating and Dating Complex," *American Sociological Review*, 2 (October 1937), 727–34, and Beth Bailey, 25–56. James R. McGovern has also argued that the social revolution in manners and morals of the 1920s actually began earlier. See James R. McGovern, "The American Woman's Pre–World War I Freedom in Manners and Morals," *Journal of American History*, 55 (September 1968), 315–33.

8. Information on the number of men she dated and the various activities she engaged in with men are culled from her two diaries, which reside at the Hoole Special Collections Library at the University of Alabama, Tuscaloosa, AL. Events are listed by date.

9. Enrollment of women at the University of Alabama can be found in Helen Delpar, "Coeds and the 'Lords of Creation': Women Students at the University of Alabama, 1893–1930," *Alabama Review*, (October, 1989), 294.

10. "A Coed Looks Back at the Campus of 1916," *Tuscaloosa News*, July 3, 1966.

11. Daphne Cunningham, May 18, 1914.

12. Daphne Cunningham, June 7, 1914, and July 14, 1914.

13. Daphne Cunningham, June 27, 1914.

14. Daphne Cunningham, July 10, 1914, July 11, 1914.

15. Daphne Cunningham, July 4, 1914; July 27, 1914; August 31, 1914; September 18, 1914. Fussing, as a term, implied some intimate interaction, though likely not to the extent of petting. It came into use in the 1890s, and applied to heterosocial activities. Margaret Lowe briefly discusses "fussing" in her analysis of college women and body image. As she writes, the term "most likely derived from its early meaning—'a bustle or commotion'—and by the turn of the century was modified into the slang 'a drinking spree, a binge, a spree of any kind.'" Regardless of the exact meaning of the term, it does suggest that men and women engaged in a considerable amount of interaction well before the 1920s. See Margaret A. Lowe, *Looking Good: College Women and Body Image, 1875–1930* (Baltimore: Johns Hopkins University Press, 2003), 93.

16. Daphne Cunningham, July 6, 1914, and July 9, 1914.

17. The war also may have affected her choices. C. W. Joplin who took her riding, to dances, and for whom she broke a date with Charlie Plyer to attend College Night with, and "was glad of it," was killed fighting in France in 1918. Both Hargrove Vander Graaf and Kid Aldridge, who were frequent companions, were decorated for their wartime service. Hargrove returned to Tuscaloosa, never married, and died suddenly in 1938. Kid Aldridge married, but committed suicide in 1942. De Vane Jones, another favored date, became a well-known lawyer in town. I could find no information about what happened to either Hugh Sherman or Edwin Goodhue after the close of her diary.

18. Daphne Cunningham, September 1, 1914.

19. Daphne Cunningham, August 11, 1914.

20. "A Coed Looks Back at the Campus of 1916," *Tuscaloosa News*, July 3, 1966.

21. "Rules and Regulations Governing the University Women Students," *Crimson-White*, October 1, 1925, 2. In 1926, at the request of the women's council, the University altered the regulations governing senior coeds. As long as they maintained passing grades, they could have dates every night, they could dine unchaperoned in hotels during the day (but not in the evening), and they could ride to certain locations at night. Senior coeds were required to pledge adherence to the new rules formally. While the council insisted that the new regulations were not compulsory, any senior female who failed or refused to sign her name to the pledge would forego the new privileges. It was a stipulation that caused an outcry among a small group of women who noted that the new rules could not be considered voluntary if failure to sign the pledge resulted in the loss of senior privileges. "Women's Council is Functioning By New System," *Crimson-*

White, October 7, 1926. Protest by eight of the coeds appeared in "Eight Girls Refuse New Rules," *Crimson-White*, February 10, 1927.

22. Hazel Goodman, class of 1929, recalled the curfew rules for women. See Hazel Goodman, Correspondence, A Century of Women at Auburn, RG 929, box 1, Auburn University Archives, Auburn, AL. Leah Watkins described the Dean of Women's attempts to enforce compliance in A Century of Women at Auburn: Blossoms Amid the Deep Verdure, p. 10, in RG 929, box 1. President Knapp's definition of late dates appears in a letter to T. A. Walthall, President of Theta Chi Fraternity, January 24, 1929, folder "1928–1929," Letters to T. A. Waltham, Knapp Presidential Records, Acc #533B, box 3, Auburn University Archives.

23. L. T. Campbell to George Denny, August 8, 1921, folder "July, August, September, 1921," Denny Papers, box 3, Hoole Special Collections, The University of Alabama.

24. F. A. Weaver to Baptist Preacher of Tuscaloosa, August 22, 1922, folder "August 14–31, 1922," Denny Papers, box 4. Weaver also wrote Denny August 28, 1922.

25. W. O. Cusman (illegible) to George Denny, July 9, 1923, folder "July 1923," Denny Papers, box 4.

26. *Rammer Jammer*, vol. 6, no. (unclear), 15. The content of the *Rammer Jammer* was scrutinized by faculty advisors who had ultimate say over its publication. One issue in 1931 was cancelled entirely by censors leading the editors to title its issue for February 1932 the "Suppression" issue.

27. These of course only included those who sought treatment, and sought it from the college doctor, and they do not specify the sex of the patient (I am making the assumption that they were at least mostly men). The college surgeon's reports included numbers of cases of VD between 1926 and 1930. See Annual Reports to the Board of Trustees in the presidential papers of Spright Dowell and Bradford Knapp, Auburn University Archives.

28. "Students Speak at Y Meeting," *Crimson-White*, November 26, 1920.

29. President Knapp to T. A. Waltham, October 10, 1928; Leland Cooper to Governor Bibb Graves, November 4, 1927, Governor Graves Administrative Files, SG 21170, ADAH; Zoe Dobbs, Dean of Women Report included in the President's Official Report to the Board of Trustees, May 19, 1930, Knapp Presidential Papers, Acc #533B, box 1, Auburn University Archives.

30. "The Both of Us," *Crimson-White*, December 13, 1922, 8.

31. "Sensations of a Summer School Girl," *Crimson-White*, June 19, 1924, 4.

32. See, for example, "Coeducation Discussed at Forum Meet," *Crimson-White*, October 25, 1923, 3. "Coed Controversy," *Crimson-White*, May, 1929, 4.

33. See, for example, *Rammer Jammer*, vol. 2, no. 1, 21, which parodied a children's song, "Do you feed your chickens corn, naughty boy, naughty boy? Do you feed your chickens corn, naughty boy? Do they stagger in at dawn, Swearing that they're off of corn? Do you feed your chickens corn, naughty boy." The women's residence at Auburn was commonly known as "the Zoo."

34. *Crimson-White*, September 18, 1924; *Crimson-White*, April 7, 1921; *Rammer Jammer*, vol. 2, No 1, 11.

35. See, for example, "Saturday Night Rules," *Crimson-White*, December 10, 1920, 3 and "Advice to Boys: How to Get a Date at the Ranch," *Crimson-White*, March 22, 1923, 4.

36. "Interpolation on Women and Other Subjects By a Mere Man," *Crimson-White*, February 14, 1924. The term "rushing," which meant to pursue a woman as a potential dating partner, and paralleled the courtship of potential pledges by fraternities and sororities, appeared in Montross and Montross, *Town and Gown*, and several other sociological studies of college students.

37. *Glomerata*, 1927, 398.

38. "How to Sew Up a Girl at the Ranch," *Crimson-White*, October 4, 1923, 8.

39. "The Etiquette of the Stag Line," *Crimson-White*, October 4, 1928. Since popularity was determined by the quantity of dates, a desirable, meaning popular, dancing partner was defined by near-continual cutting in. Getting "stuck" meant dancing with a woman with whom no other man wanted to break in.

40. "Meet Her In A drive It," *Rammer Jammer*, vol. 3, no. 3, 148.

41. *Rammer Jammer*, vol. 1, no. 4, 85.

42. *Crimson-White*, June 12, 1924, 4.

43. *Rammer Jammer*, vol. 5, no. 1, 11.

44. "Ramme Nasrah Writes of Hair, Bobbed, Or Otherwise," *Crimson-White*, July 3, 1924, 2; *Rammer Jammer*, vol. 2, no. 6, 146.

45. "The Ladies, Gentlemen . . ." *Crimson-White*, October 22, 1926, 4.

46. "And at the Ranch," *Crimson-White*, March 13, 1924, 6.

47. *Rammer Jammer*, vol. 2, no. 3, 62.

48. "Conquests of a Co-Ed," *Crimson-White*, February 2, 1922, 4. Another example is "Said the king, when his daughter was eloping, 'Be careful, knaves, else the princess gives us the slip.'" *Rammer Jammer*, vol. 4, no. 1, 19.

49. "Student Draws Date Contract With Coed," *Crimson-White*, April 10, 1924, 5.

50. *Rammer Jammer*, vol. 1, no. 1, 1924, 36.

51. *Rammer Jammer*, vol. 1, no. 3, 65.

52. "My Gal—Maybe," *Glomerata*, 1929, (no page number).

53. *Rammer Jammer*, vol. 1, no. 2, 37.

54. See, for example, *Rammer Jammer*, vol. 2, no. 3, 91. In this poem, the narrator is a female, who confirms that she kisses her date because she "loved [his] cadillac."

55. *Crimson-White*, June 23, 1921, 3.

56. *Glomerata*, 1929, Ad Section.

57. *Rammer Jammer*, vol. 6, no. 4, 14.

58. *Rammer Jammer*, vol. 2, no. 4, 81.

59. *Rammer Jammer*, vol. 2, no. 3, 59. Humor magazines frequently noted that college students rapidly learned a new vocabulary as college students. New definitions of corn, water, and tight referred to drinking, new definitions of ranch, chicken, dance, and promise referred to interactions between men and women. See *Rammer Jammer*, vol. 1, no. 1, 12; vol. 2, no. 5, 137; vol. 3, no. 1, 14; vol. 6, 7.

60. *Rammer Jammer*, vol. 1, no. 3, 68.

61. *Rammer Jammer*, vol. 3, no. 1, 95.

62. *Rammer Jammer*, vol. 1, no. 1, 11.

63. *Rammer Jammer*, vol. 3, no. 3, 144.

64. *Rammer Jammer*, vol. 4, no. 4, 17; *Glomerata*, 1929, Ad Section.

65. *Rammer Jammer*, vol. 3, no. 6, 217.

66. *Rammer Jammer*, vol. 2, no. 4, 85.

67. *Rammer Jammer*, vol. 8, no. 2, 16.

68. *Rammer Jammer*, vol. 6, no. 2, 8. While references to women being forced to walk home for refusing intimacy are not common in sociological studies of college students in the 1920s (largely, I think, because male sexual coercion was considered normal and thus unworthy of comment), there is considerably more information about women's understanding that a willingness to pet was required for getting dates. See for example, Phyllis Blanchard and Carlyn Manasses, *New Girls for Old* (New York: The Macauley Company, 1937), 62–66. Women's attitudes are difficult to determine with any certainty, because much of the doggerel that appeared in student humor publications was unsigned. It is entirely possible the sentiments expressed represented male interests. When the *Rammer Jammer* dedicated an issue to Alabama's female students, and stated that it hoped most of the contents of the issue would be written by the coeds themselves, it later admitted failure, as few female students submitted any jokes to be considered for publication. This suggests that men wrote the bulk of the humor that appeared within the magazine's pages. (See "Rammer Jammer Material Needed for Next Number," *Crimson-White*, February 12, 1925, 1.) Nevertheless, I think it

is likely that at least some women shared the attitudes of their fellow male students. There is no record that any of the humor in the *Rammer Jammer* elicited protest from female students. And the only protest that female students mustered concerned the administration's efforts to restrict dating.

69. See Fass, *The Damned and the Beautiful*, 310–24. See also contemporary sociological studies of college students, all of which addressed the problem of drinking on campuses. Certainly not all students drank, but one study estimated that approximately 64 percent of male students and as many as 56 percent of female students occasionally imbibed. (See Blanchard and Manasses, *New Girls for Old*, 67.) A study of college seniors reported that of 3,250 students, 2,178 drank at least occasionally. (J. H. Barnett, "College Seniors and the Liquor Problem," in *Prohibition: A National Experiment*, published by the Annals of the American Academy of Political and Social Sciences in 1932, p. 130–46, table on 139.) Concerns about college student life almost invariably included efforts to control student drinking, and to make sure that inebriated students did not attend college functions. See, Dorothy Dunbar Bromley and Florence Haxton Britton, *Youth and Sex: A Study of 1300 College Students* (New York: Harper and Brothers, 1938), 161–65; R. H. Edwards, J. M. Artman, and Galen M. Fisher, *Undergraduates: A Study of Morale in Twenty-Three American Colleges and Universities* (New York: Doubleday, 1928), 182–85.

70. A. A. Kirk to President Denny, January 27, 1923, folder "To Dr. Denny, February 1923," Denny Correspondence, box 4.

71. Mrs. E. H. Jewell-Loudermilk to President Denny, February 6, 1923, folder "To Dr. Denny February 1923," Denny Correspondence, box 4.

72. Anonymous letter to Governor Brandon, April 14, 1923, copy in folder "March–April 1923," Denny Correspondence, box 4.

73. Jim C. Smith to President Denny, March 28, 1923, folder "March–April, 1923," Denny Correspondence, box 4.

74. Wine made at home for one's own consumption did not violate the Volstead Act, but Prohibition's supporters hoped that community leaders would refrain from drinking any alcohol whatsoever. Carl Carmer, *Stars Fell on Alabama* (Tuscaloosa: University of Alabama Press, 1985, reprint of 1934 edition by Farrar and Rinehart), 5–7, 10. Carmer also notes the social atmosphere at the University of Alabama, the importance of dating, and profusion of dances for students including "afternoon dances, evening dances, morning dances, the latest innovation being 'early morning' dances from six to eight." Carmer, 12–15, quote on 13.

75. Amy McCandless, *The Past in the Present: Women's Higher Education in the Twentieth-Century American South* (Tuscaloosa: University of Alabama Press, 1999), 131–32.

76. An important indication of the extent of female drinking might be found in the records of the Dean of Women or in disciplinary files. Student records, however, are protected by federal privacy laws and thus unavailable to scholars.

77. See Governor Thomas E. Kilby, Administrative Files, SG 22128, folder 12, Alabama Department of Archives and History, Montgomery, AL. Auburn University officials eventually reassured the governor that the report was merely vicious rumor.

78. See for example, President Denny to T. V. Ballard, August 6, 1921, folder "July, August, September, 1921," Denny Papers, box 3; Report to the Board of Trustees, February 12, 1926, p. 16; Report of the Dean of Women, 1925–1926, p. 3, Dowell Papers, RG 533, box 1 and Social Activities Report of the Directory, May 18, 1927, Dowell Papers, RG 533, box 2, Auburn University Archives.

79. *Rammer Jammer*, vol. 6, no. 2, 27.

80. "Ten Commandments," *Crimson-White*, June 22, 1922, 1.

81. *Rammer Jammer*, vol. 2, no. 5, 117.

82. *Rammer Jammer*, vol. 3, no. 2, 132.

83. The successive stages of inebriation included, "high, tight, looping, stinking, plastered, [and] out." See *Youth and Sex*, 165.

84. *Rammer Jammer*, vol. 5, no. 1, 23.

85. *Glomerata*, 1926, 188.

86. "An Alumnus's Recollection of a Few Classy Myths," *Rammer Jammer*, vol. 2, no. 3, 54.

87. Reported in "Vulgar Dances Barred by Auburn Faculty," *Crimson-White*, July 10, 1919. *Town and Gown* included a chapter satirizing efforts to control indecent dancing, including requirements that dancing couples maintain six inches of space between them. At the end, the prudish, spinster chaperone also banned bass drums in dancing music because they encouraged savage instincts. Montross, *Town and Gown*, 185–200.

88. "University Dances," *Crimson-White*, March 24, 1921, 2.

89. Report to the Board of Trustees, May, 1923, Spright Dowell Presidential Papers, RG 533, box 1.

90. Johnnie Lee Stallworth mentions the rule in her letter to President Denny in which she compliments him on his efforts to control drinking at dances. Stallworth to Denny, January 27, 1921, folder "January 1921," Denny Papers, box 3.

Efforts to evade the rule appear in jokes suggesting couples returned to the dance hall in order to "cool off." Numerous cartoons also showed couples dressed in evening attire under trees or otherwise away from the dance hall.

91. Charles M. Boyd to President Denny, January 31, 1922, folder "January 1922," Denny Correspondence, box 4; Hill Ferguson to President Denny, January 1923, folder "to Dr. Denny, February 1923," Denny Correspondence, box 4.

92. Alden H. Snow to President Denny, February 18, 1921; President Denny to Alden H. Snow, February 19, 1921, folder "February 1921," Denny Correspondence, box 3.

93. P. W. Williams to President Denny, January 30, 1922, folder "January 1922," Denny Correspondence, box 3.

94. "They Should Be Punished," *Crimson-White*, February 28, 1924, 2.

95. Carmer, *Stars Fell on Alabama*, 15.

96. President Knapp to T. A. Waltham, January 24, 1929; President Knapp to The Committee Representing Each Fraternity, May 13, 1929, folder "Fraternities, 1929–30," Knapp Presidential Records, Acc #533B, box 3, Auburn University Archives.

97. *Rammer Jammer*, vol. 1, no. 2, 42.

98. *Rammer Jammer*, vol. 2, no. 4, 85.

99. These words were reportedly spoken by W. O. Mulkey and were reported in newspapers throughout the state. The resulting uproar even made it to the desk of the governor before Mulkey insisted, implausibly perhaps, that he had been misquoted by a young reporter. See "Mulkey Causes Big Sensation by His Recent Charges," *Birmingham Age-Herald*, May 2, 1921; "Every Item of the Mulkey Charges Denied by Denny," *Birmingham Age-Herald*, May 3, 1921.

100. P. W. Williams to George Denny, January 30, 1922, folder "January 1922," Denny Papers, box 3.

101. Report to the Board of Trustees, June 21, 1926, p. 11, Dowell Presidential Papers, RG 533, box 1, Auburn University Archives.

102. *Crimson-White*, January 24, 1929.

103. See, for example, "Be Careful," *Crimson-White*, April 24, 1925, 2; and "On Display," *Crimson-White*, April 30, 1925, 2.

104. "The Ladies, Gentlemen," *Crimson-White*, October 22, 1926, 4.

105. Nancy McLean, *Behind the Mask of Chivalry: The Making of the Second Ku Klux Klan* (New York: Oxford University Press, 1994), 92–124, quote on 103.

106. In 1930, Roy Flannigan published his tawdry novel, *The Whipping*, about a Klan flogging of a white woman who got the respectable son of a local businessman drunk. Hart Stilwell's 1950 novel *Campus Town* also depicted efforts by

the 1920s Klan to use violence against whites to enforce its vision of American values.

107. Glenn Feldman, *Politics, Society, and the Klan in Alabama, 1915–1949* (Tuscaloosa: University of Alabama Press, 1999), 92–115.

108. Quoted in Feldman, 101.

109. "Co-Ed Minstrel is Big Success: Classy Black-face Minstrel and Burlesque Tragedy Presented by Lively Bunch of Co-eds," *Crimson-White*, April 28, 1921, 2. An additional approving review of the show appeared on page 4 of the same issue.

110. "News from Dago," *Crimson-White*, June 24, 1921, 1.

111. *Crimson-White*, November 4, 1920.

112. Feldman mentions the Tuscaloosa Klan throughout his book.

113. Carmer provides an evocative description of the Klan burning a cross near the campus in *Stars Fell on Alabama*, 28–32.

114. *The Fiery Cross*, 23; "100% Americanism or Tenets of the Ku Klux Klan," 68, *The Fiery Cross*, September 1, 1924, Hoole Special Collections, The University of Alabama. This is the only known issue of the publication.

115. Carmer, *Stars Fell on Alabama*, 6.

116. *Rammer Jammer*, vol. 4, no. 1, 1927, 11.

Scepter and Masque

Debutante Rituals in Mardi Gras New Orleans

Catherine Clinton

In the efforts of full disclosure, I must confess I was not a debutante. When I was coming of age in my hometown of Kansas City, Missouri, the practice of being introduced into "society" through a series of parties culminating in formal presentation at a ball following your first year of college was far from tempting.[1] When the city fathers of Kansas City wanted to bolster tourism in the 1880s, they sent a delegation to New Orleans to come back with a plan. Subsequently, civic boosters founded a "krewe,"—the term coined in New Orleans by secret societies established in the 1850s. In Kansas City, the Priests of Pallas sponsored parades and balls, exclusive dances during which queens were crowned, a custom that prevailed from the 1880s until 1924. The Pallas parade boasted elaborate floats with annual themes that had men dressing as Greek goddesses in 1887 and even a cross-dressing Mother Goose in 1898—all in keeping with the mystery and peculiar mannerisms of one of the most fascinating carnival traditions, the Mardi Gras balls and crowning of krewe queens.

The demands and dimensions of the rituals surrounding both New Orleans Mardi Gras and the town's debutante season is really territory ripe for anthropologists as much as historians.[2] I would also venture a guess that a good 99 percent of those who are aware of Mardi Gras celebrations in New Orleans, or who attend Mardi Gras festivities, or who long to experience "Mardi Gras" have no real awareness of the debutante season connected to this tradition. (I would bet more tourists are aware of the drag queen contests than of the other kinds of "coming out" parties.) But this New Orleans cotillion culture is a rich and fascinating part of southern manners, and an overlooked dimension of "social studies."[3]

The origins of the debutante ball can be traced back to European origins.[4] Elizabeth I "began the custom of presenting eligible young women at court . . . and Queen Victoria . . . included the daughters of the rising haute bourgeoisie along with those of nobility and the gentry."[5] Court debuts of American "princesses" date back to Pocahontas's debut at the court of James I in 1616.[6] Almost as soon as the colonials broke with England they launched their own ceremonies to replicate the trappings of a formal court presentation.

In certain circles, being presented at the British court remains a high point of demonstrating that one has "arrived" for certain groups of social elites—different from the practice of debutantes applying to meet the monarch, which was suspended by the British Queen in 1958.[7] In many ways, the decorum for these court presentations was similar to the trappings required for a stateside debutante. When Abigail Adams, wife of the first American ambassador, was presented in 1785, "She wore the prescribed costume of the day: an all-white dress with a three-yard train and the ruffled cuffs signaling her status as a married woman."[8] Adams had an aversion to the court scene, and wrote home, "Nor would I ever again set foot there if the etiquette of my country did not require it."[9] However, Karal Marling points out that nineteenth-century etiquette manuals—American bestsellers throughout the nineteenth century and into the twentieth—included elaborate instructions concerning royal presentations.[10]

Even those Americans who disdained the trappings of a genuine monarch seemed very quick to replicate presentation rituals in their homegrown ceremonies launched along the eastern seaboard, most notably the Bachelor's Cotillion in Baltimore (1797), as well as the St. Cecilia Society of Charleston (which traces back to 1737, but only began formal balls in 1819).[11]

But the most complex and interesting of all debutante cultures spawned in the United States would have to remain the elaborate intersection of Carnival and cotillion that reigns in New Orleans. The origins of Carnival in New Orleans are part of a lively literature.[12] Suffice to say that we know that early Carnival customs in New Orleans stemmed from European traditions, and adaptations fit the malleable and interesting requirements of the city's evolving multicultural and multiracial heritage.

Although Mardi Gras historian Reid Mitchell claims "Mardi Gras in its modern form was thus a child of Reconstruction,"[13] early carnival traditions can be traced back to the city's Franco-Spanish roots. And by the second quarter of the century, Mardi Gras parades were firmly in place, as an 1838 newspaper noted: "The European custom of celebrating the last day of the Carnival by a procession of masqued figures through the public streets was introduced here yesterday very much to the amusement of our citizens."[14] (Some suggest it was an invasion of Cowbellians—as the oddly named parade society from Mobile was called, but I will leave these debates to the experts.[15])

We know that by the 1840s masked revelers might end their parade at a theater, taking the "theater of the streets" inside. Upon occasion, leaders of the parade would march up the aisle to join the actors onstage at the Orleans Theater, before adjourning to a ballroom, for a private celebration.[16] Many of these staged events hearkened back the to the tradition of mummers' parades, still held in Philadelphia. And like these street revels along the eastern seaboard, the festivities could result in outbreaks of violence. The antebellum New Orleans press was full of complaints about blacks and Irish, who were using the holiday as an excuse for unruly and destructive behavior.[17]

The masked men on parade did use the occasion of Mardi Gras to mock their "betters" as the custom of *entrudo* demonstrated: "Every Mardi Gras man has his pockets filled with flour, and as he passes the well-dressed stranger, who excited by curiosity gets near, throws handfuls upon him to the amusement of those bystanders who fortunately escape."[18] In 1853 one gentleman felt so injured that he had his "attacker" arrested. But this was an unusual circumstance. Most Mardi Gras disputes did not end up in the courts—as the festival was often treated as a "time out" for law enforcement during the nineteenth century (in contrast to the twentieth, when a police strike in 1979 forced the suspension of Mardi Gras parades).

The identification of Mardi Gras with violence persisted, until the New Orleans *Bee* complained, "Better no celebration of Mardi Gras than have our dreams filled with shades of murdered men and helpless orphans."[19] However, with each passing year neighborhood processions and masqued revelers became more and more elaborate, and eagerly anticipated by the townsfolk.

In order to impose order and to cash in on this annual festival, Anglo-American town fathers (as opposed to the Franco-Americans who still spoke French, intermarried, and abhorred the "yanqui" hoi-polloi) created a group known as the "Mystic Krewe of Comus." These were an elite group of thirty—all businessmen, most *slaveholders* as well. They organized an elaborate nighttime parade with blacks carrying oil lamps to light the procession. The use of black torchbearers is a striking tradition that continues into the twenty-first century. Membership was exclusive and members were sworn to secrecy on all matters Comus.

Some suggest Comus was a plot to Anglicize New Orleans high society. The group also launched a private social club, the Pickwick, in the wake of the krewe's successful festivities. The Pickwick was the second men's club in the city—a rival for the prestigious Boston Club, founded in 1841, which claims to be the nation's third oldest exclusive club. The Pickwick cherished the names and symbols of antiquity, as well as their secretive selectivity.[20] But before I get bogged down in Mardi Gras minutiae, let me move forward toward debutante rituals that blossomed after the Civil War.

There is a modest folk culture tradition of Mardi Gras, which becomes embellished and made its own by local New Orleans movers and shakers during the late 1850s. Although Yankee authorities tried to stop the festivities during their Civil War occupation, Union soldiers commented on the celebrations—most often favorably. This launches an important cultural and commercial trend: the commodification of the New Orleans exotic—its very otherness being both dangerous and alluring to outsiders, especially Yankees.[21]

Many Carnival scholars discuss 1872 as a key year because it was at this moment when a visit of the Grand Duke Alexis of Russia during Carnival season prompted initiation of extravagant parade strategies. A grand procession was sponsored by the Krewe of Rex, a group to this day that remains different from other societies. Its members were distinctly business oriented, their membership and crowned king were *not* secret, and their motto: *Pro Bono Publico—for the good of the public*—betrays a civic-minded mission.[22] By contrast, the Comus motto is *Sic volo, sic iubeo—as I wish it, thus I command*—and by custom Rex must leave his ball with his consort to attend the court of Comus and pay homage shortly before midnight of Ash Wednesday.[23]

Rex ushered in the era of the modern Mardi Gras, when a "grand parade of floats" came to symbolize the celebration—what has now become ritualized and extremely commercialized. Today a krewe's night parade costs as much as $70,000—for a start-up group, less than half this for established krewes that own the necessary equipment and are able to recycle materials.

These elaborate parades generally hire over fifty blacks to carry the torches, fifty men to carry placards for floats (announcing the themes of each float), and (in earlier times) nearly fifty more men to lead mules to haul the floats (per parade). Parades continue the musical tradition with nearly 250 musicians per parade—predominantly blacks drafted from local talent and/or high school marching bands. There are more than sixty krewes that carry on this parade tradition in twenty-first century New Orleans—and perhaps half that number that satirize the official groups and carry on an effective counter-tradition.

Carnival scholar Samuel Kinser describes an evolution of the folk festival aspect of New Orleans's Mardi Gras into a larger extravaganza, just as a newspaper complained in 1882: "The magnificent parades of Rex and of Comus are yearly increasing in splendor, but I am afraid they are doing it at the expense of the general jollity of the home parade!"[24] Kinser distinguishes between the first and second phases of Mardi Gras—its evolution from a hometown festival into a cultural landmark (and goldmine) for New Orleans—in the national and international arenas.

Reid Mitchell underscores the political issues associated with the revival of elaborate parades after the Civil War. Some other historians of New Orleans have showcased New South pride among city fathers, downplaying neo-Confederate aspects of postwar revivals. Again, much of this is not germane to debutante issues, and I must be selective in detailing the development of krewe balls and Queens for a Day, which are the focus of my investigation.

However, it would be remiss not to note the centrality of men's clubs and krewe culture to those post–Civil War battles that so distinguished New Orleans during Reconstruction. Certainly krewe members were central players in the 1874 White League Riot when a mob attacked the state constitutional convention, killing thirty-eight people, most of them black. What came to be known as the "Battle of Liberty Place" or the "Battle of September 14th" was a defining moment for white New Orleaneans. One hundred and sixteen of the one hundred and sixty-one members of the Pickwick Club fought in this uprising, and the plotters gathered to hatch their violent plans at the Boston Club.[25] This massacre signaled the defiant, supremacist backbone of krewe culture: white elites demanded total control, by violent means, if necessary.

The playful themes of Carnival parades took on an ominous cast as Mardi Gras krewes became more bold. The 1877 Comus's parade was entitled "The Aryan Race."[26] The Knights of Momus, founded in 1872, featured an equally chilling political theme in 1877 with "Hades: A Dream of Momus." Maskers portrayed New Orleans as "the outskirts of hell, populated by members of the Grant administration." The final float of their procession was called

"Ship of State," depicting a foundering vessel, sinking into a sea of fire. But these themes and topics were *unusual*, as in a survey of the more than sixteen hundred parade themes since 1857, the number one topic continues "fairy tales or children's books."[27]

Krewes may or may not parade, but all provide an invitational ball. The oldest and most traditional krewes (with the exception of Rex and Hermes) only send invitations to names approved by a screening committee. The screening committee mirrors the conservative, protectionist attitudes typifying krewe culture: secret, prideful, clannish, and male-dominated.[28]

After the parade, krewes perform a thematic tableaux at the invitational ball. At the outset, there was great competition over these displays, especially for emerging groups, such as the Knights of Proteus, who appeared in 1882. These elaborately staged playlets are performed for the benefit of a select audience, not really for "public" consumption. Only the invited members of a restrictive social circle are allowed to witness these ornate displays of conspicuous consumption—*and cross-dressing*, I might add. Only krewe members, young women (the Queen, her court of maids, and selected debutantes) and a handful of young male pages are allowed on stage—while family, friends, and special guests look on.

Carnival became the symbol of New Orleans. Descriptions of lavish Mardi Gras celebrations appeared in national periodicals, such as *Century Magazine* and *Scribner's* in the 1880s. Although it had been the richest city in the South in 1860, New Orleans was economically stagnant after the Civil War. Carnival played the central role in reviving the tourist economy. Twenty years before the war began New Orleans was the third largest city in the country, but by 1900 it was twelfth in population, outstripped by northern urban centers.[29]

In 1880 only sixty thousand tourists flocked to New Orleans, but city fathers hoped to dramatically increase this number. An aggressive campaign paid off. In 1882 *A History of the Carnival at New Orleans*, published by a railroad company, was widely distributed—full of advertisements encouraging visitors to put New Orleans on their schedule, to make a Mardi Gras visit. By the turn of the century, over one hundred thousand heeded the call. Special trains were set up to take carloads of visitors from northern cities.[30] Yankee visitors enjoyed participation in this ritualized southern boosterism, as New Orleans played on decidedly nostalgic images.

The Lost Cause became overlaid with the festivities after the end of

Reconstruction. In 1884, Comus informally created a "court" and invited the daughters of four esteemed Confederate Generals and the daughter of former Confederate President Jefferson Davis to be feted at their ball.

Mildred and Mary Lee (Robert E. Lee's daughters), Julia Jackson (General Stonewall Jackson's daughter), and Nannie Hill (General D. H. Hill's daughter), as well as Winnie Davis, were treated like royalty—showered with flowers and given the honor of first dances and the attentions of the krewe king.

Winnie Davis was presented with jewelry, and these young women were all hailed as "Daughters of the Confederacy." Later, the women would be recalled as first Queen and Court of Comus.[31] This remains confusing and imprecise—as is unfortunately too much of New Orleans carnival history—because in 1892 (by which time the krewe's crowning of a queen had become an annual invitational event) Winnie Davis was invited to become Queen of Comus. When the krewe proclaimed, "This is the first time in its history that the Krewe of Comus have ever gone outside of the historic shades of its native city to choose a partner for its king."[32]

The Presidents or chairmen of the Krewe are not honorary positions, nor is the captain of the parade. There is no way to usurp this power, and campaigns must be kept discreet within the organization—honor is bestowed by secret ballot within secret societies. The identity of the captain is kept from all but the krewe, and the invited queen, with the understanding that by being a good captain, higher reward may follow.

The public role of a king's consort was a grand privilege that became one of the most fiercely sought honors. The identity of the queen, although kept secret in advance of the ball, was revealed to the public at the event. The choice of queen, like other matters of money and politics, was controlled by "a cabal of insiders."[33] As Walker Percy, the celebrated Louisiana novelist once commented, "Queens are chosen by the all-male krewes, at sessions which can be as fierce as a GM proxy fight. New Orleanians may joke about politics and war but they don't joke about society."[34]

Because Carnival kings and krewe captains were pledged to remain covert, they sought some method to advertise prestige.[35] With the naming of a queen, krewes found a means of public display of exalted status, which stemmed directly from traditional notions of "southern honor."

The first "queen" on record for a Mardi Gras ball was the wife of a former Confederate diplomat, named as consort for the King of Rex in 1873. She was chosen as a means of honoring her husband, a visiting dignitary. However, shortly thereafter, the presentation of young women to society combined with the crowning of "Queen for a Day." Debutantes began to step up into crowns and robes, to hold court for a day at krewe balls.

When in 1874, Rex invited an eighteen-year-old debutante to be Queen, these two traditions became forever entwined. As Kinser suggests, the New Orleans carnival developed not just from European origins, but "in extenuation of the Confederate cause."[36] Elaborate protocol was necessary to distinguish and celebrate the city's elite following the defeat of "Union occupation." Power consolidated through krewe culture.

In the 1880s, Comus, the Twelfth Night Revelers, Rex, and the Knights of Momus were joined by Proteus—and another six krewes established themselves by 1900. All of these groups enjoyed clandestine activity leading up to the annual ball: "The courtly side of Carnival is fueled by secrecy, particularly by the convention of shielding the identities of the kings and queens of the top Carnival krewes every year until the last possible moment."[37]

By the last decade of the nineteenth century, this annual contest preoccupied New Orleans high society all year long. A New York reporter, visiting the city during Mardi Gras, commented, "every New Orleans girl lives in anticipation of being crowned queen of the carnival."[38] Yet the selection process remained firmly in the hands of men, many who mythologized themselves into "gods."[39] In 1915, Dorothy Collins, Queen of Comus, drank a toast "to 'Our Father' Who Art in Comus."[40]

Shortly after the crowning began, it was clear that the growing branches of the New Orleans first families required more cultivation. They needed additional perks spread around, so males devised another elaborate, complex system of distinguishing daughters of the aristocracy, with "call-outs." At krewe balls, the audience eagerly awaited the appearance of the king and his queen. Then they were joined in the first dance by maids of the court and masked krewe members. Next, men in full dress appeared and "called out" young women to dance—a limited group issued invitations and awarded regal accord.[41]

This hunger for recognition caused some "transformations" for society women. In 1880 an aristocratic southern lady's family found her name in the papers at birth and marriage, and her family might read it again, at her death—a rule rigidly applied in New Orleans. But with krewe members seeking honor through female kin, rules began to bend. Slowly, names of queens and court maids appeared in print. By 1890, even the names of women who had been sent "call-outs" were appearing in print.

The beginning of official ball season begins on January 6, the twelfth day of Christmas (the Epiphany). On this date, Twelfth Night Revelers launch their event and revelry continues through Mardi Gras which may fall as early as February 3 or as late as March 9, because the celebration falls exactly forty-seven days before Easter (and Easter is the Sunday following the full moon after the Spring Equinox of March 21.) Despite the secularization of the holiday, the carnival season conforms to Christian calendars.

But for the queens and debutantes, the season begins long before the Epiphany. Just as the krewe captains begin preparations for their Mardi Gras parade and ball the April *before* the event, so young girls are coached and prepped for their roles months and months in advance. Invitations to become a maid or queen are issued the year before—between midsummer and December. The official debutante season in New Orleans is extended for nearly eight months. The two official debutante societies, the Debutante Club and Les Debuts des Jeunes Filles de La Nouvelle Orleans, (with an August ball) launch the debutante season. Every queen must be a debutante, but not every debutante became a queen.

Of course, there are the usual stories of female infants cooed over in cribs by adoring relatives anticipating debdom and crowning, and other folkloric images. In New Orleans, queens are bred, through regal genealogy, as much as they are crowned. Descriptions of New Orleans debs in the society pages often focus on a child's pedigree—how many of her ancestors were either kings or queens of carnival balls.

Clearly a queen's reign (if only for a single night) is portrayed as the high point of a woman's life. Obituaries in the New Orleans press always mention a woman's role as former queen, and often offer a complete run-down of the deceased's connection to krewe royalty. Robert Tallant's entertaining volume on Carnival suggests: "Most Mardi Gras queens marry well, for they move in a circle wherein they are likely to do so. More than a few have married into European aristocracy, and have thus achieved real titles of a sort, but it is doubtful that many of them consider their new position of more social prominence than that they were awarded during a New Orleans Carnival." This may or may not be true, but Tallant echoes sentiments widely expressed when he concludes, "each former queen remembers her year as the most delightful of all years before or since."[42]

Certainly the unique role of debutante, and by extension carnival queen, can take hold of a young girl or a society matron's imagination. As American singing idol, Bing Crosby, suggested in the pages of *Ladies Home Journal* in

1960, "Debuts are like honeymoons. A girl may look ahead to hers for only a few years, but she will look back on it forever."[43] The singularity of the experience continues to excite comment, as David Lindsey, New Orleans hairdresser, and stylist to generations of queens, comments, "You can be married more than one time but you can never make your debut more than once."[44]

As marriage became more companionate, dependent upon woman's consent as much as family alliance during the nineteenth century, American women in general were struggling for and winning greater autonomy. This concept seems to have remained foreign to the New Orleans elite. Lyle Saxon wrote without embarrassment or apology in 1928: "Usually the young ladies were placed, so to speak, upon pedestals and left there, while the young gentlemen amused themselves in other quarters. Now a pedestal is a safe place to keep a woman, for she gives very little trouble perched high in this graceful, if somewhat constrained position."[45] This image of men in charge of placement and mobility remains in force today.

Another cynical perspective is offered by Karal Marling, who argues: "Only yesterday an insignificant schoolgirl, she is suddenly the cynosure of all eyes, the little queen for a day whose every wish amounts to a regal command. And yet she is also a sort of stalking-horse for her family, a pawn, the means whereby their social fortunes may rise or fall. If she is not the belle of the ball, she is, at the very least, expected to attract a decent suitor and spare her father the duty of supporting an elderly girl, as the post-deb spinster was scornfully called."[46]

Certainly there were rebels. Indeed, during the age of the flapper, the all-female Krewe of Iris was founded. Although established in 1922, they did not begin parading until nearly a half century later. The Krewe of Venus pioneered women on floats in 1941.[47] Before that all females depicted on parade floats were portrayed by men in women's costumes—and to this day women's roles in ball tableaux are taken on by men in drag.

Equally clear, women who challenged this krewe culture, and especially the doctrine of white supremacy, might become pariahs or exiles. This issue is raised in Rebecca Snedeker's recent documentary, *By Invitation Only*.[48] But old-line krewe culture—sexist, racist, and elitist—prevailed, because, as David Lindsey also suggests, "It's offering up the virgins to the men of the community, but it's also an *industry*."[49]

Much like the beauty pageant culture to which it bears striking resemblance, carnival queens are part of a business empire ruled by men.[50] Women have key roles—former queens can become scepter and curtsy coaches. Yet females seem to serve as interchangeable parts, as Darlene Olivo, society photographer for the New Orleans *Times Picayune* explains, "Introducing the young women to society is the cog in the wheel of what Mardi Gras is, and Mardi Gras is the loom on which the entire fabric of this city is woven on."[51] And it remains *expensive* fabric, enriching the city's economy with each passing year.

For example, during the Golden Jubilee for Comus, the 1924 Queen wore a mantle "six and a half yards long, of gold net embroidered in rhinestones with a border of golden metallic cloth trimmed with seed pearls . . . her gown was of golden metallic cloth, and her gloves were dipped in fourteen carat gold."[52] It is perhaps no surprise that this entire outfit was later donated for display at the Louisiana State Museum. Indeed, many of the gowns and jewels from carnival queens are in museums, as they represent New Orleans's unique couture.

Because of secrecy within these organizations and the reticence of New Orleans patricians to discuss financial matters, it is difficult to determine just how much money was spent on debutante seasons and queen's outfits. In 1927 the Queen of the Mystic Ball wore a gown that cost $15,000, at a time when the Louisiana governor's salary was only $7,500.[53] Judy Cobb, a dressmaker in New Orleans who specializes in ball gowns, suggests that today the average queen's dress "costs from $6,000 to $12,000."[54]

One carnival historian estimates the elite mothers and daughters of New Orleans each year spend from $3,000,000 to $4,000,000 for clothes, accessories, and hairdressing, just to attend the balls. The Queen and her maids have even more fashion expenses. One queen's mother described that as the festivities accelerated after the beginning of the Christmas season onward, girls were expected to attend two to three parties per day, with events scheduled seven days a week. The kind of extravagant wardrobe required is common for American debutantes, but surely New Orleans raises the bar.

One of the couture dressmakers in New Orleans, Heather Pennington, explains the time and effort that goes into ball gowns with some pride: a debutante gown might take twenty hours, and a wedding gown could take fifty hours. But she spends, on average, 120 hours on a queen's costume. In addition, Pennington is enlisted for her discretion, as a dressmaker must never reveal the name of a queen in advance of the ball. In one case she and her assistant gave the Queen of Comus a code name of "Trixie," lest her identity be revealed accidentally.[55] (In reality, the girl was named Muffin.)

By Invitation Only allows us a peek behind the scenes of a contemporary carnival queen. The filmmaker, Rebecca Snedeker, is the daughter of a queen, the granddaughter of a queen, and descended from nineteenth-century New Orleans royalty: her ancestor, Anita Eustis, was a maid in the court of Rex in 1881. Rebecca's maternal great-grandfather was Rex, the King of Carnival in 1935, and his granddaughter, Snedeker's mother, became queen "because this was what was expected of me." Snedeker's grandmother debuted in 1940, and became Queen of the Mystery Ball.

Snedeker interviewed her cousin Charlotte Collins about her Mardi Gras experience. Charlotte expressed that she was beholden to her family's tradition. She ascribed the secrecy and other customs to "olden times" without any working knowledge of these cultural dictates or their origins. Snedeker shadows a family friend, Emily Lacour Guiza, who is invited in 1999 to become Queen of Nereus—a secret until the night of the Mardi Gras ball in February 2000.

The persistence and necessity of tradition is echoed in interviews with a family friend, Oliver Delery II, who hosts a party for Emily during her debutante season. This image of family duty is reinforced when Lorraine, Emily's mother, explains the importance of Emily's honor:

> Both grandmothers on their deathbeds mentioned Emily's debut—we obviously told her [about Emily's selection as Queen] when we found out. She was probably the first person to know—she had emphysema, and we wanted her to know in case anything happened. But up until the end at the hospital when she decided she was tired, she wanted to go to sleep, she wanted every grandchild and every child and spouse to come and say goodbye to her, which we all did. And it was very hard, Emily was hysterical but Meemaw asked Emily how the dress was, and Emily looked and her and said Meemaw, the dress is finished. Well, at that her eyes popped up, "It's finished." So you know that's how Emily finished. She was saying goodbye to her grandmother—never see her again. And she was so glad that her grandmother asked her about the dress and Emily said, "It's finished." But both grandmothers, their last words were about Emily's debutante year. Which I think makes a big difference to Emily and she knows its tradition and she's part of it.[56]

Besides the "family tradition" harped on throughout the film, Snedeker includes intermittently the thorny problem which confronts all observers of southern culture: race. Marilee Eustis Eaves, Snedeker's mother, was presented on Thanksgiving weekend in 1962, and went on to become a queen. She married a Yankee who warmly embraced and upholds krewe traditions, even after he and his wife are divorced. None of their three daughters takes on the role of debutante or queen. Their daughter Rebecca transgresses by having a boyfriend who is black, which causes uncomfortable discussions with her grandmother who is "sad" because, "We wouldn't be able to invite you to the clubhouse."[57]

The role of African Americans and Mardi Gras is complex and combustible to say the least. Henry Rightor in 1900 in the *Standard History of New Orleans* argued "the negroes preserve in its truest essence the primitive spirit of the Carnival."[58] Perry Young rhapsodized about the African American presence in the Comus parade, "No element is more essential, or more sincerely part and parcel, that the thousand or fifteen hundred black torchbearers and mule herds, white-shrouded, cowled, that dance before the cars . . . the way is long, the asphalt hard, the blazing torches hot and heavy—but they dance . . . Not for the dollar and a half—they do it for being part of the parade."[59] This brand of romantic racialism persists, even when it's all dressed up in postmodernist lingo.[60] Putting a man in a grass skirt and crowning him King of the Zulus seems a far-fetched solution to New Orleans's racial divides. (The Zulus, an all-black krewe, had origins in a carnival marching club called the Tramps. Around 1909 the Zulu krewe formed to stage elaborate mockeries of the Rex revels. Their first Zulu queens were men in drag.[61]) The Mardi Gras Indians and Wildmen, for all of their subversion and inversion, prove equally implausible as signifiers of empowerment.[62]

The racial gulf in the City remains enormous. New Orleans may have black elected officials, but many feel power still remains in the hands of a select circle of white men, who control the city's economy. The prospects for economic growth for the city is bleak with spiking unemployment rates, especially for African Americans. Most of the city's twenty-first-century job growth stems solely from gains in the service economy.

Over the years, challenges to discrimination have been issued and New Orleans remains a city resistant to change, dragging its feet into the modern era. As carnival became a focus of modern media, the city glacially shifted.[63] Since the beginning of the twentieth century, the public spectacles included satire as well as self-glorification.[64]

The Krewe of Bacchus was founded in 1969, a populist organization aiming to please tourist concerns. There was no tableau or ball after the Bacchus parade, but a supper open to anyone who could pay admission. The King of Bacchus was an invited national celebrity—with the earliest kings figures like Danny Kaye and Bob Hope. More recently a younger set of royals have been selected, to enhance media coverage with "hip" kings—for example, Nicholas Cage. Television coverage of the Endymion Extravaganza (another new, tourist-oriented krewe without a ball) was introduced in 1987, with broadcast from the Superdome.[65] The king of Rex represented old line New Orleans—a locally elected regent. The crowning of the King of Bacchus acknowledged the national dimensions of the media circus Mardi Gras had become.[66] The blending of the two forces put New Orleans's traditions into the spotlight—and under a microscope.

In 1975, a member of the Rex organization submitted an invitation list for their annual ball that included prominent African Americans. When Rex leadership balked (invitations are issued by a club committee), Mayor Moon Landrieu (the city's last white mayor) sent a message through channels that he would not be present to greet Rex in the traditional City Hall reviewing stand on Mardi Gras day *unless* blacks were welcomed at the festivities.[67] Rex relented, and slow progress continues. Although an observer over a decade later complained, "We do not yet see blacks and whites openly riding on the same floats in their parades, much less on those of any other society, including Rex."[68]

Racial strife erupted over Mardi Gras customs when the New Orleans City Council began to question the krewe's exclusionary practices. These groups were required to obtain a permit, and the city offered police protection to select organizations. Essentially, municipal funds contributed to the costs incurred by private organizations' parades—although they were for the public festivities of Mardi Gras. (For the uninitiated, seeing the krewe members masqued and hooded—in full costume during their parades—is all too reminiscent of Ku Klux Klan regalia.)

Although the Zulu krewe has been given a free permit as well, the processions of black Second Line organizations and Mardi Gras Indian gangs were not. Thus, "Black groups . . . are required to pay exorbitant fees, upwards of $4800 per parade."[69] The battle over fairness and access began brewing in 1988, and City councilwoman Dorothy Mae Taylor introduced an ordinance in 1991 to desegregate these private clubs, because city funding required that there be non-discriminatory practices.

These 1991 City Council hearings were acrimonious, as Dorothy Taylor presided over impassioned pleas on both sides. Clearly many African American community leaders condemned the city for turning a blind eye to civil rights violations—in the name of "peacekeeping." Business leaders were alarmed at anything calculated to rock the boat. Carnival was estimated to be a $450 million business for the city by the 1990s.[70] A spokesman argued that interfering with a tradition of parades dating back to 1857 would be unwise, and warned that the "real losers will be the citizens of New Orleans and not the carnival krewes."[71]

Regardless, the ordinance passed the council unanimously. Taylor's efforts were characterized by critics as her "plot to kill Mardi Gras."[72] This proposed enforcement was extremely unpopular—as a local survey indicated the ordinance was opposed by 86 percent of white voters and 51 percent of black voters.

However, two things developed after the Council vote. The backlash resulted in a committee that pushed through softening of the language, if not the intent, of the statute. For example, proof of discrimination would rest with complainants. Second, no jail sentence for violators would be imposed; instead the krewe captains might be fined $100 to $300 for infractions (which might be envisioned as a kind of "tax").

Forty-seven krewes stepped up and revealed their membership as nondiscriminatory. However, Comus, Momus, and Proteus refused to open their membership rolls for inspection. They decided to continue their balls, but suspend their parades. In 1992, Momus formally announced: "Momus, Son of Night, god of Mockery and Ridicule, regretfully and respectfully informs his friends, supporters and his public that he will not parade the streets of New Orleans on the Thursday evening before Shrove Tuesday, 1992, as he has customarily since 1872."[73]

Unfortunately for these hardliners, even without these "gods of mockery" on parade, Mardi Gras continued to flourish. And by 1999, it would appear the mountain moved to Mohammed when Proteus signed an affidavit to obtain a parade permit from the city.

Strikingly, during these intense political battles over racial discrimination within these all-white krewes, the matter of gender discrimination was never aired with public debates. Some lame justification was offered in correspondence, arguing that women *preferred* separatism. This could be argued as well for black krewe organizations with their own black queens (which were originally married women), as well as flourishing black debutante associations.

It is very striking in addition that discussions about integration during Mardi Gras in *By Invitation Only* center on the color of escorts, rather than the racial integration of debutantes.[74] Heather Pennington, confidante to queens, asserts, "When you go to New Orleans country club the only blacks you see are the maids that work for the family for fifty years that showed up for the daughter's wedding and the people serving the food and drinks." Further, she confides, "Never ever would you see a debutante escorted by anyone out of her race. I mean, it just would not happen. Not ever. It just wouldn't happen. You can put money on it."[75]

The New Orleans debutante contest is defined by both scepter and masque. For a day, the schoolgirl is transformed into a "queen," but at what price? Her period in the cocoon of debdom is brief, but intended to stamp her for a lifetime. Modern girls need not model themselves on the sheltered vestal virgins of a previous generation, but they need to prepare to liftoff for their launch in society: "A New Orleans young lady may run with the pack, doing all things girls her age do, anything else she may feel inclined to do, but when the season starts a metamorphosis, guided by her mother, is begun."[76] She must be prepared to conform to her elders' dictates.

After years of growing up with grandiosity, she must be ready to drop everything to inherit her crown. She must drop out of college, if necessary. She must abandon unsuitable friends and activities. She must assume the mantle of her tribe. She will spend her time obsessing over appearance—getting fitted for dresses, coiffed for parties, accessorized to the max. She must purchase the proper stationery, invitations, hire the right caterers and bands. Her mother will assist her every step of the way.

She will learn her walk, her wave, her scepter skills—prepping to perfect queenly graces. She may wear her jeans and go without makeup for rehearsals, but in public she will costume herself like the future royalty she must become. She will party night and day, talking to the same people over and over again. She must chit and chat, and, when the occasion requires, give short, identical speeches and toasts. She will mix with the young men of her class and station, in hopes of a match. She will strap on a shoulder harness to carry the weight of her costume, the burdens of family responsibility, to fulfill what has been predestined. She will smile for the camera and never, not ever, forget her manners. In return, she will be cherished and rewarded by her New Orleans elders.[77]

If necessary, she must assume an invisible masque. Snedeker was unable to cloak her discomfort during the filming of her documentary, "This world of debutantes, private clubs and queens is so alluring. But I realize I end up putting on a masque for them. And becoming something else, something that's expected of me. Just for show. That's what I was trained to do. So much of what we were taught growing up was about manners. Smiling no matter what . . . I haven't been myself with these people." In a society where ancestor worship and tribalism reign, what is self, but an assemblage of roles?

A New Orleans girl must take on both scepter and masque to become queen of the carnival. She is not just born to the role, but needs to be coaxed, or in some cases bribed into it. The rituals of debdom demand that she spend months "learning manners," as a former Rex, King of Carnival confides, "You work like the devil on manners, particularly on manners . . . If you have manners I think the doors are wide open, but if you don't, the doors are going to close on you."[78] And the krewes and captains and carnival kings remain gatekeepers for much more than Mardi Gras in New Orleans. Outsiders may mistake carnival as a festive subversion, but the masquerade is *not* inversion, but *affirmation*.[79]

So during her debutante season, wearing a masque, becoming the projection of her tribe's hopes and dreams, a carnival queen embraces the grandiosity to which she, by virtue of her pedigree, feels entitled. Her crown and gown, her scepter and smile symbolize the debutante rituals of Mardi Gras—tribal rites which have been trivialized and satirized, yet continue to enthrall.

Notes

1. Coincidentally, Jewel Ball, at which I would have been expected to debut, ended up being a little over a month after the May 4 shootings at Kent State in 1970.

2. See Carol Flake, *New Orleans: Behind the Masks of America's Most Exotic City* (New York: Grove Press, 1994); Karen Leathem, "'A Carnival According to Their Own Desires': Gender and Mardi Gras in New Orleans, 1870–1941" Ph.D. dissertation, University of North Carolina, Chapel Hill, 1994; Samuel Kinser, *Carnival, American Style: Mardi Gras at New Orleans and Mobile* (Chicago: University of Chicago Press, 1990); Reid Mitchell, *All on a Mardi Gras Dray: Episodes in the History of New Orleans Carnival* (Cambridge: Harvard University Press, 1995); Lyle Saxon, *Fabulous New Orleans* (1928, reprint ed., New Orleans: Robert L. Crager, 1958); Robert Tallant, *Mardi Gras . . . As It Was* (Gretna, La.: Pelican Publishing Co., 1994); John Wilds, Charles Dufour & Walter G. Cowan, *Louisiana: Yesterday and Today* (Baton Rouge: Louisiana State University Press, 1996). Finally, I am indebted to Karal Marling, for her wonderful monograph exploring what she calls

"American Debdom:" Karal Ann Marling, *Rites and Regalia of American Debdom* (Lawrence: University of Kansas Press, 2004).

3. In both the formalized work on the history of society by scholars such as E. Digby Baltzell, or Dixon Wecter, or even in more popular work—volumes by Stephen Birmingham, among others. The dimensions of southern Jewish balls is another overlooked topic that deserves an expanded treatment, beyond the work of Eli Evans.

4. Kinser, *Carnival*, 112.

5. Julia Reed, *Queen of the Turtle Derby and Other Southern Phenomena* (New York: Random House), 120.

6. Marling, *Rites of Debdom*, 28.

7. "In 1957, the palace press secretary announced that a deb can no longer apply to meet the Queen. In fact there would be no debs. They are finished." Marling, *Rites of Debdom*, 28.

8. Ibid.,18.

9. Ibid.

10. Ibid., 19.

11. Ibid., 128–29.

12. See for example the classic work by Perry Young, *The Mistick Krewe, Chronicles of Comus and His Kin* (New Orleans, 1931) to a very modern, comparative interpretation, Kinser, *Carnival, American Style*.

13. Mitchell, *All*, 72.

14. Kinser, *Carnival*, 65.

15. Ibid., 86.

16. Ibid., 65.

17. Ibid., 90.

18. Mitchell, *All*, 41–42.

19. Ibid., 45. Ironically this attitude would shift dramatically in the late nineteenth century and into the twentieth when business at any cost was the motto for Mardi Gras boosters.

20. Flake, *New Orleans*, 233, and Kinser, *Carnival*, 94.

21. Mitchell, *All*, 59. See especially Alecia Long, *The Great Southern Babylon: Sex, Race & Respectability in New Orleans, 1865–1920* (Baton Rouge: Louisiana State University Press, 2003).

22. Kinser, *Carnival*, 106.

23. John Barry, *Rising Tide: The Great Mississippi Flood of 1927 and How It Changed America* (New York: Simon and Schuster, 1997), 217. See also Kinser, *Carnival*, 280.

24. Mitchell, *All*, 61.

25. Barry, *Rising Tide*, 217.

26. Kinser, *Carnival*, 349 n. 71.

27. Ibid., 293.

28. Need I add these groups were racist, anti-Semitic and anti-diversity. Both Italians and Jews were singled out for maltreatment—and blacks were not even considered for krewe membership until Civil Rights agitation, much later than the 1960s.

29. Kinser, *Carnival*, 136.

30. Ibid., 137.

31. Mitchell, *All*, 102.

32. Ibid., 104.

33. Barry, *Rising Tide*, 215.

34. Barry, *Rising Tide*, 216. Percy is essentially right, but Tallant tells a story about the time the Queen of Rex had been forced on the group by her social-climbing, blackmailing father, and Comus asked their queen to withdraw, so they might select "a salesgirl of good family" instead. They thought it would be the height of insult that this unworthy Queen of Rex would have to "bow to a shop-girl." So sarcasm was not entirely absent. See Tallant, *Mardi Gras*, 189.

35. Although newspapers have printed the names of "FORMER KINGS OF COMUS" and other clandestine lists have circulated in recent years.

36. Kinser, *Carnival*, 312.

37. Flake, *New Orleans*, 85.

38. Leathem, "Carnival," 103.

39. See Ibid., 110 and Perry Young, "The social system of New Orleans is run by men. Women have their place, dowagers their say, but when there's justice to be done, carnival defies the female fiats. It is generous and adamant and male." Quoted in Flake, *New Orleans*, 88.

40. Leathem, "Carnival," 110.

41. Ibid., 171.

42. Tallant, *Mardi Gras*, 199. In 1904 a queen of Nereus wrote her niece, "It is certainly a great compliment to be selected as queen, especially your first winter, and enough to last the rest of your life." Mitchell, *All*, 105.

43. Marling, *Rites of Debdom*, 195. Former Kings of Rex also have their own way of hanging on to their status, as they may display a 6 x 9 purple, gold, and green striped flag with the date of their rule embroidered on it in front of their homes for the last ten days of the Carnival season. Kinser, *Carnival*, 389 n. 16.

44. *"By Invitation Only"*: The Documentary Project. A documentary film by Rebecca Snedeker, which was screened at the Porter Fortune Jr. Symposium

on Manners and Southern History at the University of Mississippi, 6 October 2004.

45. Saxon, *Fabulous New Orleans*, 179.

46. Marling, *Rites of Debdom*, 7.

47. Kinser, *Carnival*, 125.

48. *"By Invitation Only."*

49. Ibid.

50. Marling, *Rites of Debdom*, 148.

51. *"By Invitation Only."*

52. Tallant, *Mardi Gras*, 190.

53. Barry, *Rising Tide*, 220.

54. Reed, *Turtle*, 125.

55. *"By Invitation Only."*

56. Ibid.

57. Ibid.

58. Kinser, *Carnival*, 142.

59. Joseph Roach, *Cities of the Dead* (New York: Columbia University Press, 1996), 247–49.

60. Ibid.

61. Mitchell, *All*, 151.

62. Kinser suggests that "At the very epoch when the white man eliminated them for their uncouthness, they became the soul of the second Carnival's two finest inventions, the Mardi Gras Indians and the Zulus." Kinser, *Carnival*, 159.

63. Ironically, the counterculture of gay krewes and parades has become integrated into the contemporary carnival scene—as nine all-gay krewes have been established since the 1960s. Kinser, *Carnival*, 262. Perhaps this is simply a commercial/tourist ploy, as "New Orleans has long ranked as a major gay center and mecca for homosexuals from all the American South." Mitchell, *All*, 142.

64. Kinser, *Carnival*, 259.

65. Ibid., 259.

66. Ibid., 277.

67. Flake, *New Orleans*, 204.

68. Kinser, *Carnival*, 309.

69. Roach, *Cities*, 271.

70. Wilds, Dufour, and Cowan, *Louisiana*, 160.

71. *"By Invitation Only."*

72. Roach, *Cities*, 275.

73. Flake, *New Orleans*, 239.

74. This is perhaps because there is a very elaborate and equally impressive African American debutante tradition in place in New Orleans, which is an equally compelling and even more neglected topic for historical investigation.

75. *"By Invitation Only."*

76. Tallant, *Mardi Gras*, 191.

77. Susan Buck Mayer, Queen of Comus in 1937, annually hosted a gathering of former Comus queens every Friday prior to Mardi Gras, and then the women went to lunch at the Pontchartrain Hotel. Flake, *New Orleans*, 156.

78. *"By Invitation Only."* Despite Snedeker's polished manners, doors will be closed if she attends any family social occasion with her boyfriend, who is black.

79. See Kinser, *Carnival*, 325 n. 1. See also Flake, *New Orleans*, 348.

What's Sex Got to Do with It?

Antimiscegenation Law and Southern White Rhetoric

Charles F. Robinson II

In January of 1929, the Arkansas Supreme Court reviewed a case involving an alleged violation of the state's antimiscegenation law. Martha Wilson, a white woman, and Ulysses Mitchell, a black man, both residents of Fort Smith, had been convicted of unlawful cohabitation. According to the facts of the case, Mitchell had been seen on several occasions at Wilson's home. He mowed her lawn, entertained her by playing music from an old guitar, and attended parties that Wilson had at her residence. Witnesses for the state re-called that Mitchell always came into the home and left by way of the front door, sometimes leaving as late as five a.m. On one occasion when Mitchell had left the house, Wilson came to the door in her nightclothes and called him back inside. Early one morning in August of 1928, after receiving calls from Wilson's neighbors, Fort Smith police went to Wilson's home. There, in the rear of the house, police saw Mitchell and Wilson laying in bed to-gether, and Mitchell's pants were unbuttoned. The police stormed into the room. Mitchell made no statement at all, but Wilson exclaimed, "Oh that fellow wasn't there when I went to bed!" The screen of the rear window had been cut, and upon later questioning Mitchell informed the police that he had been drinking and had mistakenly entered Wilson's residence believ-ing it to have been his own.[1]

Upon reviewing the facts of the case, the Supreme Court reversed the lower court's convictions of Martha Wilson and Ulysses Mitchell. The court held that although the weight of the evidence supported the state's position that Wilson and Mitchell frequently engaged in sexual relations with each other, the interracial sex alone did not constitute a violation of the law. In the state of Arkansas in 1929, in order for interracial couples to be in violation of the antimiscegenation laws, they had to marry or formally live together. Because evidence showed that Mitchell lived at another residence, the Supreme Court reversed the lower court's decision.[2]

The *Wilson* case was just one of many in the South in the twentieth century that clearly revealed that the prevention of interracial sex was not the primary goal of southern whites. Despite the rhetoric of the white South that commonly denounced interracial sex as the greatest societal tragedy, authorities usually focused the laws against public domestic relationships. What mattered most to whites was protecting white male privileges and preserving the social, not the sexual color line. Interracial couples, even those involving black men and white women, did engage each other sexually throughout the most racially repressive times of the twentieth century. As long as the interracial couple acted clandestinely and made no attempts to legitimize their relationships, whites often grudgingly left them unpunished. Whites attacked formal interracial liaisons because in their minds such relationships suggested equality and challenged the one true sacred grail in the South—that being white supremacy.[3]

The rhetoric of southern whites against interracial sex leaves little doubt as to its emotional importance. Seemingly at every level whites vilified interracial sex and bemoaned its consequences. Tulane Professor William Benjamin Smith called miscegenation the worst "conceivable disaster that might befall the South," and considered the prevention of it as imperative to protecting white civilization. To Smith there was no contesting the inferiority of blacks. Offering historical, anthropological, and anatomical evidence to support his position, Smith contrasted what he saw as the non-accomplishing and savage history of Africa with the august and illustrious one of Europe. He questioned whether anyone could ever sincerely believe "that the infinitely varied and beautiful elements of Greek methodology could ever by any possibility (have) emerged from the most fertile fancy of an old master of the Congo?" Smith also intimated that the marked anatomical differences of blacks gave evidence of black inferiority. Such physical differences as longer arms, flatter noses, thicker lips, larger foreheads, blacker eyes, and smaller brains suggested to Smith that blacks constituted a lower stock of humanity. For these reasons, Smith called for greater efforts to prevent interracial sex. To him, there was nothing more terrifying than the thought of the blood of whites mingling with that of blacks, for such a mixture only served to corrupt and degrade the white race.[4]

Echoing Smith's position, southern politicians railed against miscegenation. In 1938, Louisiana Senator Allen J. Ellander remarked that any attempt
to amalgamate blacks and whites would produce a "Nation of half-breeds"
and eventually spell the decay and downfall of American civilization. Also,
Mississippi Senator Theodore Bilbo, in a speech delivered to the state legislature in 1944, celebrated the racial purity of whites and enjoined them to
continue taking active steps to maintain blood purity. The alternative, Bilbo
counseled, would mean "mongrelization" and lead to the destruction of the
civilization and culture of the white race.[5]

Popular writers contributed to the invective against miscegenation. Often,
they did so by characterizing the progeny that came from interracial unions
as animalistic, lustful, criminal, and dangerous to the white race. Thomas
Nelson Page in *Red Rock* (1898), portrayed the mulatto Moses as an unscru-
pulous political brute who with his "deformed teeth, blue gums, villainously
low forehead and furtive, rolling eyes" attempted to rape a white woman.
In *The Call of the South* (1908), Robert Lee Durham illustrated the bestial
transformation that occurred in the mulatto Graham when a white woman
spurned his advances. Enraged by her rejection, Graham raped the white
woman. Also, in Norah Davis's *The Northerner* (1905), Davis described the
mulatto seductress Lesby, as "a warm, bright-colored creature, voluptuous
and passionate, as all those women are."[6]

Probably no single individual promoted the notion of the mulatto being
the great tragedy of miscegenation more than Thomas Dixon. In three novels
that spanned the first two decades of the twentieth century, Dixon portrayed
mulattos as individuals with animalistic characteristics who strongly craved
interracial sexual mixing. In *The Clansman* (1905), Dixon described Lydia
Brown, the mistress of Radical Republican leader Austin Snowman as "a
strange brown woman of sinister animal beauty and the restless eye of a leop-
ardess." Throughout the novel Dixon depicted Brown as a vicious woman
who used her charms to seduce and destroy Stoneman and the nation.[7]

In *The Sins of the Father* (1912), Dixon also detailed how a sensual mulatto
named Cleo used her bestial charms to win the affections of a noble Anglo-
Saxon, Colonel Daniel Norton. Repeatedly, Dixon referred to Cleo as a se-
ductive "young animal" whose magnetism overwhelmed Norton's practical
thinking. Norton declared: "I fought as a wounded man, alone and unarmed
fights a beast in jungle. . . . This primeval man, in the shadows with desires
inflamed by hunger meets this primeval woman who is unafraid, who laughs

at the laws of Society because she has nothing to lose. . . . The universe in him finds its counterpart in the universe in her. And whether she be fair or dark, her face, her form, her body, her desires are his."[8]

The verbal assault made by national leaders against miscegenation would have tangible consequences. One result would be the proliferation of white violence against blacks. According to a NAACP investigation, between 1900 and 1918 southern whites killed, maimed, and castrated over 1,333 blacks.[9] Although evidence clearly shows the relationship between lynching and general racial repression, southern whites explained and justified their support for lynching as a needed tool to control the "beastly" sexual desire of black men for white women. As one southern academic, George Winston, put it, "The black brute is lurking in the dark, a monstrous beast crazed by lust."[10] South Carolina Senator Benjamin Ryan Tillman echoed the spirit of this position when he declared in a speech on the Senate floor that he would rather find either of his three daughters killed "by a tiger or a bear" than to have either of them have to announce that "she had been robbed of the jewel of her womanhood by a black fiend."[11] Rebecca Felton, a southern white woman from Georgia, also believed lynching to be necessary. When Sam Hose, a black man from Newman, Georgia, fled from local authorities facing a murder and rape charge, Felton urged Georgian whites to capture Hose and lynch him. Felton fulminated, "Lynch the black fiends by the thousands until the Negro understood that there was a standard punishment for rape and he could not escape it." Ten days after the alleged incident, Felton received her wish. A white mob captured, castrated, and burned Sam Hose.[12]

The attempt to expand and strengthen antimiscegenation legislation was another tangible way that whites responded to the vituperation spewed upon notions of interracial sex. Arguing that antimiscegenation laws were necessary bulwarks against interracial sex, reformers known as progressives lobbied for the statutes at all levels of government. In cities like Fort Worth and New Orleans, progressives enacted ordinances that outlawed interracial sex within city limits and restricted the areas where black prostitutes could practice their trade.[13] On the state level progressives expanded already existing antimiscegenation provisions by providing punishments to officials who married interracial couples. They also promoted notions of racial purity by decreasing the amount of black or Indian heritage a person could have and still qualify as a white person. For example, in 1907, Alabama progressives changed the definition of mulatto from a person with African heritage to the third generation to that of a person with African heritage to the fifth generation.[14] In 1910, Virginia progressives followed suit by modifying their definition of mulattos from persons with one-fourth black heritage to those with one-sixteenth.[15] Also, in that same year North Carolina altered its definition of Negro from persons with black lineage to the fourth generation to persons with black heritage to the third generation inclusive.[16]

Southern states continued modifying their definition of Negro well into the 1920s. Responding to the tense racial atmosphere that accompanied postwar America and the growth of the eugenics movements, states made greater legislative efforts to legally discourage interracial mixing. Virginia in 1924 passed the first antimiscegenation statute in American history that firmly embraced the one-drop rule. Whites were forbidden from marrying any persons with any known racial heritage other than white. In respect for those persons who might have been descendants of John Rolfe and Pocahontas, the Virginia law allowed white persons with one-sixteenth or less of American Indian heritage to continue marrying whites. To ensure better that the law could be enforced, the legislature required all persons in the state to register their racial identities with a local registrar and made it a felony to provide false information.[17] In 1927, Georgia followed Virginia's lead by establishing a similar law. The Georgia law, however, was a bit more punitive, prescribing a penalty of two to five years in prison for deliberately making a false statement as to race on a marriage license.[18] Alabama, Louisiana, and Mississippi also passed more restrictive antimiscegenation laws during the 1920s.[19] With these provisions, whites hoped to decrease the likelihood that persons with known black heritage could "pollute" the white race by legally marrying or cohabiting across the color line.

On the federal level progressives introduced and supported attempts to establish a federal antimiscegenation law and an anti-interracial marriage constitutional amendment. Between 1907 and 1921, Congress entertained no fewer than twenty-one antimiscegenation bills.[20] One such effort came after Jack Johnson, the audacious first black heavyweight-boxing champion, married Lucille Cameron, a nineteen-year-old white woman from Minnesota. Just seven days after the nuptials, United States Senator Seaborn Roddenberry of Georgia delivered a passionate address calling for an amendment to the Constitution that would prevent interracial unions. Roddenberry fulminated: "Intermarriage between black and white is repulsive and averse to every sentiment of pure American spirit . . . no brutality, no infamy, no degradation in all the years of Southern slavery possessed such a villainous character and such atrocious qualities as the provisions . . . which allow the marriage of the negro Johnson to a woman of the caucasian strain."[21] Although many shared Roddenberry's disgust with the Johnson marriage, the amendment attempt failed.

Senator William H. Milton of Florida made one of the most interesting and exhausting attempts at convincing Congress of the need for a federal antimiscegenation measure. In January of 1909, Milton introduced a bill that prohibited the intermarriage of whites and blacks in the District of Columbia and any territories of the United States. Subsequently, the Committee on the Judiciary debated the bill. Milton, wearied with the length of time that the Committee held the bill, submitted a resolution calling for the discharge of the Committee. In a protracted oration, Milton explained that the object of the federal antimiscegenation bill "is the preservation of the Union for the sons and daughters of patriots whose life blood is the foundation for our great republic." He argued that antimiscegenation laws had always maintained almost universal support from the American people, and that the courts had on many separate occasions confirmed their constitutionality. Citing a case of a Virginia couple who married in the District of Columbia, Milton attested to the pressing need for a federal law. Milton contended that such a measure was necessary to prevent Washington, D.C., from becoming the "city of refuge for such couples" that sought to evade the sound laws of their states and marry across the color line.[22]

Milton did not simply contend for a federal antimiscegenation measure by citing the strong historical and legal foundation of the law. The Senator from Florida also presented an anthropological argument against racial mixing. Milton listed thirteen "scientifically proven" biological points of difference between whites and blacks that in his estimation pointed to the latter's inferiority. Milton cited such things as blacks having abnormal arm lengths, smaller brains, blacker eyes, flatter noses, exceedingly thick craniums, thicker skins, particularly rancid smells, and "divergent" and "prehensible" big toes as indications of their being "a distinct species." Further, he warned that the mixture of blacks with whites would result in the extinction of the Caucasian race because "one drop of negro blood makes one a negro . . . a child of the jungle."[23]

Milton insisted that his support for the bill did not in any way suggest any personal antipathy for blacks. He asserted that blacks within his state recognized him as a "friend." However, Milton elucidated that he could not allow his "kindly feeling for them" to prevent him from seeking to preserve the purity of his own race from intermixture with a people whose "presence in our land has proven a curse for the white man."[24]

In concluding his speech for a national law, Milton called for national unity. He urged northern congressmen to support the federal anti-marriage measure because he believed that such legislation advanced sectional harmony. Milton declared, "By enacting this legislation we will go far toward healing the differences between North and South and bringing back to them their common brotherhood, and strengthening their efforts for the up-building of our Nation." Apparently, northern congressmen disagreed with Milton's assertions about the positive effect of the law on national harmony because they did not provide him with enough votes to pass the bill.[25]

Although whites avowed that the primary purpose of antimiscegenation laws was to forestall interracial sex, an examination of the enforcement of the statutes reveals something else. Antimiscegenation laws rarely punished simple acts of interracial sex. In fact, in a number of cases that reached the appellate courts, interracial couples that confessed to having sex escaped punishment. For example, in *Jackson v. State* (1930), Sam Jackson, a black man, and Alexander Marksos, a white woman, admitted in an Alabama courtroom that they had had sexual intercourse. Jackson and Marksos explained that they had met on the streets of Birmingham and "by mutual agreement went to a negro house, engaged a room and had sexual intercourse" only one time. After their sexual encounter, Jackson and Marksos parted ways and did not see each other again. The lower court found them guilty, but the Alabama Supreme Court reversed their conviction. The court ruled that such a sexual encounter as that between Jackson and Marksos was not a violation of the antimiscegenation laws. In the high court's opinion, interracial cohabitation involved a "state or condition" of sex that the parties intended to continue, not one random act.[26]

In *Gilbert v. State* (1945), the Alabama Court of Appeals reversed the conviction of Myra Gilbert, a married black mother of six, found guilty of miscegenation. During the trial, Gilbert testified that she had been forced by the white man to have intercourse with him and that the act had occurred only one time. She reiterated throughout the trial, "He overpowered me and held me and told me he would kill me if I told it." For the appellate court, Gilbert's testimony along with corroborating evidence from the white male co-defendant (he claimed that he had never had sex with Gilbert) proved sufficient to reverse the lower court ruling. According to the court the state did not present evidence to show that "the named parties were living in adultery intending to continue that relationship." Therefore, despite Gilbert's admission of a sexual act, neither she nor the co-defendant was guilty of transgressing the state's antimiscegenation law.[27]

An Arkansas appellate court rendered a similar ruling in *Hardin v. State* (1960). In that case the state charged J. A. Hardin, a white man, with violating the state's law that forbade concubinage—living together as a couple without officially marrying—between blacks and whites. The state established without contention from the accused that Hardin had taken a "Negro woman to a tourist court and had sex with her." Although a lower court had found Hardin guilty, the court of appeals reversed the conviction because the state had failed to prove that "Hardin and the Negro woman ever lived together in any other way except in the act of sexual intercourse at the tourist court."[28]

Interracial couples that confessed to having merely shared a single act of intercourse might escape punishment if they claimed to have no sincere affection for one another nor any other connection that suggested a sustained intimate relationship. However, those that denied having sex but illustrated behavior that intimated that an emotional intimacy existed between them would often find themselves suffering under the weight of the antimiscegenation law. In *Lewis v. State* (1921), state authorities charged a white man named Lewis with having a sexual relationship with Bess Adams, a woman of color who reputedly helped care for Lewis's elderly parents. Josh Coleman, described as a mulatto, served as a state witness and testified that he saw Lewis holding one of Adams's children. According to Coleman, Lewis put the child to bed and said, "[I]t was his child." Tonie Evins, a white man and another state witness, confirmed Coleman's testimony about Lewis and the child. Evins added that Lewis visited the Adamses' house "once or twice a week." According to Evins, these visits often took place at night, sometimes late in the night with Lewis "sitting around" with Adams.[29]

Lewis vehemently denied the state's accusations against him and presented witnesses to refute those of the state. A number of defense witnesses testified that they never saw any improper sexual behavior between Lewis and Adams. Bess Adams also answered that one of the state's witnesses, Josh Coleman, was the actual father of the child in question. Yet despite Lewis's assertions of innocence, the lower court found him guilty. Lewis subsequently appealed to the Alabama Supreme Court but to no avail. The high court saw no reversible error in the case.[30]

In *Rollins v. State* (1922), Alabama officials used testimony from state witnesses that Jim Rollins, a black man, often brought food to the home of Edith Labue, a married, Sicilian woman, as evidence of the consistently affectionate nature of their relationship. As in the *Lewis case*, the state had no witness to any sexual encounter between Rollins and Labue. The state used statements made by the arresting officers in order to establish the sexual aspect of their relationship. On the night of the arrest, the police had found Rollins and Labue "alone together in a dark room." Upon cross-examination the police admitted that Rollins and Labue were standing and fully dressed when they kicked the door open and that there was no bed in the room. The policed stressed, however, that "the negro man and the woman were in the room together and it was dark."[31]

State prosecutors also attempted to connect Rollins to the paternity of one of Labue's three children. Police officers asserted that the youngest of Labue's children was "a dark brown child with kinky hair." To raise the possibility that Rollins might be the father, Joe Labue, Edith's husband, testified that he had gone into the army on June 24, 1918, and returned January 27, 1919, and that the child was born "in April sometime, 1919."[32]

A Jefferson County court convicted Jim Rollins, but the state high court overturned the ruling. During the trial the lower court judge had allowed into evidence a confession to police Rollins made at gunpoint. According to the high court, "[T]he manner by which the so-called confessions of this defendant were obtained was in almost every particular repugnant to the rule governing such testimony."[33] It is probable that if the lower court had refused to admit Rollins's forced confession into evidence and he had still been convicted that the appellate court would have affirmed the ruling.

The Florida case of *Parramore v. State* (1921) highlighted a consistent pattern of care without any strong evidence of sexual intimacy. Adam Parramore and Annie Brooks, a white male/black female couple, pleaded innocent to charges of violating Florida's law that made it unlawful for blacks and whites of different genders to live together "occupying the same room in the nighttime." The state displayed little evidence to support the contention that Parramore and Brooks slept in the same room during the night. Neither did the state have witnesses to any acts of sexual intercourse between the two. State witnesses did testify, however, that Parramore and Brooks lived together in the same house for several years. They confirmed that Brooks's mother lived in the home as well. These witnesses further added instances when they saw the defendants sleeping together during the day, and when

Brooks came to the door in her nightclothes while Parramore remained in the bed.[34] One other piece of evidence might have influenced the jury's decision. The state raised questions about the paternity of a defense witness named Clarence Brown. Denying it at first, Brown finally admitted that Adam Parramore's brother, Everett Parramore, was his father. With such testimony, the state probably sought to convince the jury that the Parramore family made a practice of miscegenation. Considering the times, state prosecutors probably assumed that such testimony added weight to Adam Parramore's guilt in the eyes of jurors.[35]

A Duval County jury found Parramore and Brooks guilty. The defendants entered an appeal to the Florida Supreme Court citing among many things the state questions put to Clarence Brown. The defendants considered the questions immaterial and "unnecessarily" humiliating to him "to the point of injuring the cause of the defendants." However, the Florida high court disagreed and affirmed the judgment.[36]

Fields v. State (1931) illustrated yet another instance where the state convicted a person of violating the antimiscegenation law without any strong evidence of sexual intercourse. A Colbert County Circuit Court convicted Elijah Fields of having a sexual relationship with a white woman. Both Fields and the white woman denied that their relationship was a sexual one. Evidence in the case showed that the white woman had a poor physical condition that caused her to menstruate constantly except when under the care of doctors. Fields, who claimed only to be a friend, lived near the hospital where the woman received treatment. He allowed the white woman to leave some of her clothes at his home for her convenience. He also sometimes transported her to and from the hospital because she could not walk long distances. On the night of the arrest officers saw the two, riding alone in the car together. Officers followed them to Fields's home and after knocking with no reply, forced an entrance. Once inside the policemen found Fields and the woman fully dressed, "except that the woman had no shoes." Officers also testified that the "bed was not made . . . it seemed kind of ruffled." With this highly limited evidence, a jury found Fields guilty of a felonious act. Fortunately for Fields, the state appellate court reversed the lower court decision for lack of evidence.[37]

At the completion of the lower court testimony in the *Lewis, Rollins, Parramore,* and *Fields* cases, all-white juries found the accused guilty of great social offences without any strong evidence of sexual relations having taken place between them. But, what offences? It was not the simple act of interracial sex. In fact, in each case the defendants denied that any physical intimacy had occurred. The jurors punished these defendants for transgressing an unwritten but well-established code of conduct with regard to general interracial associations. In the South, blacks and whites of the opposite sex were not supposed to be alone together in each other's homes, reveling in each other's company or helping each other as equals. They were not supposed to establish open, life-long friendships, show affection for each other's children, or shower each other with gifts of appreciation. In the minds of white southerners such examples of intimacy, care, warmth, generosity, and friendship challenged the color line and raised to the public view the possibilities of social equality. Therefore, no one had to actually see the men having sex across the color line to confirm their guilt. They were culpable because of the ease, openness, and apparent genuineness of their interracial relationships.

How do we account for the difference between what southern whites claimed to oppose and how they enforced antimiscegenation laws? Were white southerners simply being duplicitous when they declared an opposition to interracial sex but focused their legal efforts against interracial marriage and domestic relationships? Probably not. The consistency and emotional fervor with which they denounced interracial sex throughout American history suggests that for most southerners the opposition was real. However, the general opposition to interracial sex played second fiddle to the stronger desire to maintain white male privilege and control in society. Since colonial times Americans had grappled with the problem of interracial sex. Although their cultural prejudices and Christian beliefs caused them to debunk it, the institution of slavery and their determination to protect and expand the power of white masters encouraged them to tolerate interracial sex to a degree. Masters could engage their black slave women sexually in a furtive manner, but society forbade them from marrying them or making them more formal, public lovers. At the same time, the weight of antimiscegenation laws could fall more squarely on the sexual coupling between white women and black men because few white women owned slaves and could not, therefore, hide behind the cover of informality that the institution afforded white men.[38]

After emancipation Radicals in Congress erected the Fourteenth Amendment that mandated some semblance of equality before the law. Radical Reconstruction lawmakers and justices subjected anitmiscegenation laws to a tougher legal scrutiny. Although some states temporarily abandoned the statutes, most maintained them. Many southern leaders in the post-Reconstruction South understood that because of the equal protection clause of the Fourteenth Amendment, antimiscegenation laws could only survive if they punished black male/white female relationships theoretically to the same degree that they did black female/ white male ones. Since white men still wanted their sexual access to black women, more formal, domestic, intimate relationships rather than those involving simple intercourse would have to remain the targets of enforcement.[39]

The selective enforcement of antimiscegenation laws also served to buttress the post-emancipation racial caste system. Just as during slavery, when white society refused to acknowledge the personhood of slave women who became the mistresses and lovers of white men, the focusing of antimiscegenation statutes against interracial relationships denied legitimacy to black/white couples. The laws prevented the black person in interracial relationships or any biracial children from attaining the status and often the wealth of the white person involved in the coupling. Such a system reinforced notions of the inferiority of blacks. African Americans might find their way across the sexual color line, but that kind of breech would do little to augment their social standing.

Many African Americans recognized the real purpose of antimiscegenation laws. Black leaders understood that whites only wanted to prevent lawful relationships, never to erect a bona fide sexual separateness between the races.[40] Blacks in Texas protested an antimiscegenation measure enacted by the state in 1879. In a statement delivered at the Convention of Colored Men of 1883, Texas blacks criticized the new law because it made intermarriage a felony while doing nothing to augment state penalties for interracial cohabitation and sex across the color line. In the minds of Texas blacks, the antimiscegenation law endangered black women and implied that "the whole race was without morals."[41] Echoing this theme, Robert Smalls, a delegate at the South Carolina Constitutional Convention of 1895, challenged the call of white delegates for a miscegenation clause in the new state organ. Smalls introduced an amendment providing that any white person found guilty of cohabiting with a person of color should lose the right to hold office and must legally recognize any biracial child born from such a union. Although the white delegates passed the measure without Smalls's recommendation, his proposal produced some consternation among them. One white delegate, James Wigg of Beaufort County when commenting about the episode, declared that for a time "the coons had the dogs up the tree for a change and intended to keep them there until they admitted that they must accept such a provision."[42]

W. E. B. Du Bois, Frederick Douglass, and Booker T. Washington each commented on the real purpose of antimiscegenation laws. Du Bois, a talented intellectual and one of the founders of the NAACP, labeled antimiscegenation laws as "wicked devices designed to make the seduction of black women easier." Frederick Douglass, the runaway slave who became a chief advocate of emancipation and civil rights, avowed that the provisions left "the colored girl absolutely helpless before the lust of white men" and "reduced colored women in the eyes of the law to the position of dogs."[43] Booker T. Washington, the famed founder of Tuskegee College, agreed with Du Bois and Douglass. In response to a letter on the subject written to him by anthropologist Albert Ernest Jenks, Washington answered that blacks detested antimiscegenation laws because they enabled "the (white) father to escape his responsibility, or prevent him from accepting or exercising it when he has children by a colored woman."[44]

The hostility of blacks to antimiscegenation laws also derived from their belief that such measures implied the inferiority of blacks and encouraged black self-hate. Washington described the laws as "humiliating and injurious."[45] Douglass intimated that the anti-marriage provisions and public disapproval to his intermarriage threatened his "self-respect."[46] Yet it was Du Bois who best expressed this belief. For Du Bois antimiscegenation laws, as well as other Jim Crow measures, relegated blackness to a position of inferiority while raising the importance of whiteness. DuBois argued that these race-based codes actually encouraged blacks to look across the color line in a vain attempt to erase the social stigma associated with blackness.[47] In 1913, Du Bois forcefully argued that blacks who failed to oppose the laws publicly "acknowledged that black blood is a physical taint—a thing that no decent, self-respecting, black man can be asked to do."[48] In a 1920 article entitled "Sex Equality," Du Bois declared:

No Negro with any sense has ever denied his right to marry another Human being, for the simple reason that such a denial would be a frank admission of his own inferiority. . . . He could naturally say: I do not want to marry this woman of another race, and this is what 999 black men out of every thousand do say. . . . But impudent and vicious demand that all colored folk shall write themselves down as brutes by a general assertion of their unfitness to marry another decent folk is a nightmare born only in the haunted brain of the bourbon South."[49]

Interracial couples in the early twentieth century learned to circumvent antimiscegenation provisions by recognizing the difference between the application of the laws and southern white rhetoric. Many couples concealed their relationships under the guises of informality. For example the case of *Allen v. Scruggs* (1912) revealed that Ryal Noble had sustained an intimate domestic relationship with Kit Allen, a black woman, for over forty years. Allen lived on the Noble plantation, but because she appeared to be only a house maid, authorities never punished Noble or Allen despite their having five children together.[50] In *Dees v. Metts* (1944), Nazarine Parker, a black woman, won the right to inherit property worth $2,500 for the estate of the deceased John Watts, a white man. Parker secured the inheritance despite the fact that evidence showed that she had lived with Watts as his mistress for over twenty years prior to his death.[51] Also, in 1896 the state of Texas released Katie Bell, a white woman who had been imprisoned for almost two years for marrying Calvin Bell, a black man. Upon her release Katie returned to La Marque where she had lived before her imprisonment with Calvin and subsequently built a house just a few hundred feet from Calvin's home. Probably fearing further state reprisals if they lived together, the Bells maintained their separate but close residences until the time of Katie's death in 1910.[52]

Throughout much of the twentieth century antimiscegenation laws served the purpose for which they were designed. Until the Supreme Court struck down the statutes in 1967, southern states prosecuted blacks and whites who displayed genuine intimacy for one another. Interracial sex, however, never became a casualty of the provisions. In fact, antimiscegenation edicts actually encouraged those who dared to cross the sexual color line to keep their relationships informal and strictly sexual. Benevolent acts of kindness and affection subjected couples to legal penalties. In the final assessment antimiscegenation laws aided the white South in creating the kind of society it wanted—one in which black heritage was disparaged and black opportunity denied.

Notes

1. *Wilson v. State*, 13 S. W. 2nd (1929).
2. *Wilson v. State*, 13 S. W. 2nd (1929).
3. For a similar argument see Randall Kennedy, "Miscegenation Laws and the Problem of Enforcement," in Werner Sollors, *Interracialism: Black-White Intermarriage in American History, Literature, and the Law* (Oxford: Oxford University Press, 2000), 140–62. Also, Charles F. Robinson II, *Dangerous Liaisons: Sex and Love in the Segregated South* (Fayetteville: University of Arkansas, 2003).

4. William B. Smith, *The Color Line: A Brief on the Behalf of the Unborn* (New York: McClure Philips & Co., 1905), 9, 37, 47.

5. *The Development of Segregationist Thought*, ed., I. A. Newby (Homewood: The Dorsey Press, 1965), 130–40.

6. John G. Mencke, *Mulattos and Race Mixture: American Attitudes and Images, 1865–1918* (New York: Umi Research Press, 1979), 215–17.

7. Mencke, *Mulattos and Race Mixture*, 221.

8. Maxwell Bloomfield, "Dixon's The Leopard's Spots: A Study in Popular Racism," *American Quarterly* 16 (1964): 387–401.

9. See NAACP, *Thirty Years of Lynching in the United States, 1889–1918* (New York: Arno Press, 1969).

10. Martha Hodes, *White Women, Black Men: Illicit Sex in the Nineteenth Century South* (New Haven: Yale University Press, 1997), 201.

11. Francis B. Simkins, *"Pitchfork" Ben Tillman, South Carolinian* (Baton Rouge: Louisiana State University Press, 1960), 395.

12. John Talmadge, *Rebecca Latimer Felton, Nine Stormy Decades* (Athens: University of Georgia Press, 1960), 114–16.

13. For information involving violations of city antimiscegenation ordinances, see the following cases: *Strauss v. State*, 173 S. W. 663 (1915); *Brown v. State*, 266 S. W. 152 (1924); *City of New Orleans v. Miller*, 76 So. 596 (1917).

14. Peter Wallenstein, "Race, Marriage and the Law of Freedom: Alabama and Virginia, 1860s–1960s," *Chicago-Kent Law Review* 70 (1994), 406.

15. Wallenstein, "Race, Marriage, and the Law of Freedom," 407.

16. *Ferrall v. Ferrall*, 69 S. E. (1910).

17. Wallenstein, "Race, Marriage, and the Law of Freedom," *Chicago-Kent Law Review*, 409.

18. Georgia, *Acts*, 1927, 272–79. Cited in Fowler, *Northern Attitudes Towards Intermarriage*, 362.

19. Alabama, *Acts*, 1927, 219; Louisiana, *Acts*, 1920, 366, 381–82, Nos. 220, 230; Mississippi, *Laws*, 1920, 307, 214. Cited in David H. Fowler, *Northern Attitudes Towards Intermarriage: Legislation, and Public Opinion in the Middle Atlantic States of the Old Northwest, 1780–1930* (New York: Garland Publishing, 1987).

20. Rayford W. Logan, *The Betrayal of the Negro* (London: MacMillan Co., 1954), 364.

21. *Senate Journal*, 62d Cong., 3d sess., 11 December 1912, 502–3.

22. *Congressional Record*, 60th Cong., 2d sess., 1 March 1909, 3480–3483.

23. *Congressional Record*, 60th Cong., 2d sess., 1 March 1909, 3480–3483.

24. *Congressional Record*, 60th Cong., 2d sess., 1 March 1909, 3480–3483.

25. *Congressional Record*, 60ᵗʰ Cong., 2d sess., 1 March 1909, 3480–3483.

26. *Jackson v. State*, 129 So. 306 (1930).

27. *Gilbert v. State*, 23 So. 2d 22 (1945).

28. *Hardin v. State*, 339 S. W. 2ⁿᵈ 423 (1960).

29. *Lewis v. State*, 89 So. 904 (1921). Information from this section taken from trial court transcripts.

30. *Lewis v. State*, 89 So. 904 (1921).

31. *Rollins v. State*, 92 So. 35 (1922). Information for this section taken from trial court transcripts.

32. *Rollins v. State*, 92 So. 35 (1922). Transcript, 15, 17–20.

33. *Rollins v. State*, 92 So. 35 (1922).

34. *Parramore v. State*, 88 So. 472 (1921).

35. *Parramore v. State*, 88 So. 472 (1921).

36. *Parramore v. State*, 88 So. 472 (1921).

37. *Fields v. State*, 132 So. 605 (1931).

38. For works that more fully assess this dynamic see A. Leon Higginbotham Jr. and Barbara Kopytoff, "Racial Purity and Interracial Sex in the Law of Colonial and Antebellum Virginia," in *Interracialism: Black-White Intermarriage in American History, Literature, and the Law*, ed. Werner Sollors (New York: Oxford University Press, 2000); Kathleen M. Brown, *Good Wives, Nasty Wenches, and Anxious Patriarchs: Gender, Race, and Power in Colonial Virginia* (Chapel Hill: University of North Carolina Press, 1996).

39. Robinson, *Dangerous Liaisons*, 21–78.

40. Jane Dailey, "The Limits of Liberalism in the New South: The Politics of Race, Sex and Patronage in Virginia, 1879–1883," in *Jumpin' Jim Crow: Southern Politics from Civil War to Civil Rights*, Jane Dailey, Glenda Elizabeth Gilmore, and Bryant Simon, eds. (Princeton: Princeton University Press, 2000), 88–99.

41. Lawrence D. Rice, *The Negro in Texas, 1874–1900* (Baton Rouge: Louisiana State University Press), 150.

42. George Brown Tindall, *South Carolina Negroes, 1877–1900* (Columbia: University of South Carolina Press, 1952), 298–99.

43. *The Crisis*, February 5, 1913.

44. Louis Harlan and Raymond W. Smock, eds.,*The Booker T. Washington Papers* (Chicago: University of Illinois Press, 1982), 386–87.

45. Harlan and Smock, eds., *The Booker T. Washington Papers*, 386–87.

46. Philip S. Foner, *The Life and Writings of Frederick Douglass* (New York: International Publishers, 1950), 195–96.

47. Herbert Aptheker, ed., *Writings in Periodicals Edited by W. E. B. DuBois:*

Selections from the Crisis, (Millwood: Kraus-Thomson Organization Limited, 1983), 250.

48. *The Crisis*, February 5, 1913.

49. Aptheker, ed., *Writings by W. E. B. DuBois in Peridicals*, 1910–34, 34.

50. *Allen v. Scruggs*, 67 So. 301 (1912). This was a civil case in which Nobel's collateral heirs unsuccessfully challenged a will in which he bequeathed his property to his five biracial children. Kit Allen was the mother of these children.

51. *Dees v. Meets*, 17 So. 2d 137 (1944).

52. *Bell v. State*, 33 Tex. 163 (1894); *Stewart v. Profit*, 146 S. W. 563 (1912).

Civilities and Civil Rights in Mississippi

Joseph Crespino

In the 1950s and 1960s, during African Americans' historic confrontation with southern white supremacy, nonviolent civil rights protests dramatized the shortcomings of any number of white southerners' political and moral commitments: their fealty to formal declarations of democratic government; their loyalty to American values of equality and fair play; their Christian sense of brotherhood across racial lines. But the sight of well-dressed, dignified black southerners bravely asserting basic rights against vicious and violent whites also mocked the notion that most white southerners had of themselves as a peculiarly polite and well-mannered people. Civil rights struggles were, at least in part, a conflict over manners.

In 1965, the novelist Walker Percy ruminated on what he described as "the extraordinary apposition . . . of kindliness and unspeakable violence" in his home state of Mississippi, perhaps the most recalcitrant and ill-mannered southern state during these years. The problem, Percy explained, was the relative absence of any division between public and private space in Mississippi. The state was one big kinship lodge, as Percy put it. The situation gave rise to a remarkable level of affability among whites, who could show the most heart-warming kindness to people within their group, but the state lacked a developed urban setting where black and white strangers might pass each other in relative anonymity. Public life in Mississippi was like one big front porch, Percy argued, and whites dictated what amounted to the house rules. Thus, James Meredith's attempt to enter the University of Mississippi in 1962, far from an effort to put into action the law of the land, was for white Mississippians a brazen and thankless assault on the status quo, as though Meredith had employed federal thugs to push his way into their very living room. This, as much as anything, was the source of the outrage and violence among whites in Mississippi.[1]

Yet even in Mississippi, white leaders knew that bad manners were bad politics. Bad manners alienated allies in the black community. They also did not play well nationally. An important part of the civil rights fight involved public relations, controlling the images of racial confrontation, explaining to other Americans why southern segregation was reasonable, good, and proper. How else to explain Mississippi Governor Ross Barnett's bizarre comment concluding his infamous stand in the schoolhouse door, blocking James Meredith from registering at Ole Miss? After reading a proclamation in which he formally denied Meredith enrollment, Barnett announced that his conscience was clear, and handed over the proclamation to Meredith. John Doar, the Justice Department lawyer accompanying Meredith, asked Barnett a final time if he refused to let Meredith go through the door. "Yes sir," Barnett responded. "I do so politely."[2]

Barnett's comment suggests that there was an important relationship between the manners and the political power of white southerners. This essay explores that relationship and its implications for how we understand the nature of political change in the civil rights era. Manners were always intimately tied up with the operation of Jim Crow. The elaborate system of segregation laws and racial practices had developed as a way of defining appropriate behavior in public spaces shared by white and black southerners. But by the civil rights era, black southerners felt sufficiently empowered to abandon the games of racial etiquette that Jim Crow had dictated, and white southerners realized that new demands of national and international politics cast the traditional racial mores of the region in a harsh new light. In this context, the good manners of white southerners amounted to very little. Their civility was not the subtle tool by which they maintained social and political power. Instead, it was a last-ditch effort to stave off a new system of politics, one in which substance would be much more important than manners.

Paternalism and Civility in Greenville and Greensboro

Walker Percy wrote his reflection on manners and southern politics during the centennial anniversary of the Civil War, when white racism and unpunished political violence in Mississippi were subjects of national and international concern. Percy wondered what had happened to his native Mississippi. The orphaned Percy had spent his formative years in Greenville, Mississippi, in the household of his "Uncle Will," the poet and writer William Alexander Percy who was actually Walker Percy's second cousin. Like many white southern boys, Percy had been reared on the legendary bravery of Mississippi Confederates during Pickett's Charge towards Cemetery Ridge in July 1863. Surely Gettysburg was an honorable fight, Percy reasoned; the Mississippians who had fought and died there were noble men, brave soldiers with a keen sense of duty. By 1965, however, Mississippi was engaged in a different fight and white Mississippians were making a different sort of history. "If their record in Lee's army is unsurpassed for valor and devotion to duty," Percy wrote, "present-day Mississippi is mainly renowned for murder, church burning, dynamiting, assassination, night-riding, not to mention the lesser forms of terrorism."[3] Percy knew that by 1965 white Mississippians, as much as anyone, had become the very image of American hate. Images of white faces contorted by rage, spewing invective towards nonviolent protestors; of petite coeds on the Ole Miss campus shouting racial epithets at James Meredith; of cigarette-smoking, baseball bat–wielding hooligans on the edge of nonviolent civil rights marches—these became the familiar images of southern racism, testaments to the sordid underside of American democracy.

Percy knew that Mississippi had its share of responsible sorts. The most prominent among them were Percy's own relatives. Perhaps the real reason that southern whites had acted so ignobly, Percy speculated, was because the racist demagogues had shouted down what were, in effect, the "good white folks." In the hyperbole and insanity of southern massive resistance, the southerners most responsible for creating the gentile South had retreated. This may have seemed like cowardice, but for Percy—whose brother LeRoy still lived in Greenville, trying to carry on the family's planter paternalist tradition—it was a matter of mere survival. Percy's brother may not have lived up to the example of his forebears who faced down the Ku Klux Klan in Greenville, but then Uncle Will never had to face the Citizens' Councils, nor defend the Supreme Court before U.S. senators who counseled strict defiance.[4] Rather than personalize the story, however, Percy spoke in terms of Faulkner's fictional world. What had happened to the Gavin Stephenses of Mississippi—the humane and educated class? The answer: the Snopeses had won the day.

Percy still believed in a southern paternalist tradition led by men of superior education and, relatively speaking, a progressive view that placed good manners and *noblesse oblige* at the center of southern race relations. This was the tradition that the historian William Chafe, writing fifteen years after Percy, described as the "progressive mystique." Walker Percy believed that the greatest barrier to racial progress in the South was the lack of civility among southern white leaders. In his investigation of the civil rights struggle in Greensboro, North Carolina, however, Chafe concluded that, far from being the key to progress, the civility of southern paternalists was the single greatest barrier to racial justice.[5]

Greensboro, by conventional wisdom, was the heart of the progressive South, far removed from the ugly obstinacy of Mississippi. It was the first southern city to pledge to abide by the *Brown* decision. Greensboro's white elite prided themselves on being tolerant, on having a sophisticated and humane understanding of what it meant to live in a biracial society and the requirements such a society imposed on white leaders. Greensboro elites had fully embraced the paternalism of southern race relations. The city would not follow the ungainly path of resistance chartered by Deep South leaders. The irony for Chafe, however, was that the good manners of Greensboro's white elite often masked the real workings of political power, making them much more formidable opponents for southern blacks.[6] By insisting on good manners and civil discourse, Greensboro's white leaders effectively undercut any threat the black community might muster to the status quo. Civility itself became the chief means of social control.[7]

Chafe's analysis exploded the distinction that Walker Percy made between the well-mannered South and the violent South. Percy's account of the decline of white paternalism essentially recapitulated the familiar class-based formulation between the "good white folks"—the paternalistic middle-class, college-educated city leaders—and the "bad whites"—the Snopeses, or, in the civil rights era, the working class hooligans who joined right wing organizations and spread racial terror. Chafe turned the model on its head. In Greensboro, "the primary resistance to significant racial breakthroughs came from white leaders of the upper class."[8]

Chafe was not unaware of the complicated workings of civility. He admitted that one of the reasons Greensboro was the home of the sit-in movement was because African Americans in the city were less isolated; challenges to the status quo were less likely to meet the violent backlash that so often occurred in Deep South states. Yet Chafe failed to appreciate the potential for white violence, even in relatively progressive Greensboro. He dismissed as a red herring the argument that the gradualism of Greensboro's elite was a response to more violent working-class whites. In fact, the "redneck" argument, as Chafe put it, merely became another rationale for elites to preserve the status quo. "By making 'rednecks' the primary reference group on the political spectrum, those in power were able to portray any position less extreme than that of the Klan as 'moderate,'" Chafe wrote. "Poor whites did not have the power to shape policy."[9]

If poor whites could not shape policy directly, however, they surely could influence the white leaders who made policy. Chafe discounted the impact of Klan organizing on white officials, arguing that law enforcement officials had successfully infiltrated the Klan and that key Klan leaders served as FBI informants. But in the years following 1964, the Ku Klux Klan experienced dramatic growth. In no southern state was Klan activity more rabid than North Carolina. A 1967 Congressional study of the resurgent Klan movement showed that 192 klaverns with over 7,500 members operated in North Carolina between 1964 and 1966. The state with the next highest Klan membership—Georgia—paled in comparison with only 1,400 members in 57 klaverns.[10] Greensboro, moreover, was home to two separate Klan organizations as well as a third auxiliary group for Klan women. One of the key leaders in the region-wide Klan resurgence, George Franklin Dorsett, was a house painter from Greensboro who was elected the Imperial Kludd, or chaplain, of the United Klans of America.[11]

It would have taken remarkable powers of equanimity for local leaders in Greensboro not to be influenced by this extremist presence. Yet the best example of how Chafe failed to appreciate the pressures exerted on Greensboro's white elite—and the relative progress won in Greensboro—is in the area of school desegregation. Greensboro's statement of compliance with *Brown* hid the fact that in the seventeen years following the Court's decision hardly any school desegregation actually had taken place. Through the Pearsall plan and later through freedom of choice plans, Greensboro's public schools remained almost completely segregated until 1971, when the persistence of local black leaders backed by provisions written into the 1964 Civil Rights Act forced the white-dominated school board to comply. But according to Chafe, when the school board finally did adopt an aggressive desegregation plan that included sensitivity training and busing plans, it was merely another example of the cunning politics of civility. The school board's action, Chafe points out, divided middle-class black activists from more radical, working-class proponents of Black Power. The effect was to destroy "the unity so helpful to the effectiveness of black protest in 1969, 1970, and 1971."[12]

Chafe provides no evidence that white leaders focused on school integration as a strategy to divide African Americans in Greensboro. It is much more likely that white leaders caved on school desegregation as a response to increased demands by federal officials. In 1971, with twelve all-black schools in the city, the Greensboro school district was one of only five school districts in North Carolina that was still not in compliance with federal civil rights guidelines. The federal government had deferred funds to the district because of its noncompliance, meaning that the annual money from Washington had declined from $1.5 million to $423,000 a year. The point is not to nitpick about Chafe's lack of a footnote proving that whites moved on school desegregation with the express intention of dividing the black community. Even if it was not the purpose of white leaders, the school desegregation plan had the *effect* of dividing the black community. Perhaps the real power of the progressive mystique was to operate outside of intention—to undermine subversive protest even when those who wielded it were unaware of the effects.

The problem, however, is that this kind of analysis flattens out contests for power and masks the contingency present in every challenge across the color line. To his credit, Chafe does not push the analysis too far.[13] At best Chafe's analysis implies that because white leaders had greater access to power, they understood it better and knew how to wield it more effectively. Black leaders were more inexperienced, more naïve about how to play the political game. At worst, Chafe's concept of civility leans towards an almost cartoonish understanding of political power. Greensboro elites were all-knowing with epic powers of political foresight. They always were able to see through the web of details, to calculate instantly the politic dynamics involved in any given situation. They were always more politically astute than blacks, tricking them with slick talk and good manners.

The desegregation of Greensboro schools was not merely another example of the slipperiness of white civility. It was instead a critical moment in the history of black-white relations in Greensboro. After seventeen years of delay and evasion, black activists had finally closed every loophole. The integration of Greensboro public schools in 1971 was not merely a victory for the black middle class, though undoubtedly middle-class blacks benefited more from it than poor blacks.[14] This was the culmination of a process that began in 1954. To say that the vanguard of black political opinion

in Greensboro had abandoned the integrationist ethic of the *Brown* decision by the time that the full implications of *Brown* were realized in Greensboro should not detract from the achievement of Greensboro's black community. With school desegregation in Greensboro, white leaders were not
the wily and sophisticated foes who had once again slipped the blow of the
beleaguered black community. White leaders who had consistently avoided
the full implications of the *Brown* decision for seventeen years had finally
lost the fight for segregated public schools.[15]

The most important insight from Chafe's concept of civility is how it operated in the minds of Greensboro whites. They needed to believe in their
own progressiveness, in their distinction from the *true* southern racists of
the Deep South. They created an elaborate social fiction that hid from themselves and from most observers the genuine workings of racial injustice. But
in other parts of the South, we can assume, white leaders were more comfortable with the requirements of white supremacy. If the civility of Greensboro
white elites was a mere cover for social control and the continuity of racial
inequality, then in other, less civil parts of the South white hegemony should
be closer to the surface, clearer for all to see because it was unmitigated by
the "progressive mystique." In the same way, the continuity of white political power in the 1960s and 1970s should be equally obvious.[16]

It is an implicit assumption that deserves investigation. Mississippi is an
ideal place for such a comparison. Surely, if any place in the South lacked the
civility of Greensboro it was the state that gave birth to the Citizens' Councils and the Sovereignty Commission, the first state-sponsored organization
committed to the preservation of Jim Crow. Mississippi was home to some
of the most vicious acts of racial violence during the civil rights years. According to Chafe's formulation, in Mississippi we should find the more bare-
boned workings of white political power, a monolithic white community
united in its visceral opposition to racial change, and an unbroken chain of
white racial authoritarianism that persisted despite the best efforts of local
black activists and their sometime allies in the federal government.

In some ways this is the story of the civil rights movement in Mississippi.
It was in Neshoba County, Mississippi, after all, that the complicity of local
law enforcement officials with Ku Klux Klan members led to the murder of
three civil rights workers in June 1964. But whites in Mississippi, as much so
as in North Carolina or any other southern state, debated the role of civility
in the maintenance of Jim Crow. White political elites in Mississippi were
in crisis in the 1950s and 1960s and black Mississippians proved remarkably

effective in undermining traditional paternalistic patterns of race relations. In Mississippi, an examination of white civility reveals not the continuity of white political power but rather its weakness, and the relatively small but historically important successes, in turn, of African Americans in identifying and attacking the sources of racial inequality.[17]

Civilities in Mississippi

Mississippians had their paternalistic tradition as much as North Carolinians did—it was the mechanism by which white elites "managed" white supremacy. There was no better articulation of this sentiment for Mississippi or for the South than *Lanterns on the Levee*—the memoir published by Walker Percy's "Uncle Will." Blacks were dependent on the benevolence of an enlightened and educated white minority. But this paternalism was on the wane by the middle of the twentieth century, driven in greatest part by the collapse of the plantation economy in which it had first been born and later sustained.[18] By the mid-twentieth century, two ancillary developments further undermined southern paternalism: first, the growing determination among southern blacks to set the course for their own political future; and second, an increasing resentment among whites towards federal intervention in southern racial affairs—the best evidence of which came in the 1948 Dixiecrat Revolt.[19]

On the eve of the *Brown* decision, Mississippi's commitment to paternalistic politics can be seen in the debate over a massive appropriations bill to improve black public education. South Carolina already had passed legislation to equalize black and white public schools.[20] The belief was that the only way to forestall legal efforts to end Jim Crow schools was to actually make good on the pledge first articulated in the *Plessy* decision: that black public institutions not only should be separate but *equal* to those of whites.[21] The gap that white officials had to make up was wide. In any given county per-pupil-expenditure for white students was up to six times as much as for black students, though the discrepancy was particularly acute in the Mississippi Delta where black students were in the majority. In the Delta county of Bolivar, where 68 percent of the population was black, the expenditure for white students was $169 each, compared to $34 per black student.[22]

In 1953, Mississippi Governor Hugh White called a special session of the legislature to deal with the state's educational problems, or as one Jackson newspaper put it, "particularly the necessity of bringing Negro schools up to the common standard as one means of preserving segregation."[23] Backing the governor was the Mississippi Economic Council and the influential Delta Council, a kind of chamber of commerce for agricultural interests in the Mississippi Delta and the institutional voice of Mississippi paternalism. As early as 1946, the Delta Council supported a school program for blacks that included new school buildings where needed, vocational education for returning veterans, a black teachers college to be located in the Delta, and an improved pay schedule for black teachers.[24]

Equalization proponents such as White also summoned a paternalistic sense of *noblesse oblige* towards the black community, discussing the "moral obligation" to provide for school equalization. The same tone could be seen among some legislators. A legislative report was scathing in its condemnation of white oversight of black schools. Had it been written by civil rights sympathizers only a few years later, the same group of legislators surely would have dismissed it as the biased vilification of outside agitators. The report described the condition of rural black schools as "pathetic and in some cases . . . inexcusable." "Hundreds of children of the Negro race are compelled to attend school—if they attend at all—in unpainted, unheated and unlighted buildings that are not fit for human habitation and should have been condemned many years ago," the committee reported.[25] That same month, the staunchly segregationist *Jackson Daily News* published a picture of the gleaming dome of the recently completed Mississippi state capitol juxtaposed with a snapshot of an overcrowded, ramshackle classroom in an all-black elementary school in Jackson. The headline read, "From One to the Other It Is Less Than Two Miles." The accompanying text described a one-room black public school with a broken-down stove and a leaking roof. Newspaper and cardboard replaced window panes and students sat on benches of rough lumber. The only toilet was a clump of bushes behind the building. There was a gaping hole in the floor through which the State Superintendent of Education had nearly fallen in a recent visit to the school.[26]

Despite these conditions, the legislature never funded an equalization program. The expense of program and the uncertainty of the Supreme Court's decision on southern school desegregation played a major role in its defeat.[27] The most important factor in the bill's defeat, however, was the specter that white legislators would allocate the money and African Americans would still not be content with the effort. Some influential black leaders, including the president of the Mississippi Baptist Convention and the head of the Negro Educational Association, supported equalization.[28] Importantly, however, a conference of black leaders said to have represented over six hundred thousand Mississippi African Americans met in Jackson to pass a resolution stating that they supported separate schools and the equalization effort only "insofar as these bills do not violate the fourteenth amendment to the Constitution . . . as interpreted by the Supreme Court."[29] More troubling still for Mississippi paternalists, state NAACP president Amos O. Holmes said that black leaders who supported equalization did not have the best interest of the black community in mind. Holmes was not deferential and none too polite when he pledged to work until the "vicious system of segregation . . . is removed and justice is done."[30]

White paternalistic supporters of equalization took it as a great affront that some African Americans were anything less than grateful towards the school equalization effort. The Mississippi state superintendent of education denounced black leaders who opposed equalization, claiming that they did not "in the least degree represent sentiment among the real Negro leaders in Mississippi, nor the rank and file of the race."[31] They were aghast that black leaders would actually reject their beneficence. Still, the paternalistic ethos of the equalization effort contrasted sharply with the confrontational white supremacist politics that characterized Mississippi in the post-*Brown* era. What seems remarkable in retrospect was the severity with which the proponents of equalization openly criticized the white community's previous funding for black public schools. White leaders openly confessed that they had been less than upright in their role as caretakers of black interests. It was an admission that would be unimaginable only a few years later, after the "closing" of Mississippi society, when the reaction to *Brown* set loose extremist voices in the white community that denounced as treason any public statement hinting that Jim Crow race relations were less than ideal.[32]

In Mississippi, as throughout the Deep South, *Brown* galvanized the forces that would oppose the civil rights struggle.[33] The *Brown* decision, as one historian has written, "mobilized southern whites behind segregation far more effectively than it did southern blacks behind integration"; it did not begin the civil rights movement in Mississippi so much as it foreclosed paternalistic politics in the white community.[34] The force behind the new, militant voice of resistance in Mississippi was the Citizens' Councils. The organizations began in Sunflower County in the late summer of 1954 as local white

elites gathered to discuss ways of resisting the Supreme Court's school desegregation order. In little more than two years, the Councils had spread like
wildfire, counting some eighty thousand members in Mississippi.[35]

Compared to the paternalistic approach of equalization supporters, the
Citizens' Councils advocated a more confrontational approach to racial
problems. It was exactly because they believed that the NAACP and other
civil rights organizations had usurped the role of the traditional conciliatory black leadership that the Citizens' Councils formed. The idea was that
southern blacks were organizing, so southern whites better organize as well.
The Citizens' Councils pledged from the start to be confrontational but not
violent in the way of the Klan. They took pains to distinguish themselves
from the Klan.[36] They saw themselves as the modern articulation of white supremacist politics, and indeed they used all the tools of a modern public relations organization: they developed over time a fairly sophisticated monthly
magazine, they had an impressive lobbying organization at least at the state
level, and they utilized television as a way to get out their message.[37]

But the rise of the Councils led to small but important rifts among whites
in the late 1950s and early 1960s. During the height of the state's massive
resistance campaign, white leaders in Mississippi indirectly debated the role
of civility in the management of southern race relations. The public rift between white leaders reveals some of the important intersections between civility and civil rights, or more specifically, between manners and white political power. Roughly six months before Mississippi Governor Ross Barnett
would defy the federal courts and the Kennedy administration in blocking
James Meredith's entrance into the University of Mississippi—an act that remains one of the quintessential moments of southern massive resistance—a
key Barnett aide provoked controversy and consternation among hard-line
segregationists by labeling the Citizens' Councils as an extremist organization that, along with the NAACP, was needlessly polarizing race relations
in Mississippi. Erle Johnston, the public relations director of the Mississippi
State Sovereignty Commission whom Ross Barnett would later appoint as
head of that organization, criticized the Citizens' Councils for their advo-
cacy of "threats and intimidation." The main purpose of the Citizens' Councils, Johnston would later say, had become "making white people hate each
other."[38] "It would seem far better," Johnston argued, "to offer an inch of
consideration across a table of harmony than to be forced to retreat further
in an atmosphere of friction and bitterness. . . . Courtesy is better than co-

ercion, interest is better than intimidation, recognition is better than retribution, and friendship is better than force."[39]

Johnston coupled his criticisms with strong words against the NAACP, an organization, he argued, that "clamored for special privileges" and that "thrived on strained relations to strengthen their appeals for more funds from the North."[40] And Johnston did not call out the Citizens' Councils by name, though the implication was clear. Quick reaction to Johnston's speech came in Tom Ethridge's regular column in the *Jackson Clarion-Ledger*. Ethridge was a stalwart segregationist and a strong supporter of the Councils. He challenged Johnston to name the organization that Johnston felt was so deleterious to good race relations. In response, Johnston provided an analogy for his differences with Ethridge and other "hysterical segregationists," as he called them. "When I go to the post office, if a Negro is ahead of me, I speak courteously and wait for my turn to get near my box," Johnston wrote. "The hysterical segregationist shoves the Negro aside, doesn't even bother to give him a courteous greeting, and demonstrates very clearly that a Negro must get out of the way for a white man."[41] Johnston elaborated on the metaphor just in case Ethridge missed the point. "One attitude creates hate and resentment, the other, an atmosphere of harmony and respect," Johnston wrote. "Resentful citizens look to outsiders for help. But those who are treated with courtesy are more inclined to depend for guidance and progress on their local friends and neighbors."[42]

Johnston's plea for good manners was, in essence, a call to return to the paternalistic politics of the past. Avoiding resentful citizens who look to outsiders for help—this was the real motive behind what Johnston would call "practical segregation" to distinguish from the "hysterical segregationists." Johnston advocated civility, then, from a position of weakness, not strength. It was a way of avoiding unwanted outside attention and political pressure. The alternative confrontational approach of the Citizens' Councils only drew reaction from national civil rights groups and, ultimately, from the federal government. For Johnston, civility was a last-gasp effort to hold onto the reigns of southern white supremacy. Without it, southern whites ran headlong into a political fight they simply could not win.

The term "practical segregation" was not original to Erle Johnston. It was a phrase that he borrowed from J. P. Coleman, governor of Mississippi from 1955 to 1959. Coleman first used the term during his administration to distinguish his own approach to maintaining the color line from hard-liners in the Citizens' Councils, the organization that exploded in membership and political influence during the mid and late 1950s. A look at J. P. Coleman's relationship with the Citizens' Councils further explains the political context of white civility in Mississippi.

While both were committed to maintaining segregation, Coleman and the Citizens' Councils never got along. Coleman was elected in large part because he best typified what Bruce Schulman called the "New Whig" leadership of the post–World War II South.[43] By 1959, when Ross Barnett was elected governor, the sole issue in the campaign was which candidate would be the fiercest defender of white supremacy; not so in 1955, when the impact of the *Brown* decision had yet to be fully measured.[44] Coleman was an aggressive recruiter of outside industry to the state. The crowning effort in this regard was Coleman's failed attempt to hold a constitutional convention to replace the "horse and buggy" constitution of 1890 with a more modern charter that would promote economic development.[45] In race relations, Coleman's coolness towards the Citizens' Councils marked him as a moderate in the state. Moderation in Mississippi in the 1950s, of course, was on a scale that we today would hardly recognize as moderate. But the distinctions are not picayune. They reveal fault-lines among white leaders that the pressures of civil rights activism only exacerbated. By the early and mid-1960s, when local blacks in combination with the federal government forced significant changes in established Jim Crow patterns, these fissures illustrate the evolution of resistance strategies among whites.

Throughout his administration, Coleman called for "cool, clear thinking on racial problems," drawing an implicit comparison with the bombast of the Citizens' Councils.[46] Coleman's pragmatic cast of mind hardly meant that he was soft on segregation; Coleman predicted fifty years or more would pass before southern schools would willingly desegregate. "Certainly not in my lifetime," he vowed.[47] When he ran for a second term as governor in 1963 (Mississippi law at the time forbade a candidate from two consecutive terms), he proudly did so on a record that no significant integration had come to Mississippi during his watch. But Coleman, more so than Citizens' Council leaders, was mindful of how the segregation fight impinged on other political priorities. One such issue was the goal of maintaining Mississippi's and the South's role within a viable Democratic Party. Coleman had shown keen interest in national Democratic Party politics since his earliest days as a political aide in Washington where he contested for control of the Junior Congress, a political organization for Washington aides, with another young aspiring southern politico, Lyndon Johnson.[48] The early competition turned into a friendship that continued throughout Coleman's political career, eventually leading to an appointment to the Fifth Circuit Court of Appeals in 1965. After Mississippi's Dixiecrat revolt in 1948, Coleman fought hard at the 1952 and 1956 Democratic national conventions to keep a wavering Mississippi delegation in line with the national platform. The national party helped out loyal southerners like Coleman by limiting the reach of their party platforms on civil rights during the 1950s.[49]

Coleman saw the Council leaders and other last-ditch segregationists as political insurgents who were willing to provoke white Mississippians' worst fears of racial integration to advance their own political interests. While still governor-elect, Coleman made clear his opposition to the Council-backed drive to pass a resolution of nullification against the *Brown* decision. The Citizens' Council had endorsed the effort in its newspaper and prominent Council supporters such as Judge Tom Brady, Congressman John Bell Williams, and Senator James Eastland were in favor of the initiative. In an open letter to the Mississippi legislature, however, Coleman expressed dismay at the proposal and its supporters: "History teaches in a long succession of events that such efforts have always failed, and in failing have brought down terrible penalties upon the heads of those who attempted it."[50] Coleman believed that politicians like Brady, Williams, and Eastland were, like the Citizens' Councils themselves, turning Mississippi into an object of derision: "What I want to do is to preserve segregation in Mississippi. I am not trying to grab headlines."[51] Coleman again took a swipe at the Citizens' Councils' confrontational style in his inaugural address in 1956: "Those in positions of responsibility must think things through before they take positions of no return. The greatest need of the time is for cool, clear thinking on racial problems. This is not the time to let hotheads make us lose our perspective."[52]

Another Mississippi leader who agreed with Coleman on these matters was U.S. Senator John Stennis. The problem with belligerent segregationists, Stennis believed, was their inability to appreciate the "the practical side of the difficulties that confront us."[53] The leaders of massive resistance did more harm than good, Stennis believed, weakening the South's position nationally and inflaming resentments at home in the black community. Stennis's critique of Georgia Governor Herman Talmadge applied equally well to massive resistance leaders in his own state: "It seems to me that Governor Talmadge is making a severe mistake in advertising his non-compliance with the Supreme Court decision, making it a crusade of defiance." Stennis knew that white leaders in Mississippi were not going to integrate the public schools, but he also knew that "the less we advertise this the better."[54]

The week after the *Brown* decision, Stennis, in a letter to J. P. Coleman, was hopeful that the Court might still "lay down some fairly liberal ground rules in its final decree, thus making it possible to work out some plans."[55] Stennis proposed his own plan in which white leaders in each county would remind black community leaders that "whatever schools the negroes have will have to be provided by local and state taxes, which negroes themselves cannot levy, nor can the NAACP or any other outside agitator, now or in years to come." In return for a pledge not to bring desegregation lawsuits under the new ruling in *Brown*, white leaders would ensure that blacks receive "adequate and equal schoolhouses, faculties and transportation facilities."[56] Stennis ignored the fact that such a plan was merely what the federal law had, in fact, required since the *Plessy* decision. He contacted young, high-profile local leaders whom he believed would keep a cool head in the current crisis, such as the moderate state legislator William Winter of Grenada and Walker Percy's brother LeRoy in Greenville. He hoped to form a network of low-key leaders who could operate on a word-of-mouth basis, refraining from formal declarations of defiance, quietly and politely managing the school crisis—and maintaining segregation—at the local level.[57] "I still believe there are many counties in Mississippi, including your own and my own, in which the white people and the colored people could meet and work out a plan satisfactory to both," Stennis wrote to Winter. "This agreement plan would perhaps work for 15 or 20 or 25 years in many of these counties."[58] Stennis was so quiet about the school crisis that the harsher critics of desegregation wondered if he was up for the fight. Some political rumors had it that John Bell Williams, one of the most vociferous leaders of massive resistance in Mississippi, might challenge Stennis for his Senate seat in 1958.[59]

Practical segregation in Mississippi school desegregation was based on both a close reading of the *Brown* decision and, in large part, a willful misreading of the political resolve in the black community. Well-mannered pragmatists like Stennis and Coleman knew that *Brown* could take effect only if individual plaintiffs filed suit. They believed that if white leaders made polite but firm appeals to black leadership, they could avoid such suits.

They sought a common ground with black leaders that they believed represented the genuine political will of the majority of African Americans. "The great majority of our own Negroes (leaving out the paid agitators)," Coleman wrote a constituent, "know that segregation makes life much easier for them and they have no idea of attacking it."[60]

But that was the problem—black Mississippians that Coleman dismissed as "paid agitators" would, over the course of the following decade, mobilize a grass-roots campaign that directly confronted the legal and political inequalities of Jim Crow. The increased militancy of Mississippi's black community combined with dilatory but decisive action by the federal government rendered the polite, practical segregation of J. P. Coleman impotent. When Coleman ran for governor in 1963 he argued that his low-key practical segregation was more successful than the bombast of massive resistance preached by Ross Barnett and his lieutenant governor Paul Johnson. But, in fact, Coleman's unblemished record on segregation during his first term was due more to the luck of circumstance than to the effectiveness of practical segregation. It is unclear, for example, how Coleman could have practically or politely managed James Meredith's application to the University of Mississippi in 1962. The black applicant who had tried to integrate Mississippi's institutions of higher learning during Coleman's first term, Clyde Kennard, had been turned away not by Coleman's good manners and practical arguments but because state highway patrolmen imprisoned him on bogus charges.[61]

In the end, civility proved to be a very fragile hook on which to hang the future of white supremacy in Mississippi. It was a desperate effort to hold onto a pattern of white racial authority that the new black empowerment rendered obsolete. Black Mississippians understood the desperation in the paternalistic school equalization efforts of the early 1950s as easily as James Meredith saw through Ross Barnett's pathetic attempts at politeness in Barnett's stand in the schoolhouse door. The evolution of white political leadership in Mississippi, far from showing the continuity of white political power, revealed important and historic inroads that southern African Americans made in overturning established social and political patterns of white rule and in ushering in a new era of black political empowerment. This new era fell far short of the genuine biracial democracy, to be sure, but it was a new and significant departure from the exclusion and co-optation masked as white civility that had characterized Mississippi politics in the rough century since emancipation.

Notes

1. Walker Percy, "Mississippi: The Fallen Paradise," in John Meachem, ed., *Voices In Our Blood: America's Best on the Civil Rights Movement* (New York: Random House, 2001), 318–27.

2. Quoted in William Doyle, *An American Insurrection: The Battle of Oxford, Mississippi 1962* (New York: Doubleday, 2002), 83; also see Robert Canzoneri, *"I Do So Politely," A Voice From the South* (Boston: Houghton Mifflin, 1965).

3. Walker Percy, "Mississippi: The Fallen Paradise," in John Meachem, ed., *Voices In Our Blood: America's Best on the Civil Rights Movement* (New York: Random House, 2001), 318–27.

4. For an account of the Percy's confrontation with the Klan in Greenville in the 1920s, see William Alexander Percy, *Lanterns on the Levee: Recollections of a Planter's Son* (Baton Rouge: Louisiana State University Press, 1941, reprinted 1993), 225–41, and more generally, Bertram Wyatt-Brown, *The House of Percy: Honor, Melancholy, and Imagination in a Southern Family* (New York: Oxford University Press, 1994).

5. William Chafe, *Civility and Civil Rights: Greensboro, North Carolina, and the Black Struggle For Freedom* (New York: Oxford University Press, 1980).

6. In writing about the nineteenth-century urban North, John Kasson has shown how "established codes of behavior have often served in unacknowledged ways as checks against a fully democratic order and in support of special interests, institutions of privilege, and structures of domination." John F. Kasson, *Rudeness and Civility: Manners in Nineteenth-Century Urban America* (New York: Hill and Wang, 1990), 3.

7. In an article comparing university desegregation in South Carolina and Alabama, Marcia G. Synnott has described two contrasting strategies of white leadership in the 1950s South: "massive resistance" and "moderation." While "both were equally committed in principle to a defense of segregation," writes Synnott, moderates "were more successful in achieving their objectives than resisters, because they avoided sweeping federal interventions." See Synnott, "Federalism Vindicated: University Desegregation in South Carolina and Alabama, 1962–1963," *Journal of Policy History* 1, no. 3 (1989): 292–18.

8. Chafe, *Civility and Civil Rights*, 38.

9. Ibid., 69, also see 58.

10. Committee on Un-American Activities, House of Representatives, Ninetieth Congress, First Session, *The Present Day Ku Klux Klan Movement* (Washington, D.C.: U.S. Government Printing Office, 1967), 37.

11. In July 1965, Dorsett spoke before the "O. Henry" Sertoma Club of Greens-

boro in which he described the activities of what he called the "Klan Bureau of Investigation," or KBI. "The KBI investigates demonstrations and marches like the one on Selma, Alabama," Dorsett said. "We had agents in there taking pictures and making tape recordings. And we investigate politicians to see if they're shady. Our aim is to pick out the right candidates and then get out a bloc vote." At a Klan meeting in April 1965, Dorsett viciously denounced North Carolina state patrol officers who were present taking the license plate numbers of the cars of those in attendance as "storm troopers" and he boasted that there were enough Klan members there to take the guns off the troopers. At another Klan rally where policemen were performing a similar task, Dorsett lambasted law enforcement officials as "termites" and "rats" (Committee on Un-American Activities, House of Representatives, Ninetieth Congress, First Session, *Activities of Ku Klux Klan Organizations in the United States,* part 1 (Washington, D.C.: U.S. Government Printing Office, 1968), 2046, 2049, 2059). Chafe himself includes evidence of Klan terror against an African American who attempted to integrate an all-white Greensboro neighborhood, which was intended as a message as much to white leaders as to the black community. Chafe, *Civility and Civil Rights,* 161–63, 201.

12. Chafe, *Civility and Civil Rights,* 244.

13. As Chafe carries his analysis into the late 1960s and early 1970s, when black power advocates increasingly outflanked traditional NAACP leaders in their protest of institutional racism in Greensboro, the seams start to show in Chafe's social control thesis. He asserts the notion that civil actions by Greensboro white elites are co-optive and strategic much more tentatively than in earlier parts of the book. Thus, Chafe writes that the Community Unity Division (CUD), the interracial offshoot organization of the Greensboro Chamber of Commerce, played "a pivotal role in Greensboro's future racial politics," but he leaves unresolved for the reader whether this activity was "for the purposes of subtle social control or radical social change" (212). Equally evasive, Chafe refuses to say whether the white leaders' adoption of desegregation plans was intentional or unintentional in the way that it divided the black community (231).

14. Chafe implies that more radical activists of the late 1960s actually spoke for "the people" in a way that middle-class, establishment NAACP leaders did not. It is an assumption not always born out by the evidence and it is not unique to Chafe. See Alan Draper's critique of John Dittmer in *Conflict of Interests: Organized Labor and the Civil Rights Movement in the South, 1954–1968* (Ithaca: ILR Press, 1994), 203–4.

15. It is possible to discuss certain continuities between the 1950s and the

1980s in Greensboro race relations without submitting to Chafe's thesis about the uses of civility in maintaining white hegemony. In the seven years following public school integration in Greensboro, public school enrollments decreased by five thousand students. The vast majority of the losses were in the white student population. The ratio of white to black students in Greensboro schools during the same time shifted from 68/32 to 55/45. Chafe estimates that 25 to 30 percent of this loss represented a move by whites to private schools. Another factor was the movement to white suburbs (Chafe, *Civility and Civil Rights*, 242). It is right to ask how this pattern of white flight to private schools and the rejection of metropolitan desegregation plans that created nearly all-white suburban school districts bringing majority black inner-city school districts differed significantly from the Jim Crow patterns that had come before. An important distinction is in the spatial transformation of white urban areas and the ideologies of white elites that justified such segregated patterns. While Chafe shows change over time in the black community, as more radical black activists increasingly challenged middle-class NAACP leaders, he fails to appreciate similar changes in the white community. White leaders who presided over the integration of the schools in 1971 were of a different generation and operated from different ideological foundations than the ones who adopted the Pearsall plan in the 1950s. By the 1970s, a rising generation of middle-class, increasingly suburbanized whites found new ways to avoid the impact of desegregation that had less to do with the accommodation and subterfuge of paternalistic civility than with what the historian Matthew Lassiter calls "color-blind" conservatism rooted in a white suburban, middle-class consciousness. White middle-class suburbanites in North Carolina articulated a disenchantment with liberal civil rights policy that would echo across the nation and would lay the groundwork for the conservative political triumphs of the 1980s. See Matthew D. Lassiter, "The Suburban Origins of 'Color-Blind' Conservatism: Middle-Class Consciousness in the Charlotte Busing Crisis," *Journal of Urban History* 30, no. 4 (May 2004): 549–82. Also see Lassiter, *The Silent Majority: Suburban Politics in the Sunbelt South* (Princeton: Princeton University Press, 2006) and Kevin Kruse, *White Flight: Atlanta and the Making of Modern Conservatism* (Princeton: Princeton University Press, 2005), 234–66. For more on the resegregation of southern public schools, see Gary Orfield and John Yun, "Resegregation in American Schools," The Civil Rights Project, Harvard University, June 1999, http://www.civilrightsproject.harvard.edu/research/deseg/reseg_schools99.php and Erica Frankenberg and Chungmei Lee, "Race in American Public Schools: Rapidly Resegregating School Districts," The Civil

Rights Project, Harvard University, August 2002, http://www.civilrightsproject.harvard.edu/research/deseg/Race_in_American_Public_Schools1.pdf).

16. For more on the debate between continuity versus discontinuity during the civil rights era, see Hugh Davis Graham, "Since 1965: The South and Civil Rights," in Larry J. Griffin and Don H. Doyle, eds., *The South as an American Problem* (Athens: University of Georgia Press, 1995), 145–63. This essay argues that the investigation of civility and power in Mississippi shows the discontinuity in power relations across the color line. This is not to imply that the civil rights movement ushered in a new era of racial equality in the South, only one that was significantly distinct from what had come before.

17. Implicit in this analysis is a reminder that we should be careful not to overemphasize the degree to which civility acts as a function of political and economic power. It is important to remember that as a mode of power, civility often has acted as a replacement for more explicitly violent, and therefore, inefficient regimes. This, I would argue, is one of the implicit, if unstated, points of one of the earliest scholars of manners, Norbert Elias, in his classic investigation, *Power and Civility* (New York: Pantheon, 1982). The civility of the courtier class came as a replacement for the explicit power of the warrior class. If civility functioned as a more indirect exertion of political and economic power, it derived, in part, out of a need for a more efficient mode of administration. For an example of how civility replaced more explicitly violent regimes in the post–emancipation but pre–Jim Crow South, see Jane Dailey, "Deference and Violence in the Postbellum Urban South: Manners and Massacres in Danville, Virginia," *Journal of Southern History* 63, no. 3 (August 1997): 585.

18. On the collapse of the plantation economy, see Pete Daniels, *Breaking the Land: The Transformation of Cotton, Tobacco, and Rice Cultures Since 1880* (Urbana: University of Illinois Press, 1985); James C. Cobb and Michael V. Namorato, eds., *The New Deal and the South* (Jackson: University Press of Mississippi, 1984); James C. Cobb, *The Most Southern Place on Earth: The Mississippi Delta and the Roots of Regional Identity* (New York: Oxford University Press, 1992); McMillen, ed., *Remaking Dixie: The Impact of World War II on the American South* (Jackson: University Press of Mississippi, 1997); Nan Elizabeth Woodruff, "Mississippi Delta Planters and Debates Over Mechanization, Labor, and Civil Rights in the 1940s," *Journal of Southern History* 60 (1994): 263–84.

19. On the end of paternalism in Virginia, see J. Douglas Smith, *Managing White Supremacy: Race, Politics, and Citizenship in Jim Crow Virginia* (Chapel Hill: University of North Carolina Press, 2002). On the rise of black militancy in the

1940s, see Payne, *I've Got the Light of Freedom*, 29–66; Dittmer, *Local People*, 1–40; Fairclough, *Race and Democracy*, 106–34. On the Dixiecrat revolt, see Kari Fredrickson, *The Dixiecrat Revolt and the End of the Solid South, 1932–1968* (Chapel Hill: University of North Carolina Press, 2001).

20. William D. Smyth, "Segregation in Charleston in the 1950s: A Decade of Transition," *South Carolina Historical Magazine* 92, no. 2 (1991): 99–123.

21. For a more detailed examination of the equalization campaign in Mississippi, see Charles Bolton, "Mississippi's School Equalization Program, 1945–1954: A Last Gasp to Try to Maintain a Segregated Educational System," *Journal of Southern History* 66, no. 4 (2000): 781–814. Bolton argues the equalization effort was a fundamentally regressive effort in the dying days of Jim Crow. It was also, however, an attempt to hold on to a kind of paternalistic politics that the overt activism of local and national civil rights organizations would render impotent by the mid-1950s.

22. "Is This Separate but Equal Education?" *Christian Century*, April 22, 1953, 469; *Memphis Commercial Appeal*, March 15, 1953.

23. *Jackson Daily News* (hereinafter referred to as *JDN*), September 22, 1953, 1.

24. V. O. Key, *Southern Politics*, 235, footnote 11; For the Delta Council resolution, see B. F. Smith to John Stennis, May 17, 1951, folder 39 Delta Council, box 2, Series 39, JCSP; for the MEC and the Citizens' Council for Education resolution, see Mississippi Economic Council, "Our State's School Crisis", c. 1951, subject file: Economic Council, 1949–1955, Mississippi Department of Archives and History (hereinafter referred to as MDAH).

25. *JDN*, November 1, 1953, 1.

26. *JDN*, November 11, 1953, 2.

27. A large number of legislators openly admitted the state's hypocrisy in their pledge of "separate but equal," but the majority preferred to wait to see if the Supreme Court would be content with that standard. When the session ended two days before Christmas 1953, no clear plan remained for how the state might come up with the money for equalization (*JDN*, December 24, 1953, 1). The most conservative estimate predicted an equalization program would cost $100 million over the next twenty years (*JDN*, November 2, 1953). Hopes for an equalization package were set back even further at the end of November 1953. U.S. Attorney General Herbert Brownell issued an *amicus curiae* brief in support of school desegregation. Legislators promised to push ahead with equalization plans despite Brownell's decision, but other Mississippi leaders began preparing for what increasingly seemed like the inevitable (*JDN*, November 30, 1953, 1).

28. *JDN*, October 8, 1953, 1; *JDN*, November 6, 1953, 9.

29. *JDN*, November 4, 1953, 1.

30. *JDN*, November 7, 1953, 1.

31. *JDN*, November 4, 1953, 1.

32. James W. Silver, *Mississippi: The Closed Society* (New York: Harcourt, Brace & World, 1966); Charles Eagles, "The Closing of Mississippi Society: Will Campbell, the $64,000 Question, and Religious Emphasis Week at the University of Mississippi," *Journal of Southern History* 67, no. 2 (2001): 331–72.

33. For more on the role of *Brown* in fueling white backlash, see Michael Klarman, "How Brown Changed Race Relations: The Backlash Thesis," *Journal of American History* 81, no. 1 (June 1994): 81–118.

34. Quoted in Bartley, *New South, 1945–1980*, 186; Michael Klarman, *From Jim Crow to Civil Rights: The Supreme Court and the Struggle For Racial Equality* (New York: Oxford University Press, 2004); Fairclough, *Race and Democracy*.

35. For more on the organization of the Citizens' Councils, see Neil McMillen, *The Citizens' Councils*; Numan Bartley, *The Rise of Massive Resistance*, 82–107.

36. Tom P. Brady, "Notes on *Black Monday*" (Winona, Miss.: Association of Citizens' Councils, 1955).

37. See Joseph Crespino, "Strategic Accommodation: Civil Rights Opponents in Mississippi and Their Impact on American Racial Politics," (Ph.D. Dissertation, Stanford University, 2002), 28–52.

38. Quoted in Silver, *Mississippi*, 42; quoted in Smith, *Congressman From Mississippi*, 274.

39. *Scott County Times*, May 30, 1962; also quoted in Erle Johnston, *Mississippi's Defiant Years: An Interpretive Documentary With Personal Experiences* (Forrest, Miss.: Lake Harbor, 1990), 138–39.

40. *Scott County Times*, May 30, 1962.

41. See Tom Ethridge, "Letter from Erle Johnston, Jr.," *Jackson Clarion-Ledger* (hereinafter referred to as *C-L*), undated, found in folder 2, box 135, m191, Paul Johnson Papers, University of Southern Mississippi.

42. See Tom Ethridge, "Letter from Erle Johnston, Jr.," *C-L*, undated, found in folder 2, box 135, m191, Paul Johnson Papers, University of Southern Mississippi.

43. Bruce Schulman, *From Cotton Belt to Sunbelt* (New York: Oxford University Press, 1994).

44. Johnston, *Defiant Years*, 32.

45. Bill Minor, *Eyes on Mississippi: A Fifty-Year Chronicle of Change* (Jackson, Miss.: J. Prichard Morris, 2001), 35.

46. Quoted in editorial, *St. Petersburg Times*, April 25, 1956, 6.

47. W. F. Minor, "Mississippi Schools in Crisis," *New South* 25, no. 1 (1970): 31–36.

48. Robert A. Caro, *Means of Ascent: The Years of Lyndon Johnson* (New York: Knopf, 1982), 336–37.

49. J. P. Coleman, interviewed by Orley Caudill, November 12, 1981, Oral History Program, University of Southern Mississippi.

50. J. P. Coleman to Members of the Mississippi Legislature, December 15, 1955, folder 2, box 80, series 4, Sillers Papers; "Coleman Rejects Idea of Nullifying High Court Ruling," *Memphis Commercial Appeal*, December 15, 1955; "Politicians Divided on Nullification Idea," *JDN*, December 15, 1955.

51. J. P. Coleman to Members of the Mississippi Legislature, December 15, 1955, folder 2, box 80, series 4, Sillers Papers.

52. Inaugural Address of Governor James P. Coleman, Journal of the House, 1956, regular session, 65; "Coleman, at Inaugural, Pledges to Keep Segregation," *C-L*, January 18, 1956.

53. Oliver Emmerich to John Stennis, February 20, 1948, folder C-4, box 1, series 29, John C. Stennis Papers, Mississippi State University, hereinafter cited as JCSP.

54. John Stennis to Hugh White, June 4, 1954, folder C-34, box 1, series 29, JCSP; John Stennis to Thomas J. Tubb, June 4, 1958, folder C-34, box 1, series 29, JCSP.

55. John Stennis to J. P. Coleman, May 20, 1954, folder C-33, series 29, JCSP.

56. John Stennis to J. P. Coleman, May 20, 1954, folder C-33, series 29, JCSP.

57. John Stennis to LeRoy Percy, May 10, 1955, folder C-39, box 1, series 29, JCSP.

58. John Stennis to William Winter, March 15, 1954, folder C-32, box 1, series 29, JCSP. Stennis wrote J. P. Coleman with a similar plan in the days after the *Brown* decision; see John Stennis to J. P. Coleman, May 20, 1954, folder C-33, box 1, series 29, JCSP.

59. Tom Ethridge, "Mississippi Notebook," *C-L*, May 2, 1956, 4.

60. J. P. Coleman to C. C. Smith, April 10, 1958, folder 5, box 12, series 5, Coleman Papers.

61. John Dittmer called Mississippi state officials' harassment of Kennard "the most tragic of the decade." A year after his arrests on the University of Southern Mississippi campus, Kennard was arrested again under dubious charges of complicity in a plot to steal chicken feed. He was sentenced to seven years in the state penitentiary, the maximum sentence. See Dittmer, *Local People*, 79–81; also David Oshinsky, *Worse Than Slavery: Parchman Farm and the Ordeal of Jim Crow Justice* (New York: Free Press, 1996), 231–33.

Remarks

Jane Dailey

There are two broad areas of intersection among these papers. Three of them speak explicitly of gendered ideals of manners, three of them speak of raced codes of manners, and one crosses those boundaries to consider, at some points, gendered aspects of what the author calls racial etiquette. I want to consider the papers individually, grouped broadly into these two categories, inserting, at suitable intervals, some more general historical and methodological remarks about the topic of manners and southern history.

Let me begin with Lisa Dorr's investigation into white heterosexual dating conventions at the University of Alabama and Auburn between 1913 and 1933, "Fifty Percent Moonshine and Fifty Percent Moonshine: Social Life and College Youth Culture in Alabama." I found this entertaining and well-told story, particularly Dorr's description of the close correlation between drinking and dancing, instantly recognizable: not of college youth culture of the 1920s, of which I know little, but of the social world of the average Southern Historical Association Meeting, of which I know more. Fortunately, what was true in the 1920s seems also to be true for the SHA today: to wit, that because of all the drinking, "no one remembers who was there or what happened at the dance . . . and, as a result, many reputations will be saved."

The behavior of college coeds might seem less worthy of scholarly explication had not the Ku Klux Klan decided to meddle in it and, as Dorr describes it, attempt to put an end to the new social practices of middle-class white youth. What business was it of the Ku Klux Klan how students constructed their social world? In order to understand the Klan's stake, and the real revolution in manners that occurred on Alabama's secular university campuses in the quarter century between 1913 and 1930, we need to recall at least in shorthand a few of the main points of scholarly writing on manners.

The historical sociology of both manners and honor is derived from a model of the civilizing process in which the individual subjugates his own passions, will, and desires and plays instead a longer-term strategic game whose rules (manners, civility, courtliness, and, for women, chastity) become internalized into a new subjectivity: a subjectivity that differentiates between a person's exterior and her interior, and that accepts the rules of the group for herself. This process is particularly descriptive of honor societies, in which the discourse of honor functions to stabilize "the cohesion, standing, regularity and furtherance of the life processes" of a social group, and it does so by instilling in the individual "the conviction that the maintenance of his honor constitutes his most intrinsic, most profound, and most personal self-interest."[1]

The point I want to stress here is this process of internalization that is intrinsic to the formulation and successful reproduction of a culture of manners such as an honor society. Manners are not some external code that lies between an individual and society; rather, manners are the core values of a society that are internalized in the individual. Individual identity, in this understanding, melds with group identity and interest, until the two are virtually indistinguishable.

So far, so good: nice middle-class white girls in Alabama are sent to college to meet nice middle-class white boys who are suitable marriage partners. Boy meets girl, girl keeps her legs crossed and becomes adroit with her elbows, boy proposes: parents are happy, culture is reproduced. But something different happened in Tuscaloosa and Auburn in the years Dorr focuses on, and that something seems to have been a genuine revolution in manners. Sometime between the time of Daphne Cunningham and the writing of "The Tired Girl's Diary," many middle-class white Alabama college women (aided and abetted by their male classmates) reevaluated their relationship to conventional expectations of white womanhood, particularly conventional expectations of female sexuality, and rejected them in favor of a new set of rules. What had once been considered the core of an unmarried white woman's honor—her sexual innocence—was traded for a new value, sexual experience. At a certain level, it might be said that middle-class college girls finally discovered something that urban working-class girls (and, indeed, their aristocratic sisters) had known all along: that sex had commodity exchange value and also—possibly—that female pleasure was worth something as well. In any case, the new youth culture naturalized and legitimated women's sexual desire, and what had once been hoarded was transformed into a means of exchange. That this shift in manners was both real and noticed is evident from the Klan's response, as well as the frantic efforts of parents and university officials to contain it.

Had they been born fifty years earlier, Dorr's free-spirited Alabama college girls might well have become the "she-rebels" described by Anya Jabour in her paper "Southern Ladies and She-Rebels; Or, Femininity in the Foxhole: Young Women in the Confederate South." Jabour's jaunty essay portrays the Civil War as a major crisis in culture, with slaveholding women "forced to choose between their identity as ladies and their identity as rebels." Certainly the Civil War opened up new possibilities for female behavior (as the Revolution had done three generations earlier), possibilities that many elite women viewed with both interest and alarm. And it seems clear, as Jabour puts it, that "many young women in the Confederate South weighed the value of ladylike behavior against the ethos of southern nationalism and concluded that Confederate loyalty was of greater worth than good manners."

I am entirely convinced that the war changed the behavioral expectations of elite southern women (both within their own heads, and in the world outside the family), and further that some slaveholding women took the opportunity of secession to redefine their own social roles. I am less sure, however, about some of Jabour's broader assertions regarding the relationship between female submission and slavery, and female rebellion and the war. Jabour argues that "In their display of Confederate—as opposed to simply southern—loyalty, southern white women often acted in ways that contradicted their assigned role as passive supporters of the system." My trouble with this sentence lies in the word "passive." Surely there is a wealth of scholarship (including, of course, Catherine Clinton's *The Plantation Mistress*) elucidating white women's very active role in slavery and, indeed, as supporters of the Confederacy. Whether disciplining house slaves or keeping a plantation's books, white slaveholding women participated actively in the peculiar institution, and they felt their own interests, as well as those of their menfolk, threatened by Lincoln's election and protected by Jefferson Davis's new government. As Mary Chestnut put things with typical lucidity, "This southern Confederacy must be supported now by calm deliberation— & cool brains."[2]

In her paper, Jabour raises the issue of the centrality of the idea of the southern lady to the defense of slavery. Following George Fitzhugh, Jabour sees slavery and female submission as mutually dependent and mutually constitutive. It is true that Fitzhugh "saw domestic slavery as just another variety of subordination, in a world where power and subjection [were] intrinsic to social relations." But it is not sufficient to rest such large claims on an author whose chief trait as a thinker, Michael O'Brien has recently reminded us in his magisterial two-volume history of southern intellectual thought, was idiosyncrasy.[3] Female submissiveness was linked to slavery insofar as it naturalized bondage by being part of the same system of rank and subordination. But we go too far, I think, when we assert that female subordination and slavery are linked causally, and that "the myth of the southern lady" was a "vital foundation" of the slaveholding South. In the absence of war (to throw in a quick counter-factual), would a sudden uptick of uppitiness on the part of white southern women have brought the peculiar institution crashing down around the shoulders of white men? To use a reverse example that actually happened, there was no great flowering of women's rights in the North before the war, despite the lack of slavery there, and despite the robust efforts of antislavery women to link slave and female emancipation.

Turning again to the definition of manners outlined already—in which individuals internalize the behavioral expectations of the larger group in order to pursue mutual interests—it becomes possible to see the merit in Jabour's denomination of the Civil War as a "war of manners." The war, as Jabour explains, "provoked many southern women to abandon their prewar standards of behavior," prompting a sort of war of manners within elite southern women themselves. In a revolutionary moment, standards of behavior change. This was as true in 1861 for Confederate women as for Confederate men. That standards of ladylike behavior did not change all at once, or even uniformly across the Confederacy, is to be expected, as is the conflicted response of many women to new standards of womanliness. But there was a certain degree of overlap, particularly where the womanly ideal of submission was concerned. Rather than being irreconcilable, submissiveness and rebellion can join happily: particularly when the she-rebel is following her father, uncle, and brothers in rebellion!

The fact that so many of the descendants of Jabour's "she-rebels" remain willing to drop out of college and spend a year learning how to glide while wearing a tiara in order to, as Catherine Clinton puts it, "assume the mantle of their tribe," suggests the constant repositioning of southern women vis-à-vis societal expectations of southern "ladyhood." In her paper "Scepter and Masque: Debutante Rituals in Mardi Gras New Orleans," Clinton gives us a glimpse of the race politics and degree of female role-playing that undergird New Orleans's largest tourist attraction and hence, to a significant degree, its economy.

This paper (and Rebecca Snedecker's marvelous documentary film upon which it was based) addresses several issues of concern to us today. Following Samuel Kinser and Reid Mitchell, Clinton identifies Mardi Gras with the Confederate cause and with violence. This is, of course, far more true of the Krewes than the debutantes (if, that is, we don't count waxing as a form of violence). Certainly the correspondence between anti-Reconstruction political violence and the elite post–Civil War Krewes was more than coincidental: as Clinton notes, the Pickwick Club fought almost to a man in the "Battle of Liberty Place" in 1874 (in which thirty-eight people, most of them black, were massacred at the state constitutional convention). Mardi Gras, Clinton argues, was a way of controlling New Orleans society in the face of economic change and outside political pressure. Whereas leading whites in other southern cities responded to black political power and Yankee economic imperialism with political violence and street riots, New Orleans whites seem to have been unique in using a cultural event to recapture lost social and political capital.

Clinton's focus is more on the debutante season affiliated with Mardi Gras than on the events of Mardi Gras itself. As concerned with defining social status in twentieth-century New Orleans as during the reign of Elizabeth I, the Mardi Gras cotillion season remains central to the reproduction of elite society. Clearly linked with the Confederate cause in the Jim Crow era, the cotillion's role in maintaining racial hierarchy in an age of a reinvigorated Fourteenth Amendment is less clear. Whereas the all-male krewes have been opened to African American membership through use of the law, the couples at the cotillions remain locked in racial symmetry: Clinton quotes a source who asserts that "never would you see a debutante escorted by anyone outside of her race. It just wouldn't happen." Clinton argues convincingly for the ultimately reinforcing cultural meaning of this: "Outsiders may mistake carnival as a festive subversion, but the masquerade is not inversion, but affirmation": of an all-white, "by invitation only" elite.

At this point, I would like to ask a broader question about whether or not manners is the right descriptive hook on which to hang a discussion of southern history. Is this really a useful category of analysis when considering the American South? I don't want to insult the conference organizers, but I do think this is a question worth asking. The discourse of manners as an analytical language for historians and sociologists developed originally to describe an explicitly non-coercive regime: a regime whose powers are so hidden that they seem to become the most cherished values of the individual, and become internalized as those values, which reinforces the regime. According to this theory (as propagated by thinkers from John Stuart Mill to Freud), through the mediation of manners, and the creation of this new subjectivity, civilization replaced violence and individual desire. The point that should be stressed here is that manners are not a coerced and external set of rules: manners are internalized rules, and the process of internalization creates a new kind of subject. (The classic example of this is Freud's description of the Super-Ego.) This process as a sociological phenomenon is particularly descriptive of honor societies. It is the ability to internalize the values of the group in the individual that makes the concept of honor, as Georg Simmel put it, "one of the most marvelous, instinctively developed expediencies for the maintenance of group existence."[4]

Caveat: Now, we have all learned from Foucault that everything is a product of a discourse of power, even the manners of the bourgeoisie that seem to be so self-empowering. But we have to admit that there are gradations: that the regime of power presents itself very differently in the case of a white coed for whom manners are a performance of self-identity and a black man for whom manners are a legally imposed form of submission, and the subjectivities that go with that are going to be different. There is a moment in southern history that can be legitimately described as part of the civilizing process: I mean, of course, the Reconstruction years, during which the freed-people internalized many of the norms of the broader society, but they also expected white southerners to play by those rules. In this as in so much else, black expectations were disappointed. These were the years during which Whitelaw Reid, for instance, found whites ready to kill blacks for the tiniest of social transgressions. Nothing less "gunpowery" than violence, or the credible threat of violence, could compel African American acquiescence in white dominance in the immediate postwar South: in everyday social interactions as much as in politics.

Jennifer Ritterhouse—surely one of the most intelligent cultural historians of the Jim Crow South—sees segregation as a "fall-back position"; the people who wrote the Black Codes would certainly have agreed. Another way of viewing the Jim Crow segregation laws is to see them as an admission of the failure to develop a manner society in the post-emancipation South. Segregation ended any possibility of manners becoming a meaningful mode of communication in the period: coerced deference does not communicate internalized civility, which is why, as Robin D. G. Kelley reminded us in his seminal essay, "'We Are Not What We Seem': Rethinking Black Working-Class Opposition in the Jim Crow South," police departments, vagrancy laws, extralegal violence, and the mutilated bodies of black men and women were such an integral part of the landscape of black life in the segregated South. The Jim Crow South was a regime of stipulated coercion, and it produced a much more double-voiced subject (what Du Bois meant when he referred to the "veil") and a sharper split between surface performance and interior desire, than a manner society would have.

This emphasis on state coercion—through the law and its enforcers—explains why I am dubious about Ritterhouse's claim that "unwritten rules of racial 'etiquette' . . . were the chief form of everyday social control in the segregated South." The issue here is in great measure one of emphasis. I do not deny the importance of such rules, and I agree that taking a close look at these relations provides a revealing perspective on the important roles white women played in policing segregation, roles often overlooked by those who use a wider lens. And I agree that the unwritten rules of racial etiquette shaped southern culture, perhaps even as much as the formal rules did. But there is an analytical, as well as a political, pitfall in overemphasizing "manners" or etiquette when studying the Jim Crow era, and that is that when our analytical language is itself the product of the values of the period we are studying, it is easy to miss the degree to which those values are being contested. I do not want to push this point too strongly, but it seems to be mainly whites who talk about manners, as such, in the Jim Crow context (both in the sources and in the historiography). When white historians adopt the terms of manners to describe the violent history of Jim Crow, we implicitly assume a position closer to that of Jim Crow's champions than its opponents to analyze that society. Focusing on manners effectively pushes the coercive state apparatus of the police and the law out of sight.

Given the importance of violence (legal and extralegal) and the law in mandating and maintaining segregation, can the categories of manners and civility, which were developed to make sense of court and bourgeois societies, really help us think about the Jim Crow era? Can this model make sense of race relations in a situation where manners are legally stipulated and coerced? Ritterhouse's marvelous example of the white housewife who charged Eloise Blake with "disorderly conduct over the phone" reveals beautifully Stuart Hall's remark that "hegemonizing is hard work." The truth is, the Jim Crow South was a society in which everyday conduct was legally controlled, and was not internalized by blacks, except in an oppositional mode. Can we really regard a society that generates such a robust culture of opposition as a manners society?[5]

Despite all that has come before, I think that we can—but only if we acknowledge explicitly that we are adopting a white southern perspective when we do, and reveal the irony of white southerners convincing themselves that they inhabited a manners society. The Jim Crow South may not have been a manners society—but white southerners told themselves it was. This in itself is important, and deserves explication. But this story must be told with a heavy dose of irony and from a critical stance. Certainly it is worth investigating the worldview of the white citizens of Natchitoches, who in 1927 erected a statue to "the good darkies of Louisiana" that depicted a black man with stooped shoulders and doffed hat in the act of bowing.[6]

To change the topic slightly, in her paper Ritterhouse makes the intriguing argument that white southerners "lost their ability even to imagine a world in which black and white were not separated in the public sphere." I am not so sure about this, probably because I have spent so much time recently with Virginius Dabney—the long-time editor of the *Richmond Times-Dispatch*, a founding member of the Southern Regional Council, and a committed segregationist. In November 1943, two months after a police shooting of a black soldier in uniform sparked a riot in Harlem, Dabney did something unusual: he proposed (in print) that Richmond repeal its laws segregating streetcars and buses. Originally passed to lessen racial friction, the laws, Dabney argued, no longer worked and actually heightened racial tensions because of war-related overcrowding and attendant jostling for position. Under these circumstances, Dabney considered segregated public transportation counterproductive, and therefore a danger to the broader system of segregation, which he embraced. "I am entirely opposed to the elimination of segregation as a general proposition," Dabney wrote in a letter to a Richmond banker, "but this is one area where segregation doesn't segregate."[7]

Recognizing that civility itself was a barrier to integration, Dabney was willing to sacrifice segregated transportation in order to restore a measure of public decorum. An acute observer of human behavior, Dabney recognized that not only had black Richmonders not internalized white norms of public deference, but that when meeting the letter of the law allowed aggression, that was what happened. This kind of aggression was dangerous—especially in the context of the war—and Dabney was concerned above all else with limiting the potential of violence. There was no failure of imagination involved here: Dabney was all too capable of imagining life after segregation, which is why he and others like him worked so hard to humanize Jim Crow through the equalization of teachers' salaries, by fighting lynching, and in general by arguing the utility of making "separate but equal" truly equal. In the end, as Ritterhouse points out, segregation was really more about dominance than separation—which was why Dabney was willing to sacrifice the latter to shore up the former.

Dabney's attempt at limited desegregation failed when Virginia governor Colgate Darden—a man described by a writer for the *Baltimore Afro-American* as the only man he knew "who can pronounce 'Negro' with a small 'n'"—worried publicly that repeal of the public transportation laws might threaten other legislation proposed "for the benefit of the colored people."[8] But Dabney is immediately recognizable as what Joe Crespino might dub a "premature practical segregationist." The post–World War II South was stocked with these characters, particularly as it became clear that the federal government—through the courts and the executive—was willing to take steps to alter the racial balance of power in the South. From James Byrnes in South Carolina to Sheriff Pritchett in Albany, a considerable group of white southern leaders understood, as Tony Badger has argued recently, that civility and half-measures could, in themselves, prove an important means of preventing change.[9]

In his extremely interesting and nuanced paper, "Civility and Civil Rights in Mississippi," Joe Crespino outlines the choices available to white leaders trying to chart a middle course between capitulation to civil rights activists (dubbed "outside agitators") and radical white supremacists. Rather than representing a position of strength, Crespino argues that the use of civility as a political weapon by elite whites in Mississippi reveals a revolutionary moment of white weakness. In embracing a vision of themselves as civilized, white Mississippi leaders foreclosed certain violent options, and thereby limited the range of their response to the Black Freedom Struggle. This strategy was opposed, vociferously, by that portion of Mississippi whites who created the Citizens' Councils—in a direct critique of their public representatives. This rift among local whites did not escape the notice of black Mississippians, who promptly set to work to widen and exploit it.

Focusing on the post-*Brown* era, Crespino notes that the Supreme Court decision "galvanized the forces that would oppose the civil rights struggle,"[10] although he argues against those who suggest that the school decision "foreclosed paternalistic politics in the white community."[11] Rather than foreclosing paternalist politics, *Brown* made it harder to pursue them by spurring the creation of the Citizens' Councils—which advocated a much more confrontational approach to demands for black civil rights than most elected officials did. Still believing that race relations could somehow be "managed" and willfully misreading the political intentions of local blacks, many of Mississippi's white leaders—prominent among them Governor Hugh White and Senator John Stennis—preferred to compromise on an issue-by-issue basis rather than commit the state wholeheartedly to a strategy of massive resistance. Like Virginius Dabney, who was willing to sacrifice some aspects of segregation to save the rest, "The logic of racial troubleshooting, in sum, was that sometimes you have to give up a little to save a lot."

This was a tactic that could work, in the short term. Even some African Americans adopted it—witness the original, limited goals of the Montgomery Improvement Association. The trouble was, black Americans were not much interested in pursuing a path of incremental change that might, someday, tidy up some of Jim Crow's messier rooms while retaining the basic structure. In the spring of 1945, a panel of experts consisting, in the words of a critic, of "one buck negro, one Jew, one New York social service official and Congressman H. Jerry Voorhis, of California,"[12] was asked to discuss the question, "Are We Solving America's Race Problems?" on the popular radio show "America's Town Meeting of the Air." The "buck negro" referred to was Richard Wright who, as usual, spoke directly to the point. "At once let's define what we mean by a solution of the race problem," he advised. "If the race problem were solved, we would have no Black Belts, no Jim Crow army or navy, no Jim Crow Red Cross blood banks, no Negro institutions, no laws prohibiting inter-marriage, no customs assigning Negroes to inferior positions. We would all simply be Americans, and the nation would be the better for it."[13]

This was exactly the sort of broadcast that caused Virginius Dabney to lay awake nights. Desegregated public transportation was not going to satisfy Richard Wright. Richard Wright wanted equality: nothing more, nothing less. It is to Virginius Dabney's credit that he understood this—although it was precisely this understanding that underlay his resistance to substantive change in the South. Dabney opposed school integration—even the integration of the graduate school at the University of Virginia, a question that arose in 1935—because he believed that integration would lead to "racial amalgamation." Such a position has been dismissed by scholars as the standard shibboleth of the white supremacist South; as one wrote last year,

Dabney "continued to express his own personal disapproval of miscegenation, no doubt a comforting position for a man who never recognized that African American aspirations had nothing to do with interracial marriage and sexual relations."[14]

But African American aspirations did have to do with interracial marriage and sexual relations, and these aspirations informed the organizations that African Americans formed to fight for their freedom. W. E. B. Du Bois wrote the right of freedom of association into the pledge of the Niagara Movement, the predecessor to the NAACP. Roy Wilkins upheld that pledge when he insisted that blacks and whites belonged "on a plane of absolute political and social equality." And Martin Luther King could not have been clearer when he said on television in 1958 that "The thoroughly integrated society means freedom. When any society says that I cannot marry a certain person, that society has cut off a segment of my freedom."[15]

In his paper "What's Sex Got to Do with It? Antimiscegenation Laws and Southern White Rhetoric," Charles Robinson investigates the barriers to bonds of intimacy and sympathy created by antimiscegenation laws in the post-emancipation South. Arguing that antimiscegenation laws "rarely punished simple acts of interracial sex," Robinson surveys a number of cases at the appellate level in which people who admit to having participated in interracial sex in violation of the law are let off scot-free. Concluding that one-time-only individual acts of interracial sex were of about as much interest to the courts as acts of prostitution—they were bad for the social fabric, but they didn't undermine society unduly—Robinson zeroes in on a group of fascinating cases in which people who did not, apparently, engage in sex across the color line were nonetheless punished under antimiscegenation laws.

Surveying four cases in which it was not proved to the satisfaction of the appellate courts that the defendants had ever violated any antimiscegenation laws (one of which—*Parramore v. State*—rivals *Loving v. Virginia* in the category of Most Appropriately Named Lawsuit), Robinson concludes that local jurors "punished these defendants for transgressing an unwritten but well-established code of conduct with regard to general interracial associations. In the South, blacks and whites of the opposite sex were not supposed to be alone together in each other's homes, reveling in each other's company or helping each other. They were not supposed to establish open, life-long friendships, show affection for each other's children, or shower each other with gifts of appreciation. In the minds of white southerners, such examples of intimacy, care, warmth, generosity, and friendship challenged the color line."

My response to this argument is: yes and no. As long as such interactions across the color line occurred within the proper class framework, they were fine: indeed, as Jennifer Ritterhouse and others have pointed out, middle-class whites were constantly at home alone with African American domestics, and they often formed deep and lasting attachments. Robinson gives us a good example of this rule in action when he discusses the case of *Allen v. Scruggs*. Ryal Noble, we are told, sustained an intimate domestic relationship with Kit Allen for over forty years, during which time four children were produced. This relationship was tolerated by Noble's neighbors, it seems, because Allen gave the appearance of being Noble's domestic servant. Because the man was white and the woman was black, and because both were discrete and upheld some of their society's cultural norms while trampling over others, they were left in peace.

The *Lewis, Rollins, Parramore* and *Fields* cases are fascinating examples of the peril people who did not conform to the unwritten rules of segregation faced. But I am not convinced that these cases prove that "benevolent acts of kindness and affection subjected couples to legal penalties" in the Jim Crow South. Certainly some couples seem to have been penalized for this (although the evidence is messy, as there were ambiguously-raced children involved in the *Parramore* and *Lewis* cases). What is made clear in this paper is the flexibility of the laws, and their strategic use both by defendants and by prosecutors. Southern whites were not, as Robinson notes, duplicitous in their selective enforcement of the antimiscegenation laws, because the purpose of those laws was far greater than the mere policing of interracial sexual relationships. Antimiscegenation laws were the bulwark of the entire Jim Crow system, the logical base from which all the other segregation laws derived. This was so clear to white and black southerners alike that they often forbore to mention it. In 1955, for instance, C. Vann Woodward published *The Strange Career of Jim Crow*, which traced legal segregation back to the post-emancipation era and argued that southerners could amend a social system so recently inaugurated (and not, as southern traditionalists insisted, rooted in the lost sands of time). Designed to buttress the *Brown* decision and considered by Martin Luther King Jr. "the historical Bible of the civil rights movement," perhaps the strangest thing about *Strange Career* was its complete omission of southern laws restricting sex and marriage across the color line.

With this reference to Woodward's politic silence in 1955 (and not any failure of imagination on his part), we return to the question of manners. I will not belabor the point any further, but I remain wary of applying the historiographical sociology of manners—either as theory or simply via terminology—to the Jim Crow South (although I do think that we can usefully apply both to the Reconstruction era). Once we are talking about the Jim Crow South we are talking about two codes of manners, not one; about competing and oppositional cultures. That whites have been slower to recognize this circumstance than blacks is as much a product of this oppositional culture as anything else. As Zora Neale Hurston put it so well in 1935, "The Negro, in spite of his open-faced laughter, his seeming acquiescence, is particularly evasive. You see we are a polite people and we do not say to our questioner, 'Get out of here!' We smile and tell him or her something that satisfies the white person because, knowing so little about us, he doesn't know what he is missing."[16]

Notes

1. Georg Simmel, *Soziologie*, 5th ed. (Berlin, 1968), 403–6; see also Ute Frevert, *Men of Honor: A Social and Cultural History of the Duel* (Cambridge, MA, 1995), 47.

2. C. Vann Woodward and Elisabeth Muhlenfeld, eds., *The Private Mary Chestnut: The Unpublished Civil War Diaries* (New York, 1984), 3.

3. Fitzhugh was, O'Brien says, "a man half-in, half-out of what his world thought"; a strange mixture of "conventional ideas, startling insights, and avant-garde philosophy." Michael O'Brien, *Conjectures of Order: Intellectual Life and the American South, 1810–1860*, vol. 2 (Chapel Hill: University of North Carolina Press, 2004), 972, 974.

4. Simmel, *Soziologie*, 403–6.

5. Robin D. G. Kelley, "'We Are Not What We Seem': Rethinking Black Working-Class Opposition in the Jim Crow South," *Journal of American History* 80 (June 1993): 75–112; Stuart Hall quoted in George Lipsitz, "The Struggle for Hegemony," *Journal of American History* 75 (June 1988): 148.

6. Adam Fairclough, *Better Day Coming: Blacks and Equality, 1890–2000* (New York: Viking, 2001), 167.

7. "To Lessen Race Friction," *Richmond Times-Dispatch*, November 13, 1943; Virginius Dabney to Warren M. Goddard, November 19, 1943, "Segregation Correspondence 1943" file, box 4, Virginius Dabney Papers, #7690, Alderman Library,

University of Virginia. John Temple Graves quote from *Birmingham Post*, September 20, 1958, in box 13, Papers of Virginius Dabney, #7690-m, Alderman Library, University of Virginia. J. Douglas Smith, *Managing White Supremacy: Race, Politics and Citizenship in Jim Crow Virginia* (Chapel Hill: University of North Carolina Press, 2002) anticipates Crespino's "racial troubleshooters" argument in his formulation of "managed race relations." On Dabney and "liberalism," recall that he published *Liberalism in the South* in 1932 (New York: AMS Press, 1970, orig. pub. 1932). For a useful example of the willingness of scholars to adopt their sources' terminology see John Michael Matthews, "Virginius Dabney, John Temple Graves, and What Happened to Southern Liberalism," *Mississippi Quarterly* 45 (Fall 1992): 405–20. (Although Matthews does allow, 406, as how some white southern liberals "made the transition to another sort of liberalism" during and after World War II. See as well Morton Sosna, *In Search of the Silent South: Southern Liberals and the Race Issue* (New York: Columbia University Press, 1977); and John T. Kneebone, *Southern Liberal Journalists and the Issue of Race, 1920–1944* (Chapel Hill: University of North Carolina Press, 1985).

8. Clipping, *The Afro-American*, August 28, 1943; "Negroes, Clippings, 1942–43," box 4, Virginius Dabney Papers, University of Virginia; VD to Dr. Robert H. Tucker (Dean of Washington and Lee), January 13, 1944; both in "Segregation Correspondence, 1943" file, box 4, Dabney Papers.

9. Tony Badger, "From Defiance to Moderation: South Carolina Governors and Racial Change," The Citadel Conference on the Civil Rights Movement in South Carolina, March 5–8, 2003, paper in the author's possession.

10. For more on the role of Brown in fueling white backlash, see Michael Klarman, "How Brown Changed Race Relations: The Backlash Thesis," *Journal of American History* 81, no. 1 (June 1994): 81–118.

11. Quoted in Numan Bartley, *The New South, 1945–1980* (Baton Rouge: Louisiana State University Press, 1995), 186; Michael Klarman, *From Jim Crow to Civil Rights: The Supreme Court and the Struggle For Racial Equality* (New York: Oxford University Press, 2004); Adam Fairclough, *Race and Democracy: The Civil Rights Struggle in Louisiana, 1915–1972* (Athens: University of Georgia Press, 1995). For more on the civil rights movement in Mississippi before Brown, see John Dittmer, *Local People: The Struggle for Civil Rights in Mississippi* (Urbana: University of Illinois Press, 1994), 1–40; and Charles Payne, *I've Got the Light of Freedom: The Organizing Tradition and the Mississippi Freedom Struggle* (Berkeley: University of California Press, 1995), 7–66.

12. Letter, L. C. Christian, Houston, TX, May 5, 1945, in box 26, Critical T. M., Moderator, Speakers file, "America's Town Meeting of the Air," Town Hall

Inc., Records, New York Public Library. In addition to Wright and Voorhis (Democrat of California), the panel included Elmer A. Carter, the former editor of the Urban League's magazine "Opportunity" and a member of the Unemployment-Insurance Appeals Board of the New York State Department of Labor; and Irving M. Ives, the Majority Leader of the New York state assembly and coauthor of a recent anti-discrimination bill.

13. "America's Town Meeting of the Air," box 26, May 24, 1945, NYPL.

14. J. Douglas Smith, "'The Ordeal of Virginius Dabney': A Southern Liberal, the Southern Regional Council and the Limits of Managed Race Relations," Paper for the Southern Regional Council and the Civil Rights Movement Conference, University of Florida, Gainesville, FL, October 23–26, 2003.

15. King quote from Mike Wallace Interview, June 25, 1958, in The Papers of Martin Luther King Jr., Stanford University, http://www.stanford.edu/group/King/publications/papers/vol4/580625-012-Interview_by_Mike_Wallace.htm.

16. Zora Neale Hurston, *Mules and Men* (Philadelphia: J. B. Lippincott Co., 1935), 2–3.

Taking Manners Seriously

John F. Kasson

> It is because subjects do not, strictly speaking, know what they are do-
> ing that what they do has more meaning than they know.
>   —Pierre Bourdieu[1]

Manners and southern history: the terms nestle as sweetly together as honey and biscuits. To speak of manners and *southern* history seems so unproblematic that we might begin to pry open the subject by considering how comparatively unlikely it would be to have a symposium on manners and midwestern history, to take my own native region as an example. For the Midwest is not commonly thought of as having a distinctive set of manners, an especially distinctive history, or even a distinctive sense of regional identity, and the South is thought to have all three. The first question this symposium raises, then, is what is the relationship among these three elements? To what extent are manners a constitutive part of southern identity and a defining element in southern history?

The notion that southerners possessed a special—and superior—set of manners is both venerable and enduring. It goes at least back to the tidewater planters of the eighteenth century, though they vied among themselves as to which colony was most cultivated in this regard (and Virginians and South Carolinians agreed that North Carolina, the place I have called home for over thirty years, was not a contender). By the antebellum period, however, such local rivalries were increasingly subordinated in favor of a larger regional identity. It was not just southerners, however, who regarded their region as distinguished by its gracious manners. As William R. Taylor noted in his classic study, *Cavalier and Yankee*, the belief that white southerners represented a distinctive type with manners much more cultivated than their grasping Yankee cousins became a cultural myth promulgated by northerners and southerners alike.[2] To a remarkable extent that conviction has persisted.

It was the rock on which in 1930 the Nashville Agrarians took their stand against the unholy forces of industrialization, modernization, and Yankee "progress."[3] And, it remains part of what the sociologist John Shelton Reed has called "the enduring South." The consensus shared by northerners and southerners that the South is especially mannerly and polite, he has shown, persists despite all the forces of homogenization and modernization.[4] Thus, to suggest that, say, New Yorkers are unmannerly (however gross or unjust this characterization might be) would be to utter only conventional wisdom; to impugn the manners of southerners as a group, however, would surprise most Americans and deeply insult most southerners.

Precisely because good manners have been such a central part of southern identity, within the South they also became a point of invidious comparison, tension, and division. Manners served as a way of mapping regions (such as tidewater and backcountry), classes (for instance, "good" families and no-accounts), education (learned and ignorant), gender (gentlemen and ladies, blackguards and hussies), and, above all, race (a self-respecting white man, for example, but an uppity black one). Most strikingly, manners became a way that dominant social elites covertly conducted politics, enlisted support, patronized subordinates, and quelled dissent. Much of what the Italian Marxist Antonio Gramsci theorized in a Fascist prison about the workings of hegemony was known intuitively by many a southerner, white and black. They would have appreciated, too, the insight of the late French sociologist Pierre Bourdieu, "The concessions of *politesse* always contain *political* concessions."[5] In their own ways, too, southerners knew about the possibilities of resistance. Manners, so frequently the weapon of choice by the powerful in any social duel, could at times be dexterously used against them, as in the civil rights movement of the 1950s and early 1960s.

Thus, southerners, white and black, know and always have known, in ways that many Americans from other regions may have not, that, far from trivial, manners are political; indeed, they are often a matter of life and death. From William Faulkner and Richard Wright on, much of twentieth-century southern literature is premised on this recognition. And it is the awareness of the high stakes of manners, the myriad ways that they go to the heart of southern politics and identity, their coercive uses and resistant possibilities, that so animate the papers of this symposium.

I remember once being shown through a historic townhouse in Savannah by a gracious white-haired docent. "Of course, they had slaves," she said brightly, "so there were many willing hands to do the work." A key task for any social and cultural order is how to perform its dirty work, literally and figuratively, while pretending such arrangements are consensual and "natural." In different ways all these essays illuminate this process, which manners are often intended to conceal, and expose the central role race has played in it.

In Anya Jabour's entertaining and thoughtful essay, "Southern Ladies and 'She-Rebels'" an early generation of privileged white southern women were taught to see their exalted social position and the "willing hands" that made it possible as the ultimate vindication of a way of life based on slavery. Jabour focuses on the transformations wrought by the Civil War on these proper and privileged white southern belles. In her analysis, the Confederate secession brought conflict on many levels. The one that interests her most is the "war of manners" fought by these young Confederate women against the Union occupation. As she points out, this was a war within the Confederacy as much as a war on its behalf. Young southern women devoted to the Confederate cause found themselves forced to choose between the dictates of ladyhood, which preached submission, modesty, and meekness, among other tenets, and the cause of Confederate resistance, which prompted demonstrations of rebellion, disrespect, and anger. George Fitzhugh, the idiosyncratic theorist of conservative southern patriarchy and a disdainer of any concept of "natural rights," gloried in the southern lady's abject dependence: As quoted by Jabour, Fitzhugh declared, women's "weakness is her strength, and her true art is to cultivate and improve that weakness. . . . [I]n truth, woman . . . has but one right and that is the right to protection. The right to protection involves the obligation to obey. . . . If she be obedient she stands little danger of maltreatment."[6]

Even in his own day and society, Fitzhugh hardly represented the mainstream of white southern opinion, and one can imagine how mordantly Mary Chesnut might have commented on his reassurances of protection—let alone what Harriet Jacobs might have said. But if we accept Fitzhugh's declaration of white women's tremulously slender and sole "right," "the right to protection," as one vouchsafed by white southern men to white women as a whole, there remained the dilemma of how such women should conduct themselves when they lost that protection, as they did during the Civil War.

Jabour vividly depicts the surge of conflicting emotions that swelled within the bosoms of her erstwhile ladies-turned-"she-rebels." Women's duty to suppress anger, after all, like much of the concept of ladyhood, was not simply a southern ideal but an obligation equally extolled by northerners. For example, *The Young Lady's Own Book,* published in Philadelphia in 1833, pronounced "an enraged woman . . . one of the most disgusting sights in nature."[7] Nonetheless, the occupying Union forces provided what Jabour calls a "provisional cultural sanction for the expression of anger." Suddenly released to a degree from their emotional corsets, these young she-rebels seem to have felt a transgressive thrill in their new freedom, which provided emotional release and potentially a new public role. Although the immediate target of their anger was the despised Yankees, Jabour's account thoughtfully raises the question whether they might not have also seethed because of the failure of the southern patriarchy to provide the protection Fitzhugh and others had promised. These young women meted out their own punishment for such anger, as this essay makes clear. But it is notable that the shame they felt lay in their metaphoric fall from southern Christian ladyhood. Significantly, they seem to have felt impervious to shame in the eyes of their Union enemies. The firm sense of honor that they had imbibed from their position at the top of a rank-ordered, locally based society did not falter with the arrival of occupying troops. For "honor," as Bertram Wyatt-Brown has written, "resides in the individual as his understanding of who he is and where he belongs in the ordered ranks of society," adding "when society has pretensions that there are no ranks, honor must necessarily be set aside or drastically redefined to mean something else."[8] Outside the Old South, honor might be yielding to respectability, but even in the waning days of the Confederacy, it was what these self-styled "she-rebels" ultimately defended.

The defense had its inner costs, nonetheless. This essay reminds us of the power of manners to dictate not simply what one should do but what one should feel, even who one should be. These southern ladies struggled with what the sociologist Arlie Russell Hochschild has called "feeling rules" encoded in the "deep etiquette" of situation and deference.[9] Such rules are not easily suspended, and the new demands of feeling that war inevitably required took their toll on all concerned. The pedestal of white southern ladyhood was especially lofty, resting as it did on the backs of almost four million enslaved African Americans. But northern women also struggled in the constraints of their "separate sphere," and for them, too, the Civil War had ambiguous implications. Having to climb down from the pedestal in the cause of the war effort, neither would fully ascend it again.

A key difference historically distinguishing southern from northern codes of manners was the South's greater stress on honor and deference. This emphasis, in turn, rested on the fundamental importance of a racial caste system as a principle of social hierarchy. Although that hierarchy was the ultimate basis of the privileged position of Anya Jabour's young white southern ladies, they did not feel the need to police it intensely. Like so much other dirty work, they left it to others. In "The Etiquette of Race Relations in the Jim Crow South," Jennifer Ritterhouse provocatively discusses how and why the color line of racial deference and distinction was maintained from the post-emancipation period to the Second World War.

The great effort of southern whites after emancipation was to establish new codes of racial dominance and deference to replace those of the old slave South. In establishing and maintaining the racial politics of everyday life, those who did the dirty work, Ritterhouse emphasizes, were women as well as men, children as well as adults. The elaborate machinery of Jim Crow was an important element in the maintenance of this racial politics.

Even so, Ritterhouse persuasively argues, to speak of a "culture of segregation" overemphasizes the uniformity of practices of racial subordination, when in fact segregation was always riddled with exceptions. Complete separation of the races was never a possibility. Instead, segregation was intended to promote performances of racial superiority on the part of whites and performances of deference on anyone defined as non-white, performances that, together with all the other inculcations of racial etiquette children learned literally at their mothers' knees, were intended to be daily enacted on both sides of the color line, lest anyone forget one's proper role and the approved racial scripts. In such ways, the racial etiquette of white domination daily inculcated and perpetuated what various sociologists, including Pierre Bourdieu, have termed a *habitus*, the "socially constituted system of cognitively and motivating structures" that form the ideas, beliefs, dispositions, and sense of possible actions and choices with which one views and acts in the world. Bourdieu emphasized that habitus includes one's emotional blinders, the possibilities not glimpsed or even imaginable, as well as those consciously entertained and rejected. He also stressed the deeply historical character of such dispositions and the formative power of practices and outlooks acquired in childhood.[10] It is hardly surprising, then, that the racial etiquette of the Jim Crow era had long-lasting effects. In shaping this sense of the world and one's place in it, the deep etiquette of deference, deportment, and feeling is much more powerful than we customarily acknowledge. This is the splendid insight of Ritterhouse's essay.

The themes of southern honor, a prime consideration in Anya Jabour's paper, and continuity and change in social rituals, key to Jennifer Ritterhouse's essay, converge in Catherine Clinton's "Scepter and Masques: Debutante Rituals and Mardi Gras New Orleans." The modern Mardi Gras queen, Clinton's paper makes clear, figuratively wears a very long train, first fashioned by women like Anya Jabour's erstwhile "she-rebels" in the 1870s under the close direction of their Klan-robed male relatives and intended to perpetuate the honor and splendor of the Lost Cause and the New Orleans social elite. The history of these krewe queens, then, is one of the "invention of tradition"[11] through rituals of class, cultural, and genealogical legitimation, and that tradition now weighs heavily on the heads and shoulders of the young women who prepare so assiduously for the role of carnival queen-for-a-day. Building on Rebecca Snedeker's inspired documentary, *By Invitation Only*, which traces the backstage preparations for the great event, Clinton shrewdly analyzes the politics of this invention.

In descriptions of New Orleans's three-week carnival season that reaches a climax with Mardi Gras, much ink has been spilled analyzing symbolic inversions, transgressions, and subversions, but Clinton regards such claims skeptically. In any case, for the debutante ball queens, license does not exist. Rather, the demands to conform to prescribed roles affirming symbolically the status of family and class are at their most rigid. In the words of one young woman in *By Invitation Only*: "This world of debutantes, private clubs and queens is so alluring. But I realize I end up putting on a masque for them. And becoming something else, something that's expected of me. Just for show. That's what I was trained to do. So much of what we were taught growing up was about manners. Smiling no matter what . . . I haven't been myself with these people." That, Catherine Clinton argues, is just the idea. In a critical rite of passage from girlhood to womanhood designed to serve as a template for all girls of this class and social circle, the young queen must pledge her own fealty to her family's values, aspirations, and pretensions, charted by men, instilled by women. "Smiling no matter what," she must demonstrate both the ritual competence and emotional management intended to ease her transition into an elegant, courteous, and compliant upper-class wife.[12]

A problem that economic and social elites in the United States have always faced is how to preserve the appearances of distinction that set them apart from others, how to convert their economic capital into social and cultural capital.[13] The South has a deeper tradition of rank and status to draw on in this enterprise, one preserved and defended, in the last resort, by the doctrine of white supremacy. The private Mardi Gras balls are one of the most spectacular instances of this effort. In the quest for cultural capital, the exclusive white male krewes might be said to mint their young queens as glittering gold sovereigns and to demand from all concerned (not just invited guests) a symbolic tax. No wonder they horde their treasure and refuse to risk their circulation in a free-market social economy in which, in accordance with Gresham's law, the bad might drive out the good.

In his meticulous and illuminating paper, "What's Sex Got to Do with It?" Charles Robinson studies a subject that outwardly contrasts markedly with Catherine Clinton's Mardi Gras krewes and queens but which inwardly affirms many of the same dynamics of race and gender, genealogical legitimation and illegitimacy, in southern history. The virulence with which white southern politicians demanded strict antimiscegenation laws as an essential part of the construction of the Jim Crow South is well known. Nonetheless, the rhetorical excesses that Robinson cites are startling. If leading white southerners cared so deeply about the threat of miscegenation that they wished to enshrine its prohibition in a constitutional amendment, then why, Robinson asks, did a number of judges shrink from enforcing the letter of the law?

His answer is intriguing, surprising, and, I think, convincing. Southern state courts plotted a checkered course in their views of what constituted miscegenation. Although for some, to catch a couple *flagrante delicto* was sufficient, superior courts at times overturned convictions if the relationship appeared casual and opportunistic. What the courts would not countenance, he argues, were interracial couples that appeared to have established ongoing bounds of intimacy and affection, even if no direct evidence of sexual intercourse was forthcoming. Sex itself was not the issue, he argues, or at least sex without the possibility of loopholes by which white men might wiggle out was not the overriding goal. "In the final assessment," Robinson concludes, "antimiscegenation laws aided the white South in creating the kind of society it wanted—one in which black heritage was disparaged and black opportunity denied." It is an assessment that accords well with that of Jennifer Ritterhouse in her analysis of the racial etiquette of the Jim Crow South. The color line, their two papers contend, was never rigid and inflexible because it did not need to be. Exceptions were made daily, mostly to facilitate the convenience of white southerners—and, in matters of sex and power especially, white southern men. As such men well knew, the line could be lowered or raised by a white court depending on circumstances. In certain extremities, courts could be dispensed with entirely, and the line tightened into a noose.

Lisa Lindquist Door's sprightly paper on the rise of a new youth culture at the University of Alabama and other Alabama white state colleges in the second and third decades of the twentieth century puts privileged young women in the symposium's spotlight once again. But whereas Catherine Clinton's young debutantes must carefully don the masques and precisely perform the parts their families have assigned them, Door's college women delighted in their freedom to experiment with new social roles in which dating, petting, drinking, and motoring played conspicuous parts, while evading parietal rules and anxious parental inquiries. In contrast to Clinton's queens, who perform the laundering of economic and social capital into cultural capital under the careful inspection of their families, Dorr suggests that her Alabama coeds evaded adult oversight in order to spend their sexual capital instead of saving it. Still, one must observe that their choices were not wide open. A certain liberty for college women and a generous latitude for college men were socially sanctioned in the 1920s, even if their precise boundaries were a matter of contention. Perhaps one might say that, in this more elastic dispensation for college youth, white southerners became "modern" in a key respect: they dealt with behavior and identity less as matters of honor and more as matters of reputation. The quotation from the University of Alabama humor magazine, the *Rammer Jammer*, with which Dorr opens her paper suggests this shift: "The only time a girl does not want the spotlight on her is when she is on a wild party." Indeed, it might be more accurate to say that young college women and men became concerned with *reputations* in the plural rather than a single unitary image. Seeking to maintain an upright image in the eyes of parents, clergy, and, to a degree, college administrators (the last at times supported by an "honor code"), they simultaneously sought to cultivate a more hedonistic, "popular" image among themselves. As Dorr observes, adumbrations of this new youth culture predated the First World War and the 1920s. Historians such as Kevin White and Sharon Ullman have pointed to the advent of "the first sexual revolution" from the beginning of the century, led by the young.[14]

Yet it would be too easy, I think, to celebrate uncritically the growing "agency" of these young women—or that of the daring young men. Here again, Pierre Bourdieu's concept of habitus may be illuminating. The choices these college students saw before them were not nearly as open-ended as they might have thought; they were, in many respects, a rather narrow set of transgressive practices and gestures—including the terms of heterosexual dating, drinking, and driving—that bore the name, more than the reality, of "freedom." College women, in particular, found in their social events, their male dates often set the terms and expectations to which they were pressured to conform. But college men experienced considerable pressures to prove themselves as well in accordance with standards as demanding in their own way as the Victorian expectations of their fathers. At the same time, they nervously looked over their shoulders to evade the moral police of a revived Ku Klux Klan.

As Joseph Crespino reminds us in his fine essay on "Civility and Civil Rights in Mississippi," civility and violence have long been the right and left hands—one courteously extended, the other clenched in a fist—of white southern resistance to African Americans' demands for civil rights. Through much of southern history, the work of those two hands has been carefully coordinated. However, in the wake of the *Brown* v. *Board of Education* decision, even in Mississippi, debate over which hand to extend first consumed much of the white political and social order. Advocates of the paternal hand of civility, such as Governor J. P. Coleman, Senator John Stennis, and Erle Johnston of the Mississippi State Sovereignty Commission, defended their strategy as "practical segregation." Their objections to the violent tactics of the white Citizens' Councils and other advocates of massive resistance were fundamentally on political grounds. Such violence would inevitably attract attention and counterattack, they feared. Seeking to placate local African American leaders by paternalistic concessions, they offered to give the old edifices of segregation a new coat of paint but not to pull them down.

One could say that such white paternalists found themselves in a tragicomedy of manners of their own devising, but for many others it was tragedy, pure and simple. These "practical segregationists" consistently overestimated their ability to control both white advocates of massive resistance and local black community leaders pressing for integration. Not only did these paternalists believe their own propaganda that "outside agitators" were responsible for the commotion; they also had no comprehension of the grass-roots power of the civil rights movement.

In Walker Percy's appalled reflections on the state of civilities and civil rights that Mississippians had reached by 1965, with which Crespino begins his paper, Percy feared the demagogues had shouted down "the good white folks." There were, indeed, good white folks in Mississippi, then as now, and Crespino is right to ask us to understand their position. But as for the "practical segregationists" who felt that "good manners" could prevail in brokering a paternalistic compromise, this essay makes clear, beneath their gestures of politeness was a profound sense of white ownership and rule as the fundamental basis of southern society. They extended their right hand cordially because it had so rarely failed them in the past. The power of the civil rights movement, of course, was to refuse to be satisfied with such gestures and publicly to insist that there was a deeper moral and political debt that must be paid.

The challenge of civility in the South in the 1960s was a variation of the challenge the United States has faced from its beginnings as a democracy: to move from codes of etiquette, rituals of deference, and embodied histories of inequality and ascribed inferiority to codes, forms, and habitus that are more fully democratic, mutually respectful, inclusive, and just. Some, such as the sociologist Richard Sennett, have celebrated the metropolis as the best place to create new forms of civility, precisely because the need to negotiate on a daily basis among strangers with diverse interests, backgrounds, and customs takes individuals beyond localism and trains them to live in a pluralistic, impersonal society.[15] Still, if a great city, such as New York, might provide one model of manners and civility, we may find another in the South with its countryside and small towns as well as its cities. A full sense of the part it might play in the future must begin with re-examinations of its history, such as those we have heard at this symposium. This history, as we know, has been deeply contentious, and the greatest element of contention has always revolved around race. At the same time, this history teaches us that immense change is possible, and that agreements that seemed unimaginable for generations can sometimes be achieved with surprising speed.

Thus, we might reflect that one of the young legislators whom Senator John Stennis contacted in his effort to find a conciliatory tack while maintaining "practical segregation" was his former assistant, William Winter. Winter went on to become one of the state's most distinguished governors, and the centerpiece of his administration was the Education Reform Act of 1982, addressing deep-seated deficiencies and inequities. Now, half a century after *Brown* v. *Board*, the University of Mississippi houses the William Winter Institute for Racial Reconciliation, which seeks to address some of the most painful chapters in the state's history in order to provide a basis for a more truly civil society. Such work reminds us that one of the great tasks of history is to disturb amnesia and complacency, so as to uncover new possibilities. The goal is not to make the dirty hands of the past clean; rather, it is to engage in a deep struggle with the past so as to create a more humane future.

Notes

1. Pierre Bourdieu, *Outline of a Theory of Practice*, trans. Richard Nice (Cambridge, UK: Cambridge University Press, 1972), 79.

2. William R. Taylor, *Cavalier and Yankee; the Old South and American National Character* (New York: Braziller, 1961).

3. *I'll Take My Stand: The South and the Agrarian Tradition* (New York: Harper, 1930).

4. John Shelton Reed, *The Enduring South: Subcultural Perceptions in Mass Society* (Lexington, Mass.: Lexington Books, div. of D. C. Heath, 1972), 24–25. Reed bases his characterizations on analysis of a 1957 Gallup Poll.

5. Bourdieu, *Outline of a Theory of Practice*, 95.

6. George Fitzhugh, *Sociology for the South* (Richmond: Morris, 1854), 214–15.

7. *The Young Lady's Own Book* (Philadelphia: Key & Biddle, 1833), 201. See the discussion of anger as treated in early and mid-nineteenth-century marriage manuals and popular fiction in Carol Zisowitz Stearns and Peter N. Stearns, *Anger: The Struggle for Emotional Control in America's History* (Chicago: University of Chicago Press, 1986), 36–68.

8. Bertram Wyatt-Brown, *Southern Honor: Ethics and Behavior in the Old South* (New York: Oxford University Press, 1982), 14, 20.

9. Arlie Russell Hochschild, *The Managed Heart: Commercialization of Human Feeling* (Berkeley and Los Angeles: University of California Press, 1983), 57 and note 3, 250–51.

10. Bourdieu, *Outline of a Theory of Practice*, 72–95, esp. 76.

11. See Eric Hobsbawm and Terrence Ranger, ed., *The Invention of Tradition* (Cambridge, UK: Cambridge University Press, 1983).

12. On emotional management, see Hochschild, *Managed Heart*.

13. The concept of social and cultural capital is most fully developed in Bourdieu, *Distinction: A Social Critique of the Judgment of Taste*, trans. Richard Nice (Cambridge, Mass.: Harvard University Press, 1984).

14. Kevin White, *The First Sexual Revolution: The Emergence of Male Heterosexuality in Modern America* (New York: New York University Press, 1993); Sharon R. Ullman, *Sex Seen: The Emergence of Modern Sexuality in America* (Berkeley and Los Angeles: University of California Press, 1997).

15. Richard Sennett, *The Fall of Public Man* (New York: Knopf, 1977), 349.

Contributors

CATHERINE CLINTON teaches history at Queen's University, Belfast. She is the author of numerous works, including *Harriet Tubman: The Road to Freedom* (2004), *Civil War Stories* (1998), *Tara Revisited* (1997), and *The Plantation Mistress* (1982), and editor or coeditor of several collections of scholarly essays such as *The Devil's Lane: Sex and Race in the Early South* (1997), *Southern Families at War: Loyalty and Conflict in the Civil War South* (2000), *Southern Women and Women Historians* (1998), and *Battle Scars: Gender and Sexuality in the American Civil War* (2006). She is also the editor of *Fanny Kemble's Journals* (2000) and Susie King Taylor's *Reminiscences of My Life in Camp: An African American Woman's Civil War Memoir* (2006).

JOSEPH CRESPINO teaches history at Emory University. He is the author of *In Search of Another Country: Mississippi and the Conservative Counterrevolution* (2007).

JANE DAILEY teaches history at the Johns Hopkins University. She is the author of *Before Jim Crow: The Politics of Race in Postemancipation Virginia* (2000) and a coeditor of *Jumpin' Jim Crow: Southern Politics from Civil War to Civil Rights* (2000).

LISA LINDQUIST DORR teaches history at the University of Alabama. She is the author of *White Women, Rape, and the Power of Race in Virginia, 1900–1960* (2004).

ANYA JABOUR teaches history at the University of Montana. She is the author of *Marriage in the Early Republic: Elizabeth and William Wirt and the Companionate Ideal* (1998) and editor of *Major Problems in the History of American Families and Children* (2005).

JOHN F. KASSON teaches history and American studies at the University of North Carolina. He is the author of *Civilizing the Machine: Technology and Republican Values in America, 1776–1900* (1976), *Amusing the Million: Coney*

Island at the Turn of the Century (1978), *Rudeness and Civility: Manners in Nineteenth-Century Urban America* (1990), and *Houdini, Tarzan, and the Perfect Man: The White Male Body and the Challenge of Modernity in America* (2001).

TED OWNBY teaches history and southern studies at the University of Mississippi. He is the author of *American Dreams in Mississippi: Consumers, Poverty, and Culture, 1830–1998* (1999) and *Subduing Satan: Religion, Recreation, and Manhood in the Rural South, 1865–1920* (1990) and editor of *The Role of Ideas in the Civil Rights South* (2002) and *Black and White: Cultural Interaction in the Antebellum South* (1993).

JENNIFER RITTERHOUSE teaches history at Utah State University. She is the author of *Growing Up Jim Crow: How Black and White Children Learned Race* (2006) and editor of Sarah Patton's *The Desegregated Heart: A Virginian's Stand in Time of Transition.*

CHARLES F. ROBINSON II teaches history at the University of Arkansas. He is the author of *Dangerous Liaisons: Sex and Love in the Segregated South* (2003).

Index